1495

'With the Sharpened Axe of Reason'

'With the Sharpened Axe of Reason'

Approaches to Walter Benjamin

Edited by
Gerhard Fischer

BERG
Oxford • Washington, D.C.

First published in 1996 by
Berg
Editorial offices:
150 Cowley Road, Oxford, OX4 1JJ, UK
13950 Park Center Road, Herndon, VA 22071, USA

Berg is an imprint of Oxford International Publishers Ltd.

Library of Congress Cataloging-in-Publication Data

A catalogue record for this book is available from the Library of Congress.

British Library Cataloguing-in-Publication Data

A catalogue record for this book is available from the British Library.

ISBN 1 85973 044 2 (Cloth)
1 85973 054 X (Paper)

Printed in the United Kingdom by WBC Bookbinders, Bridgend,
Mid Glamorgan.

To make arable areas where up to now only madness is rampant. Advancing with the sharpened axe of reason and without looking left or right in order not to fall prey to the horror luring out of the depth of the jungle. All ground had to be made arable once by reason, had to be cleared from the undergrowth of madness and myth.

[Gebiete urbar zu machen, auf denen bisher nur der Wahnsinn wuchert. Vordringen mit der geschliffenen Axt der Vernunft und ohne rechts noch links zu sehen, um nicht dem Grauen anheimzufallen, das aus der Tiefe des Urwalds lockt. Aller Boden mußte einmal von der Vernunft urbar gemacht, vom Gestrüpp des Wahns und des Mythos gereinigt werden.]

Walter Benjamin, *Arcades Project*

Contents

Contents

Introduction:
Benjamin the Centenarian

Gerhard Fischer

I

On the Fourth of July, 1934, Walter Benjamin, who was then visiting Bertolt Brecht in Skovsbostrand near Svendborg, wrote a letter to a Danish Committee which had made it its task to provide financial support for foreigners living in Denmark, usually German intellectuals who had fled from Hitler's regime, and who were without income or other means of support.[1] Exiled for over a year, Benjamin was facing an uncertain future. His letter is a plea for help written by a destitute refugee in a desperate situation. It is also an attempt to reflect on his life and to take stock of his achievements; it contains a curriculum vitae, a list of publications, and it mentions some of the projects he was working on at the time. Addressed to Professor Aage Fris who chaired the committee, the letter reads, in part:

> In order to support the petition which I take the liberty of addressing to you at the end of this letter, I allow myself to make the following observations about myself:
>
> I, a German citizen, 41 years of age, had to leave Germany in March 1933. Due to the political upheaval I was not only robbed all of a sudden of the basis of my means of existence, but also – although a dissident and not a member of any political party – I was no longer certain of my personal freedom. In the same month, my brother was severely mistreated and kept in a concentration camp until Christmas.
>
> From Germany I went to France, as I hoped to find a possible field for my activities there on the basis of my previous scientific work.
>
> In the following I provide the most important dates of my education and scientific activity: after completing the classical-liberal *Gymnasium*, I studied literature and philosophy in Germany and Switzerland, and I graduated as doctor of philosophy in Bern in 1919 with the grade *summa cum laude*. After my return to Germany, I concentrated on literary criticism in the areas of German and

French literature. In order to secure the necessary economic basis for this research, I also worked as a regular literary contributor and reviewer of scientific publications for the *Frankfurter Zeitung* and Southwest German Radio in Frankfurt. In addition, I contributed occasionally to a few respected journals which appeared in the German language area between 1920 and 1930. I should like to mention above all the *Neue Schweizer Rundschau* and *Neue Deutsche Beiträge*.

The editor of the latter journal was Hugo von Hofmannsthal, with whom I was allied in a bond of friendship during the last seven years of his life, and who regarded my writings with particular appreciation. A testimony to my work on French literature, apart from critical essays, is my translation of the work of Marcel Proust; two volumes were to appear just before the political upheaval (Verlag R. Pieper, München). I also published a translation of the *Tableaux Parisiens* by Baudelaire (Verlag Richard Weißbach, Heidelberg), which contains a voluminous theory of translation as an introduction.

In the following, Benjamin provides a list of his published works: *Der Begriff der Kunstkritik in der deutschen Romantik* (1920), *Ursprung des deutschen Trauerspiels* (1928), *Goethes Wahlverwandtschaften* (1924/25), and *Einbahnstraße* (1928). He also mentions his article on Goethe in the *Great Russian Soviet Encyclopaedia*, as well as a volume of essays of literary criticism for which a contract had been signed but which could not appear due to the political events. The letter ccontinues:

As a result of my hurried departure from Germany, my collection of reviews of my work was left behind in Berlin; I hope to get hold of a comprehensive description of my work which was published in the *Frankfurter Zeitung*, and I shall take the liberty of submitting it to you at a later date.

My hope to establish an independent existence in Paris could, unfortunately, not be fulfilled. None the less I was able for some time to gain the most basic means through publications that appeared under pseudonym in the *Frankfurter Zeitung* (signed Detlef Holz or K.A. Stempflinger). By the end of spring, this possibility was also closed to me. I was forced to leave France because the stay there was too expensive for me. In Paris, I decided, in co-operation with the great collector and cultural historian, Eduard Fuchs, who was also forced to escape into exile, to write a comprehensive and definitive study of the basic lines of his life work, of which the documentary material has been confiscated and largely destroyed by the Berlin police. It is this study that I am presently working on.

In Denmark I found provisional lodging with my friends, the Brecht family. However, I can claim the hospitality of the Brecht family only for a short period. Otherwise I am completely without means; my sole possession is a small working library which has found a place in the house of Herr Brecht.

I have taken the liberty of presenting these facts to your committee in the hope that it may be possible for you to relieve my present situation in some way.

II

It seems appropriate to begin this collection of scholarly essays dedicated to the work of Walter Benjamin by including an account, in his own hand, of his extraordinary life story. It is a testimony to the fate of a writer whose posthumous fame today stands in stark contrast to the lack of recognition he suffered during his lifetime. Benjamin's curriculum vitae of 1934 is a document devoid of all pathos and sentimentality, a testimony to the quiet and proud dignity of a man in the face of an adversity that seems beyond human capacity to endure. It is also a poignant reminder that Benjamin's career, beset more often than not by rejection and misunderstanding, failure and despair in his own time, underwent a remarkable turnaround in the post-war era: the nearly forgotten literary critic, philosopher of aesthetics, language and history and social theorist of Wilhelminian, Weimar and Nazi Germany; re-discovered and re-claimed as an unorthodox – and the 'most peculiar' – Marxist thinker by the New Left of the 1960s and early 1970s as 'our' contemporary; acclaimed and revered to a level reaching almost 'cult figure' status by the participants in academic discourses on postmodernism in the present age of electronic culture some twenty years later.

Benjamin's tragic suicide on 26 September 1940, so full of quiet, unpathetic heroism, again encapsulates the contradiction that characterizes the reception of his work. He had chosen to leave the prison that Europe had become in 1939 through the last open gate to freedom; but perhaps his decision came too late because of an instinctive fear that cutting off his cultural roots in Europe would rob him of the vital necessity of continuing his work. His passing away – all but unnoticed at the time – appears to us today as one such 'single moment' repeatedly evoked in his writing, of the 'crystal of all that has taken place', the memory of which will remain forever etched in the consciousness of readers of his work in the *choc* of recognition he so vividly described.

Benjamin, then, the contemporary of modernity, of postmodernity, *our* contemporary? Why is it that the essays of the centenarian are today prescribed reading in university courses around the world, most notably in 'advanced' subjects such as media and communication studies, and why do so many of today's 'avant-garde' critics and artists feel so distinctive an affinity with the paradoxical theses and striking observations of an unlikely guru, whose major works concentrate on German baroque literature and the history of the nineteenth century? The evaluation of Benjamin's contribution as well as the explanation for his success remain a challenge that seems today no less daunting than at the beginning of the Benjamin renaissance. To be sure, the Benjamin industry that has come into existence since the 1970s – philological, biographical as much as critical scholarship – has covered a great deal of ground during the last two and a half decades or so, accelerated and urged along by the publication of the *Werkausgabe* of his *Gesammelte Schriften*, which, controversial though the underlying editorial policy and its history might be, has for the first time made available the great bulk of his work with thorough documentation and commentary.

Yet it would be an obvious oversimplification to claim that we have managed to make Benjamin *our own*: it is not only that great gaps in interpretative scholarship remain to be filled; more importantly, the nature of Benjamin's work itself – that peculiar and sometimes frustratingly puzzling mixture of aphorism and paradox, allegory and fragment, metaphor and dialectical image, Marxian theology and Messianic materialism, theory and fictional narrative, history and political pamphlet (the list goes on), this unique literary *collage*:, which attracts as much as it keeps you at bay – does not in the end combine to make the individual pieces of the mosaic disappear within the harmony of the whole. How could it be otherwise with the reception of his work?

III

The essays collected in this volume make a modest attempt to contribute to a fuller understanding of Benjamin and to complement existing knowledge about his work. They were written and delivered, for the most part, on the occasion of an international conference at the University of New South Wales in Sydney, Australia, devoted to the commemoration of the author and his work on the centenary of Benjamin's birth. By the time the present collection appears, some of the essays will have been published in journals in Australia (Roberts, Hollington, Milfull)[2], while two contributions from Germany are edited versions of essays published in their original language (Weigel, Mattenklott)[3].

The essays address a number of areas central to the concerns of scholars and students of Benjamin, most notably the debate on modernity and postmodernity. Others topics covered have been less exhaustively treated in Benjamin scholarship: for example, the analysis of feminist themes, contributions on children's literature, children's culture and pedagogy, or the exploration of Benjamin's theory and practice of epistolography and literary criticism. The essays aim to provide decidedly critical perspectives. They attempt to avoid the kind of adulatory-identificatory approach, by way of empathy with the peculiar metaphorical quality of Benjamin's thinking and language, which is sometimes characteristic of Benjamin criticism. The temptation to write in a Benjaminian *style* can be strong, given the imaginative power of his writing, but criticism must be informed above all by a commitment to employ what Benjamin himself calls the 'sharpened axe of reason'. The essays in this collection share the common aim of demonstrating a commitment to such 'sharp' intellectual analysis. They do so on the basis of their own individual methodological frames of reference and critical-theoretical perspectives. The contributors' interdisciplinary interests and wide-ranging research questions reflect the plurality of Benjaminian discourses, in social and cultural criticism, in literary studies, and in aesthetics and art history, rather than representing a single and unifying conceptual and methodological-theoretical frame. Taking up Benjamin's metaphor, the general idea of the present collection of essays is to approach Benjamin's work from a number of different areas and critical positions, using the 'sharpened axe of reason' to open different paths of scholarship towards the central clearing of illumination in his work.

In his opening piece in the section on Modernity/Postmodernity, David Frisby (Chapter 1) analyses Benjamin's work on the nineteenth century as an attempt to identify the basis of modernity as *Vorgeschichte* or, indeed, *Urgeschichte*, and he takes the proponents of a Postmodernist theory of history to task for not establishing the case for a 'prehistory' of postmodernity, a task for which Benjamin's own model in the *Arcades Project* could be considered as a very useful preliminary study. Frisby's focus on the *Ursprung* (origin) of modernity also features prominently in Bernd Hüppauf's essay (Chapter 2) on Benjamin's imaginary-intellectual landscape, which deals with changes in the perception and representation of space. Hüppauf's point of departure is a discussion of urban culture and the *nomadic*; drawing on a number of literary sources on nomadism (Kafka, Spengler, Deleuze/Guattari); he sees Benjamin's topography as essentially ambivalent, mingling elements of modern urbanity, aspects of Utopian nature and, particularly, the landscape of the front of World War I, which is defined as a 'place of continual decodification' and the 'point of culmination of the dissolution of the nineteenth century'.

David Roberts's essay (Chapter 3) draws on Gernot Böhme's *Ecological Aesthetics of Nature* to ask about the role, not of art, but of nature in the age of mechanical reproduction, thus linking Benjamin's central theory to a question that is at the centre of contemporary ecological concerns. While Critical Theory, in particular Adorno's negative Utopia of 'nature reconciled', is seen as the 'most extreme expression of alienation from nature', the culmination of a development that begins with Hegel, Roberts finds in Benjamin's concept of aura the reciprocity between nature and man ('the recognition of the one human and natural lifeworld') which is at the same time, as in Critical Theory, the emblem of the unbridgeable gap, both infinite closeness and distance, and thus of the impossible reconciliation with nature. Roberts points to Habermas's and Böhme's proposals for a new aesthetic education of man as complementary *rescuing critiques* of the 'sublime political-aesthetic paradigm of redemption in modernity'.

John Docker (Chapter 4) focuses on another ambivalence in Benjamin's work, namely his attitude to the question of mass culture. According to Docker, the writings of F.R. and Q.D. Leavis establish a paradigm in the discussion on modern art and literature in which a 'low' or popular culture is linked to a realm of femininity, whereas 'high' literary modernism is described in notions of masculinity. This pattern is seen as a paradigm for subsequent modernist analyses of mass culture, including the essay by Horkheimer/Adorno on the *Culture Industry*. Benjamin's position is seen as 'hermaphroditic', both embracing Adornoesque positions, but also challenging and subverting them. Benjamin's interest in allegory as fragmentation, for example, or his 'heteroglossic' method that is 'pulled by contrary movements, centripetal, centrifugal', anticipates diverse Poststructuralist and Postmodernist features (Docker cites Bakhtin, Lyotard and Derrida, among others).

Docker's essay also provides a link to the chapters of the second part, which focus on gender and the Utopian aspects of Benjamin's philosophy. Sigrid Weigel (Chapter 5) reads Benjamin's writing on the intellectual-historical topography of the modern city, comparing it to Franz Hessel and Italo Calvino, and their use of images of femininity. Both Benjamin and Calvino are seen as practising deconstructive forms of writing; but whereas Calvino's descriptions of *Invisible Cities* thematize the power of the imaginary, and images of the city (as desire for the feminine repressed into the unconscious) are related to foundation myths and to the (male) process of civilization and of writing, Benjamin arrives at a 'semiotic of feminine places' within a topographical writing that seeks to 'decipher the visual and physical space of the city.' Margaret Mahony Stoljar's essay (Chapter 6) deals with Benjamin's use of gender images in the *Arcades Project*: the work of the historian as penetration of the past in a figurative language that employs 'the erotic and the feminine as key concepts' is explained with regard to the peculiar methodology of historical analysis that results in 'multiple resonance...as an index of Benjamin's complex existential and intellectual positions'. Benjamin's work is criticized as disturbing, sexist and, in the end, counterproductive, because it 'cuts through the dynamics of his own text', bringing its 'dialectic to a halt' and extinguishing 'the woman reader's ability to engage with the text'. Stoljar's conclusion implies a sobering question: what does it mean to our reading of Benjamin that 'the hero of all subversions' should have been 'blind to the critical category of gender'?

Michael Hollington's Chapter 7 traces the similarities in lines of reception of Fourier by Benjamin and Barthes, with the work of Klossowski as intermediary. Benjamin's interest in the ideas of the 'nineteenth-century pioneer' as a *frère semblable*, as well as his fascination with Surrealism, connect with similar preoccupations of Barthes, particularly with regard to the Utopian dimensions of Fourier's work in a number of areas (elaborating further on points discussed in earlier chapters): the affirmation of sexuality, both male and female, and the celebration of the pleasure principle, the emphasis on 'matriarchy' (i.e. Benjamin's reading of Bachofen's fashionable work in order to enlist it in the ideological struggle against fascism), the 'rehabilitation' of the status and power of women, the notion of play and creative imaginative force, and a denial of progress seen in terms of a 'conquest of nature'. In all these aspects, Fourier stands at the threshold of the nineteenth century, a transitory figure who allows for the discovery of 'origins' and the analysis of the past as much as for the possibility of looking into the future (of modernity).

John Milfull's Chapter 8 focuses on the Utopian aspect of Benjamin's Messianic dream, as it appears in historical hindsight after the watershed of the final collapse of the inheritors of the Stalinist regimes of Eastern Europe. Reflecting on the 'strange solidarity' and 'friendship' of Western intellectuals, like Milfull himself, with the 'embattled protagonists of the vanished world of state socialism', Milfull turns to Benjamin's *Theologico-Political Fragment* as a paradoxical, and paradoxically comforting, paradigm of a 'logic of reversal'. This paradigm is seen as similar in kind to the characteristic experiences of German and Jewish (and German-Jewish) intellectuals in pursuit of historical 'redemption' from the outset of the Enlightenment to the catastrophe of the 'millenium of the man from Braunau' or the finally crumbled 'edifice that Stalin built'. To Milfull, the lesson of history is to 'free ourselves from the lure of the Lurian, the Messiah complex', and to reject the metaphor of the flight of Benjamin's angel: the imperative is to walk, so as not to lose sight of the road of the present (which is in need of 'our critique') by way of a fixation with 'time travel' that overlooks 'that there are no ends of history but those we reach ourselves'.

Manfred Jurgensen (Chapter 9) begins Part III, on literature and literary criticism, with an overview of Benjamin's work as literary critic. Benjamin, who plays a prominent role in the transition from academic to journalistic criticism, is seen both as a representative and authoritative critic, and yet as one who is outside the mainstream of twentieth-century German literary criticism. Benjamin's insistence on historical thinking and on detailed and objective philological research puts him at odds with the emerging subjectivity that is characteristic of 'the new type of literary critic' (in Hans Mayer's terms). Jurgensen discusses some of Benjamin's reviews as paradigmatic models of a materialistic analysis of literary culture, and he analyses at some length Benjamin's critical language: the 'metaphorical analogies', his 'intellectual parallelisms' (e.g. in the apodictic comparisons of authors), as well as his 'manneristic search for stylistic balance'. Jurgensen finds both a 'conservative, essentially Romantic attitude' and a 'structure of analysis' that emphasizes 'progression of understanding through interrelationships, linking concepts and judgements in such a away that a new logic of reason emerges'. The ultimate aim of Benjamin's literary analyses, according to Jurgensen, is 'renewal, an artistic regeneration and revaluation in the historical context of sociocultural developments'.

In contrast, Benjamin's early essay on Goethe's *Wahlverwandtschaften* appears in Anthony Stephens's analysis (Chapter 10) as a piece that suffers from the 'essential vulgarity' of its author passing moral judgement on fictional characters 'as if they were real people'. Benjamin is criticized for eliminating the novel's manifold ambiguities – for example, in his interpretation of the *Novelle* as 'simple reversal' of the fate of the central characters – and for imposing arbitrary and seemingly axiomatic concepts, such as 'guilt' or 'myth' or 'destiny', without either explanation or justification. The result is, on the one hand, an overloading of the novel with metaphysical-theological construction that is quite unlike the novel itself, and on the other hand, a 'leap outside history', leaving the reader (at least the one unfamiliar with Benjamin) bewildered and confused. To Stephens, this is part of a strategic and not so subtle 'powerplay' to establish the 'superiority of the critic', *vis-à-vis* the reader, other critics (in this case, Gundolf and his influential interpretation of Goethe), and lastly, of the author himself. Stephens admits there is some value in Benjamin's reading of the classical novel, if only because some elements of his critique 'tend to undermine his [Benjamin's] own dogmatism', but in the end Stephens insists on the category of the 'vulgar' to describe a critic, and his claim, expressed with great pathos, to have unveiled the 'truth content' of a work. Entertaining as any good *Verriß* ought to be, Stephens nevertheless draws attention to a problematic dimension of Benjamin's work.

Another Benjamin altogether emerges in Gert Mattenklott's essay (Chapter 11): the correspondent, the theorist of the letter and of epistolography, the editor of a justly famous collection of letters of *Deutsche Menschen* seems far removed from the image of the manipulative critic (which Stephens suggests). Mattenklott emphasizes the connection with a tradition of letter-writing by Jewish authors in German literature, and thus with a spiritual dimension that implies a highly moral attitude derived from its closeness to metaphysical imperatives. To Benjamin, letter-writing is more than just communication to exchange information; instead, he sees its destinctive feature as an 'exchange in the afterlife of letters', i.e. correspondence as *Fortleben* which 'provides an opportunity, or rather more compels a writer, to construct the shape of his or her own afterlife which has to be invented anew with every letter and perhaps always in a different shape'. Mattenklott stresses the notion of testimony: letters do not merely belong to a pragmatic, biographical lifeworld, rather 'they are testimonies of an intellectual life', a 'true medium...that testifies to the possibility of a balance between nature and intellect'. It is in the 'performative nature' of letter-writing that a new reality is created (as a kind of 'non-sexual form of productivity') and where the two spheres can be reconciled. Mattenklott finds a number of affinities to Benjamin's ideas: to George and his circle, to the *Jugendbewegung* prior to World War I, but particularly to the aesthetic-idealist and moral programme of German classicism. Characteristically, it is Goethe who is the most important example of a correspondent for Benjamin: his praise of Goethe's correspondence (its 'noble, unerring certainty') is also 'a glorification of the form in general.'

Klaus Doderer, finally (Chapter 12), discusses Benjamin's varied interests in children's literature: his work as a collector of illustrated children's books, his writings for children, especially the radio plays and features for young listeners which continue the story-telling traditions of *Kalendergeschichte* (of authors like Hebel, in particular) within the new medium, and finally Benjamin's theoretical essays on children as readers and on children's literature which amount to a fragmentary theory *in nuce* of a literature for young readers.

Doderer's concerns with the new media, as well as with children and with the notion of performing for them, provide a link to the last part of this collection. The next two chapters deal with the same text, Benjamin's *Programme of a Proletarian Children's Theatre*, a neglected essay which experienced a brief phase of prominence, particularly in Germany, during the days of the student revolt of the 1960s, in the context of a debate on an alternative educational theory and practice. Hans-Thies Lehmann (Chapter 13) explores the philosophical context of Benjamin's article with reference to other texts on education and childhood, focusing on some of the central concepts of the *Programme*: observation as the 'genius of education', the rejection of 'theoretical moralism', and the concept of the 'child as dictator'. Lehmann argues that, in political terms, Benjamin's views on children are 'anarchic' rather than Marxist (as they had been misunderstood in the 1970s), and he emphasizes the central thesis of 'suspension of all norms' and of 'the thetic approach as such' at the core of his educational philosophy. Lehmann also traces the meaning of the concept of 'gesture', relating it in particular to the 'radicalization' of theatre in Brecht's didactic plays (*Lehrstücke*), where 'mimesis and the representation of knowledge take a minor role in favour of participation...and the "acquisition" of knowledge', a shift seen by Lehmann as the decisive aspect of a profoundly altered idea of communication.

My own contribution (Chapter 14), by contrast, while suggesting an influence on Brecht by Benjamin that can be traced to the *Programme of a Proletarian Children's Theatre*, emphasizes the essential difference to Brecht's 'cool', epic-rational theatre of a 'scientific age', in comparison with the anarchistic release of 'wild' energy described by Benjamin. My chapter proposes a relationship to Freud's thesis on artistic creativity and creative imagination, as in the article on 'The Poet and Day-dreaming', and it emphasizes again the Utopian quality of a non-prescriptive, non-ideological education that is at the same time a *theatrum mundi et vitae*. In the concluding chapter of this volume, Andrzej Wirth returns to Benjamin's famous thesis on the reproduction of art in the context of technological development, claiming that it is in need of correction with regard to performative artwork. Wirth distinguishes between a purely technical reproduction and the reproduction of an artistic procedure. In terms of theatre as performance art, the reconstruction of a production (through multiple stagings, international marketing, revivals, model productions and the like) stands essentially in contradiction to the unique event of a show, with its unrepeatable, interactive quality (the exchange between actor and spectator) which provides an 'aura' of authenticity and charisma. Wirth cites the work of Robert Wilson (and other artists) as examples of a highly-developed high-tech multimedia theatre; in particular, Wilson's installation at the Pompidou Centre in 1991 is seen as an instance of 'technical and artistic self-reproduction of theatre' by an artist 'obsessed with a Utopian goal of reproducing his own images globally'. While Wirth insists, in principle, on the impossibility of reproducing theatre as artwork, he points to new developments which may yet prove Benjamin right: namely, the use of interactive multimedia devices driven by computer, as they are currently being employed in CD-ROM documentation of the work of Wilson. The electronic process creates a possibility not only of programming, documenting and storing artistic processes (thus allowing for their reproduction), but also allows the 'spectator' the chance of individual creative interaction, of participating in a 'unique' event in his or her own *virtual reality*.

NOTES

1. Walter Benjamin, *Gesammelte Schriften*, ed. R. Tiedemann and H. Schweppenhäuser, 7 vols (Frankfurt/Main, 1974–), VI, pp. 220–2. Translated by Gerhard Fischer.
2. Cf. David Roberts, 'Aura and an Aesthetics of Nature', *Thesis Eleven* pp. 127–37; Michael Hollington, 'Benjamin, Fourier, Barthes', *AUMLA – Journal of the Australasian Universities Language and Literature Association*, 81 (May 1994), pp. 33–54; John Milfull, 'The Messiah Complex: The Angel of History Looks Back at Walter Benjamin from its Perch on the Ruins of "Socialism as it Existed in Reality"', *Australian Journal*

of Politics and History, 39, 3 (1993), pp. 381–5. The permission of the publishers to re-print these articles is gratefully acknowledged.

3. Cf. Gert Mattenklott, 'Benjamin als Korrespondent, als Herausgber von "Deutsche Menschen" und als Theoretiker des Briefes', in *Walter Benjamin*, ed. Uwe Steiner (Copyright 1992 by Peter Lang Verlag, Bern, Frankfurt, New York), pp. 272–82; Sigrid Weigel, 'Traum – Stadt – Frau: Zur Weiblichkeit der Städte in der Schrift', in S. Weigel, *Topographien der Geschlechter: Kulturgeschichtliche Studien zur Literatur* (Copyright 1990 by Rowohlt Taschenbuch Verlag, Reinbek bei Hamburg), pp. 204–27. The permission of the publishers to re-print edited versions of these articles in English translation is gratefully acknowledged.

I
Modernity/Postmodernity

Walter Benjamin's Prehistory of Modernity as Anticipation of Postmodernity? Some Methodological Reflections

David Frisby

I

Walter Benjamin, in his *Arcades Project*, was convinced of the necessity of providing not merely a presentation or representation of modernity but a 'prehistory of modernity'. No such necessity or obligation has befallen those who, over the past two decades, have announced the arrival of postmodernity, Postmodernism, the postmodern condition, and the like. In so far as such announcements have also been accompanied by the declared arrival of posthistory, such a necessity or obligation has been rendered redundant and superfluous. Does posthistory require a prehistory that is not history? Yet, at the same time, many of these delineations of postmodernity do make reference to aspects of the work of Benjamin as anticipations of the postmodern condition (most often in relation to cultural production and reproduction), just as the most frequently cited philosopher in such discourses is Nietzsche, one of the most devastating critics of modernity and, one might add, orthodox historiography.

Any acquaintance with Benjamin's *Arcades Project*, with his prehistory of modernity, reveals that it, too, is not conceived as an orthodox history of modernity. Indeed, as many commentators have pointed out, his prehistory of modernity has some affinities with his earlier project, *The Origin of German Tragic Drama*, which was published in January 1928, at a time when he had already commenced work on his *Arcades Project*. As its title suggested, it was concerned with the 'origin' of the neglected seventeenth-century *Trauerspiel*. As Benjamin declares there:

origin [*Ursprung*], although an entirely historical category, has, nevertheless, nothing to do with genesis [*Entstehung*]. The term origin is not intended to describe the process by which the existent came into being, but rather to describe that which emerges from the process of becoming and disappearance. Origin is an eddy in the stream of becoming...Origin is not...discovered by the examination of actual findings, but it is related to their history and subsequent development.[1]

This means that actual research findings are neither left 'unarranged and unordered (inductionism)' nor are they projected 'into a pseudo-logical continuum (deductionism)'. Rather, Benjamin proceeds monadologically, on the assumption that 'every idea contains the image of the world', that relevant findings are those whose 'innermost structure appears to be so essential as to reveal it as an origin'. Methodologically, this commits Benjamin to a search for 'that which is *exemplary,* even if this everyday character can be admitted only in respect of the merest fragmen'.[2]

The constellation of images that impress us in reading Benjamin's *Vorrede* to the *Trauerspiel* study are those of the fragment, the monad, the mosaic, the redemption of phenomena and the search for origin. Its substantive treatment of the seventeenth-century German *Trauerspiel* brings together a constellation or configuration of melancholy, allegory and the ruin. All return in a different guise in his prehistory of modernity. To take the example of allegory and ruin, Benjamin seeks to establish that 'an appreciation of the transience of things, and the concern to rescue them for eternity, is one of the strongest impulses in allegory', and that 'allegory establishes itself most permanently where transitoriness and eternity confronted each other most closely'.[3]

Later, Benjamin suggests that, it may have been Balzac who was 'the first to speak of the ruins of the bourgeoisie', and Surrealism 'which first allowed its gaze to roam freely over them'.[4] And it was surely Benjamin whose archaeology of modernity excavated the ruins of the nineteenth century and all that was still attached to them. But it was Baudelaire who dramatically defined modernity as precisely that explosive constellation and confrontation of transitoriness and eternity which Benjamin so closely associated with allegory. 'By modernity', Baudelaire declared, 'I mean the transitory, the fleeting, the fortuitous, the half of art whose other half is the eternal and the immutable'. Modernity, for Baudelaire, constitutes both a 'quality' of modern life as well as a new object of aesthetic activity, both associated with experience of the newness of the present 'in trivial life, in the daily metamorphosis of external things'. The painter of modern life must be able to capture its fleeting beauty in order to become 'the painter of the passing moment and of all the suggestions of eternity that it contains'.[5]

Yet Baudelaire was not a social theorist intent on exploration of the origins of modernity, despite his own perceptive grouping of the metropolis, the crowd, fashion, the *flâneur* and the modern hero around his concept of modernity. None the less, the first half of his definition of modernity does provide us with a concept of modernity as signifying the discontinuous experience of time as transitory, space as fleeting or ephemeral, and causality as fortuitous, contingent and arbitrary. In turn, these three dimensions of modern experience indicate, respectively, experience of an eternal present, an indeterminacy and destruction of space, and the absence of historical necessity. Extended in this manner, they find some resonance at least in three dimensions of modernity indicated by Baudelaire's contemporary, Karl Marx (in his *Communist Manifesto*, *Capital*, *Grundrisse*, and elsewhere): as the revolutionary new destruction of the past, the ever-new destruction of the present, and the ever-same reproduction of the 'socially necessary illusion' of the commodity form as a barrier to a qualitatively different future. Experience of modernity thus manifests itself to us as the destruction of the past (though traces remain) and the forgetting of historical specificity, as a disintegrating present (in part, through the universalization of the commodity form and urban destruction necessary for the acceleration of the circulation sphere), and as the illusions of the surface, particularly in 'the daily traffic of bourgeois life', in the sphere of circulation and exchange of commodities.[6]

And, with respect to the origin of modernity, both Marx and that other critic of modernity, Nietzsche, shared the view that a significant feature of modernity is fear of origin. The absolutely new does not wish to explore origin. Despite the incomplete and sketchy account of the origins of capital accumulation in Marx's *On Primitive Accumulation* – more accurately *On Original Accumulation* – its predominant features in no way corresponded to the mythical origins of accumulation provided either by what Marx termed 'Crusoeades' or assertions of the 'natural' existence of capital by vulgar economy. Similarly, it was Benjamin, in *Central Park*, who pointed to one dimension of Nietzsche's response to questions of origin and future when he claimed that 'the significance of the notion of the Eternal Return lies in the fact that the bourgeoisie no longer dares to look the impending development of the mode of production which it set in motion in the eye. Zarathustra's notions of the eternal return and the motto of the cushion cover, "Just a short nap", complement one another.'[7]

Of course, Nietzsche's critique of modernity (and we should not forget that he declares, in *Beyond Good and Evil*, that 'this book...is in all essentials a critique of modernity' – an intention equally apposite for many of his other works) moves in many other directions, including a critique of historicism and the predominance of 'the unhistorical'. There is, too, the delineation of entrapment in an immediate, superficial present. The culture of modernity is preoccupied with the newest fashions, inward hasty grasp and exploitation of ephemera, indeed of the momentary: and absolutely nothing else! As a result, it is embodied in the heinous nature of journalists, the slaves of the three M's: of the moment [*Moment*], of opinions [*Meinungen*] and of fashions [*Moden*]; and the more an individual has affinities with this culture the more will they look like journalists.[8]

For Nietzsche, albeit in a more muted manner than Marx, things in the world of general circulation (opinions, fashions, etc.) are experienced as dissociated and dislocated. The fragmentary chaos of the surface of life calls forth another characteristic of modernity for Nietzsche – the 'preponderance of the dealer and intermediary persons' (the *Vermittler*): a fourth 'M', the mediator (concerned with means, with *Mitteln*).[9]

Even such limited aspects of the work of Baudelaire, Marx and Nietzsche should indicate not merely that there are many themes in their work which Benjamin could draw upon for his own prehistory of modernity, but also that these and other themes are present in current theories of postmodernity. Indeed, some of the experiences of modernity reappear in accentuated form as putative experiences of postmodernity.

II

Just how little Benjamin's prehistory of modernity was a celebration of modernity can be seen immediately from two of his 'definitions' of modernity: 'The world dominated by its phantasmagorias...this is modernity' (V, 77), and 'The new in the context of what has always been there' (V, 1010). Both focus upon representations of the world and the world of things. The first statement has affinities with Marx's notion of 'socially necessary illusion', an illusory world created by the commodity form and its fetishisms. The second statement could also be interpreted with reference to the commodity form, to the commodity's ever-new face; but it can also be fused with Nietzsche's notion of the ever-same in such a manner that the ever-new masks the ever-same. At all events, Benjamin's prehistory of modernity goes in search of the phantasies, the nature of their representation, the sources of their domination, and the sources of newness, the absolutely new that hides the old.

Benjamin explores modernity in such dialectical images as those of modernity and antiquity, the masses and the city, the new and the ever-same, in order to build up a constellation of interrelated dimensions of modernity. In these and other dialectical images there is a conscious abandonment of linear progression from the premodern to the modern: antiquity, for instance, is recognized as lying in modernity itself. Antinomies are dissolved in dialectical images. The arcade is constituted by both interior and exterior space. Further, each object of Benjamin's attention is viewed multidimensionally: the metropolis is both the site of the circulation of commodities and the circulation of individuals (including individuals as commodities); at the same time, the metropolis is examined as the locus of representations not merely of decreptitude and antiquity but of dreams and desires. Similarly, when Benjamin seeks to explicate his methodological intentions in exploring the prehistory of modernity, he often has recourse to figures who themselves are multidimensional: the archaelogist of the topography of Paris must also be an allegorist; the collector is both the collector of fragments of high culture and the rag-picker; the *flâneur* as investigator of urban experience and its traces can become the detective. And the author of the *Arcades Project* himself participates in the activities of these figures.

What is Benjamin's starting point? It is the Parisian arcade as the 'historical signature of modernity', as one of 'the phenomenal forms of the dreaming collectivity of the nineteenth century'. The arcades which concern Benjamin are located in Paris as the capital of the nineteenth century, Paris as *the* city of modernity. Why Paris and not, say, London as the centre of capital itself? Benjamin's choice of Paris indicates a crucial feature of his project, a political intention to force or explode the origins of his modernity into our present, indeed, as Kracauer suggested, in order 'to wake the world from its dream'.[10] One of Benjamin's dialectical images makes this connection between modernity and Paris: 'That which is modern stands in opposition to the ancient, the new in opposition to the ever-same. (Modernity: the masses; antiquity: the city of Paris)' (V, 164–5). For Benjamin, there are two Parises: the one is the Paris of capital, of lethargy trapped in the mythical forces of the commodity, of fashion (as natural phenomena) and in its myth-laden monuments to itself; the other is the Paris of revolts and revolution (1789, 1830, 1848, 1871), as an active historical volcano. It is this second dimension that is more difficult to discover for London, especially after the defeat of Chartism, in contrast to this dialectical juxtaposition of the mythological, static representations of the city (for Baudelaire, the city as decor) and the activity of the masses as locus of social movement (Blanqui and a social movement opposed to the 'evil new').

Within this city of Paris, then, are the arcades – 'constructions or passages which have no outside – like the dream'. The entrance to the arcades is a threshold to illusion and fantasy, an entrance to 'the world of the secret life of the commodity', to 'the primal landscape of consumption' (already explored in Aragon's *Paris Peasant*). Its glass-covered passage is an interior that is exterior. It is part of the paradigmatic ensemble of arcade, panorama and mirror which enclose newness, fashion, the theology of modernity, fantasy (including sexual fantasy and prostitution). Arcades are the temporal space (*Zeitraum*) of the nineteenth century as a temporal dream (*Zeittraum*). The arcade is both an edifice (*Häuser*) and passage (*Gänge*), a transit without transition, the atemporal location of society at a standstill. The uncertainty and variability of its lighting gives the sense of entering an indeterminate spectral realm. By extension, the panorama in which the exterior landscape or prospect is located in the interior more fully accords with the notion of a monad. It is an interior within whose windowless edifice the truth appears to reside. But whereas the proper role of the monad is reflection or manifestation, that of the panorama is projection (of an exterior). In fact, it is the edifice within which the projection of history, fixed in a moment of time, is housed. In turn, the proliferation of the mirrors of the arcade, cafe, bar, restaurant, constitute a dilation of space, thereby producing a multiplicity of perspectives, a surreal labyrinth.[11]

If we were to follow through this constellation of edifices and techniques of representation, we would move through the shop windows of the grand boulevards, the vertical stratification of its façades, the horizontal stratification of its developments as we move from its central edifices; the seemingly transient iron and glass constructions of glass houses and then world exhibition centres (displaying their dead commodities at a standstill); the early department stores with layered balconies and glass canopies and acceleration of circulation of the mass article (and accompanying circulation of images and individuals), and today, the modern shopping mall, multilayered and with multiperspectives, a mixed form of the department store and the earlier arcade, with a return of the relatively highly-priced commodity and a rapid circulation of customers. For its part, the panorama and its many variants is the early form of technology associated with changing representations of the exterior, and was to be extended with the development of film and the cinematograph, and later the private monad of the television set (for some, the average number of hours spent before this newest monad – which communicates monologically – signified the arrival of postmodernity). It was Benjamin's intention to extend his analysis from the arcade to the whole Parisian metropolis of the Second Empire. How was this possible methodologically?

Benjamin's starting point is the exploration of the remains of modernity; 'the trivia, the refuse' of modernity are to be extracted from the 'encrusted surface' of reality. The concern is thus with the surface phenomena, however insignificant: 'The rags, the refuse: I will not describe but rather display them' (V, 1030). Yet the early aim of a 'literary montage' of fragments was already to be distanced from Aragon's surrealist montage: 'Whereas Aragon stands firmly in the realms of the dream, here the constellation of awakening is to be found...The aim here is the destruction

[*Auflösung*] of mythology in the historical realm. Of course, this can only take place by means of the awakening of a still unconscious knowledge of what has taken place.' (V, 1014) The search for origin and destruction are ultimately connected. This deconstructionist intention of reducing the world to rubble accords with a task of 'the destructive character' who 'reduces what exists to ruins, not in order to create ruins, but in order to find the way that leads through them'.[12] As in his early work, Benjamin holds on to the monadological significance of the fragment. His method is 'to build up the major constructions out of the smallest and precisely manufactured building blocks. Indeed, to discover in the analysis of the smallest individual elements the crystal of the totality of what exists' (V, 1014).

The fragments are to be analysed with the aid of dialectical images, the critical constellation of the past and present moment, in which the dialectical image explodes the past into 'now time' (*Jetztzeit*), the 'tiger's leap' into the present. In a positive sense, the dialectical image of the past constellation that is our present is intended to shock us into recognition of our world as a dream world, as a world of masks, façades, illusions, indeed of phantasmagorias.

The exploration of the prehistory of modernity must also dispose of one of the strongest narcotics of the nineteenth century and beyond: historicism. Historicism places all elements of the past in a reified continuity and views the present as a linear continuum from the past. For Benjamin, 'the materialist presentation of history leads the past to place the present in a critical condition', by breaking that continuum through an exploration of 'the numbered group of threads that represent the weft of the past as it feeds into the warp of the present'.[13] The destructive element of shattering the continuum of history is decisive.

One way of illuminating Benjamin's method with regard to his exploration of the site of modernity is to refer to three figures whose significance extends beyond the metaphorical: the archaeologist/critical allegorist, the collector/refuse collector; the *flâneur*/detective. They all are concerned with the analysis of fragments, whether as fossils, as refuse or as urban signs and interactions.

It has been suggested by Sagnol that Benjamin's prehistory of modernity has affinities with Foucault's archaeology of modernity.[14] Certainly, it can be argued that Benjamin, too, is an archaeologist of modernity, one who retains his links with his earlier monadological procedure, but now directed, for instance, at the arcade as monad, as a world in miniature. In 'Excavate and Remember', he states that 'whoever seeks to gaze more closely at one's own buried past must proceed like a person who excavates' (*Ausgraben und Erinnern*; IV, 400). This involves locating the fragments, examining the layers of earth/history/intepretations above them that have encrusted and obscured them, and requires, too, proceeding with a plan, creating a topography. Thus, the archaeologist not merely deciphers the signs and traces of the past, but also the dream and fantasies: 'the dream – that is the earth in which the finds will be made which provide evidence of the prehistory [*Urgeschichte*] of the nineteenth century' (V, 140). The excavation of such dreams requires, too, that the archaeologist also be a critical allegorist.

However, for Benjamin, the dreams are also located in urban structures themselves: that is, above ground level in architecture, streets, the interior. The archaeologist must excavate 'the dream houses of the collectivity: arcades, winter gardens, panoramas, factories, waxworks, railway stations', etc. (V, 511). A critical topography of his archaeological site of Paris is Benjamin's aim: 'To build up the city topographically, 10 times and 100 times over out of its arcades and its gates, its cemeteries and brothels, its railway stations' (V, 134–5). It is an activity that decisively breaks with historicism. As Anna Stüssi has commented:

> For Benjamin, the past never lies merely 'behind' – it has not been disposed of – but rather 'below' in the depths. In the present it lies subliminally contemporaneous...the city still stands in whose ground its own past lies hidden. The present-day city transforms itself in the light of remembrance into an excavated one that bears testimony to the time of the past. Archaeology takes place on the showplace of modernity.[15]

The exploration of the complex labyrinths of the showplace of modernity by the archaeologist of modernity forces a recognition of antiquity in modernity: 'Modernity possesses antiquity like a nightmare that creeps over it in slumber' (V, 309). The examination of 'the phenomenal forms' of the showplace of modernity also requires means to penetrate them. Benjamin refers to the 'ultra violet knowledge' of the city provided by the photograph, which captures the individual element and image, and the 'ultra red knowledge' of the city provided by the city plan, which captures the whole topography.

In the case of the individual element, the fragment, how can they be brought into meaningful connection with one another? Here, the ambiguous figure of the collector is instructive. Collecting itself is, for Benjamin, 'a form of practical remembrance': 'the true method of making things contemporaneous is to conceive of them...within our space: this the collector does' (V, 273). Fragments, individual objects, are re-assembled by bringing them into contact with those things with which they have affinity in order to restore their meaning. But the collector, like the archaeologist, must be aware of the traditions (socially constructed) through which the fragment or object has been received and handed down.

The fragment therefore 'bears historical scars which must be of interest to critical observers'.[16] The collector is active, however, in a different though related sense, as the rag-picker, picking – with a strong tactile sense – through the insignificant refuse of modernity.

The rag-picker's location is the alleys and byways of the labyrinth of the city. The figure who most fully explores the wider labyrinth of the metropolis is the *flâneur*. The *flâneur* goes 'botanizing on the asphalt' in order to seek out 'images wherever they are housed' (III, 196). The *flâneur* passes through the labyrinthine world of the arcade, the streets and 'the newest labyrinth', the masses. It was suggested by Bloch that the *Arcades Project* itself was a 'documentarium', a collection of seemingly miscellaneous documents that were 'viewed by a *metaphysical flâneur*' – Benjamin himself.[17] The *flâneur*'s search for images, urban signs, fleeting interactions, suggests that the more earnest the figure becomes, the more the flâneur is transformed into the detective (Benjamin, too, may be seen as detective in the Bibliothèque National). At all events, the *flâneur* is to be distinguished from the mere idler or stroller: 'Distraction and amusement as contrast to *flânerie*. The *badaud* of the distracted. Isolation and nonconformity of the *flâneur*. Contemplative residue transformed into the armed watchfulness of the hunter' (VII, 743).

Although the *flâneur* was originally associated with the arcades, the figure became one who explored the whole metropolis. If we now return briefly to *Paris, Capital of the Nineteenth Century*, we can indicate in summary form some of the dimensions of the metropolis as showplace of modernity which Benjamin excavates. The order in which they are presented here is not that which he intended in any of his own topographical plans.

If the arcade is the starting point of Benjamin's project, then it is only one of the 'fully insignificant places where dreams come into their own...The labyrinth of buildings in the city resembles consciousness in broad daylight'. That labyrinth is crucially structured by the social space of circulation, the streets themselves. The streets can appear as monuments, as when Haussmann unveiled new sections of the grand boulevards; in turn, the boulevards could appear as security against revolution and civil war; they could also constitute a new kind of interior for the bourgeoisie – an open arcade, as it were, a showcase of modernity; the streets could also be the home of the masses, their permanently fought-over public sphere.

However, the place of maximum security appeared to be the bourgeois *interieur* itself, an inner retreat populated by myths and dreams. Benjamin suggests that 'the *interieur* of this period is itself a stimulus to intoxication and the dream', and that to live within it is to be trapped 'within a spider's web that dispersed the events of the world, hung up like the dried out bodies of insects' (V, 286). The interior, in seeking to hide the traces of transitoriness, was full of styles and masks (Egyptian, Persian, etc.) and casings (the source of clues for the detective who emerged at the same time).

But, returning to the city, to the exterior, Benjamin explores the significance of the mass as 'the newest and least researched labyrinth' (V, 559), an object that is crucial, too, for Baudelaire: 'For Baudelaire, Paris stands as a testimony of antiquity, in contrast to its masses as testimony of modernity' (V, 437). The streets are therefore not merely decor for the showplace of modernity but, away from the grand boulevards, the home, even the interior, of the collectivity. This collectivity appears in three forms. It appears as the crowd, an abstract collectivity of individuals whose unpleasant proximity of confrontations is hidden by physiognomies, as counterforces to the shock experience of the electric force of the crowd; it appears as mass of consumers with the development of the department store where 'consumers began for the first time to feel themselves as a mass' – a mass consuming the mass article; and finally, the mass periodically appeared on the streets of Paris as a mass movement: social movement in opposition to movement of the commodity.

As Benjamin's project developed, it was the commodity form which acquired an increasingly prominent position in his prehistory, and especially in the dialectical image of the new and the ever-same. His project had commenced with the phenomenal life of the commodity, from its auratic life in the arcade, through its mass life in the department store, its public, frozen life in world exhibitions (including instruction for the masses: 'look at everything, touch nothing') and its public, human life in prostitution (the human commodity).

It is this seemingly trivial thing, the commodity (for Marx, the economic 'cell form' of capitalism), which Benjamin analyses in the dialectical image of the new and the ever-same; the ever-new face of the commodity highlighted by fashion and advertising, and the ever-same realization of exchange value and the maintenance of the social relations necessary for the permanent production of the ever-new. Modernity itself is explored as the techniques for the reproduction of the ever-new and the continuous shock of the new. The commodity signifies both the phantasmagoria of modernity (its allegorical effect) and the new in the context of what has always been there.

III

Benjamin's prehistory of modernity was a project firmly located in his own experience of modernity (including the vanguard city of Weimar Berlin, Paris of the Popular Front and outbreak of war and, at a distance, Nazi

Germany and its posthistorical, antimodern project).[18] In what sense can we say that Benjamin's prehistory of modernity has affinities with, or can be identified with, a prehistory of postmodernity? There is, as yet, no prehistory of postmodernity as a project understood in Benjamin's sense. That which is deemed postmodernity must, however, have a history that is located in modernity itself. Indeed, it may be that, as Calinescu and others have argued, postmodernity should be viewed as another new face of modernity itself, an accentuation of dimensions of existence already found in modernity.[19]

Such a location for postmodernity is, of course, rejected by all those who see postmodernity as a reaction to and break with modernity. Benjamin, searching for the prehistory of modernity, did not succumb to the need to put a precise date on those origins. Today, however, it is perhaps ironical that those who assert the existence of posthistory as a constituent feature of postmodernity should wish to be precise. The most extreme version of this is Charles Jencks's assertion, in *The Language of Postmodern Architecture*, that Modernism in architecture terminated on 15 July 1972 with the demolition by explosives of a housing estate in St Louis, Missouri.[20] Elsewhere, Jencks argues more cautiously that Postmodern architecture emerged around 1960 as a set of plural departures from Modernism.[21] Others suggest the break came in the early 1950s, when the average US adult spent four or more hours a day before a television set. Jameson associates postmodernity with changes in the nature of modern capitalism: 'The case for its existence depends on the hypothesis of some radical break or *coupure*, generally, traced back to the end of the 1950s or the early 1960s'.[22] Lyotard argues that the postmodern condition 'designates the state of our culture following the transformations which, *since the end of the nineteenth century*, have altered the game rules for science, literature and the arts' and ushered in an 'incredulity towards meta-narratives', towards the grand narratives of the objective spirit, Enlightenment, social totality, absolute beauty, liberation.[23]

Such imprecision also characterizes many of the debates on modernity and modern society, associated sometimes with its emergence around 1500,[24] or identified at others with the Enlightenment and the late eighteenth century.[25] Many of the discourses on modernity and postmodernity are grounded in particular conceptions of the nature, development and transformation of capitalism. Thus, Benjamin assumes, often implicitly, that Marx, in *Capital* at least, is writing about mature or high capitalism (Baudelaire is a lyric poet in 'high' capitalism). The end of modernity might then be associated with the demise of 'late' capitalism. But what if we assume that capitalism as a socio-economic formation is only at its beginning? Then would it not be appropriate to see modernity in the same light? Such a shift in perspective would then also challenge the connections between changes in 'late' capitalism and modernity/ postmodernity.

At all events, a change in the nature of capitalism is one of the features posited by discourses on postmodernity. Most radically, it has been argued that we live in post-capitalist societies; more often, postmodernity is associated with a posited post-industrial or post-production society. A possible meaning of the latter is that what is associated traditionally with industrial production now takes place elsewhere, outside the metropolitan core (e.g. no longer in the USA but increasingly in South-East Asia or elsewhere). Yet capitalism as a *world system* can function perfectly well where a major part of the production of commodities takes place outside metropolitan areas (the core). The metropolitan core can then concentrate on the production of comodities associated with the sphere of circulation, exchange and consumption (from a variety of services, from financial to personal, leisure, images, and a technology necessary for the maintenance of a world system).

The presumed shift away from the centrality of the production sphere to the centrality of the sphere of circulation, exchange and consumption (and the growing significance of leisure and/as consumption) is one which has attracted considerable attention from postmodern theorists. The implications of this shift extend also to other features of postmodernity, such as a preoccupation with the surface of existence, the existence of self-referential systems and the centrality of an apparently autonomous aesthetic sphere.

If we return to Benjamin's prehistory of modernity, and to his multilayered, cross-referenced notes for the *Arcades Project* (listed A to Z), we find that there is no entry for production, but a number of entries associated with consumption and circulation (of commodities, individuals and capital), e.g. A: Arcades, department stores, calicot; B: Fashion; E: Haussmannisation (in part); G: Exhibitions, Advertisements; M: *Flâneur* (in part); O: Prostitution, Gambling; U: Saint Simon, Railways; G: Stock exchange, economic history (V, 81). The longest section of notes is on Baudelaire, who is located in relation to almost all the topics of Benjamin's compendium. And the majority of the entries are related to issues surrounding *representation*. Indeed, we can go further and suggest a closer connection with our present theme. Benjamin notes that Baudelaire's social experiences of modernity 'nowhere derive from the production process – least of all in its most advanced form the industrial process – but all of them originated in it in extensive roundabout ways...The most important among them are the experiences of the neurasthenic, of the big-city dweller, and of the customer.'[26]

Despite the crucial exceptions of the author as producer and cultural production and reproduction (also of representations), Benjamin's three experiences ascribed to Baudelaire are instructive. The neurasthenic denotes the individual inner experience (*Erlebnis*) of the private individual and is thus associated with the interior, inward retreat, inner response to the metropolis and the commodity, (and the speed and shock of circulation of both) and a dream world. The big-city dweller denotes the constellation of experiences in the metropolis, the city and its façades, dream edifices, its population, the masses. The customer denotes experience of consumption, circulation of individuals, the commodity and its various housings.

Further, in so far as the experience of capitalism focuses upon the sphere of circulation, exchange and consumption of commodities, it denotes the most common experience of the phenomenal forms of capitalist society. It is one which veils class divisions and the social relations necessary for the phenomenal forms to appear in the manner in which they do so. Marx refers to it as 'the daily traffic of bourgeois life', a 'movement which proceeds on the surface of the bourgeois world', in which 'the motion of exchange values, their circulation, proceed in its pure form'.[27] It is a form without content. Benjamin suggests that 'the devaluation of the world of objects in allegory is outdone within the world of objects itself by the commodity'.[28] It is this sphere in which the commodity as allegory resides; it is one in which we experience the re-enchantment of the world (contra Max Weber's thesis on *Entzauberung*), in which the commodity is enveloped in 'mystery', in 'magic and necromancy'. A new 'veil' is created around social relations in which 'the participants in the capitalist process live in a bewitched and distorted world'. The sphere of circulation and exchange is a seemingly autonomous sphere, devoid of permanent referents: Benjamin noted that the stock exchange can represent anything, the crystal palace can be used for anything.

A second feature of postmodernity which has already been intimated is the end of grand narratives, the end of history, and the end of society as totality. In this context, Benjamin was unceasing in his attack upon the continuum of history generated by historicism and its associated grand narrative of progress, crucially distorting social movements intent on social transformation. More generally, Benjamin's prehistory of modernity presupposes no pre-existing totality, rather it starts out from the fragments (in contrast to the Hegelian-Marxist analyses of Lukács and Adorno).

The putative end of history as grand narrative is responded to in a variety of ways, according to postmodern theory: a plurality of styles that play, often ironically, with past styles (most noticeably in architecture); a new historicism associated with imaginary museums of the past and nostalgia. A prehistory of postmodern architecture, in this context, might focus upon nineteenth-century historicism (with its multi-layered historical façades that hide the purpose of buildings). The sense of loss of tradition is responded to by the search for a non-existent past, for artificial communities. Again, Benjamin takes the historicism of the nineteenth century as symptomatic for a thirst for the past that is realized in masks, museums, façades and the like.

A presumed feature of postmodernity is the shift from differentiation to de-differentiation.[29] The most significant dimension of this shift has been viewed as the collapse of the difference between high and low culture. It is here that Benjamin's work on the reproduction of the work of art and the accompanying loss of aura is most often cited: 'Within mass production there is one thing of quite unique significance for the decline of aura: this is the massive reproduction of images' (V, 425). Certainly, Benjamin was one of the earliest theorists of the reproduction of works of art and images. It remains an open question, however, as to whether the collapse of the high/low culture divide has come about (studies such as those of Bourdieu suggest that the issue is more complex and that cultural reception and consumption is still differentiated).[30]

A dimension of postmodernity sometimes associated with the dedifferentiation process is the disintegration of the modern personality, the presumed fragmentation of the human subject (into narcissism, schizophrenia). More apposite might be an analysis which developed Benjamin's reworking of the distinction between individual, inner, lived-out experience (*Erlebnis*) and concrete social experience (*Erfahrung*), the former characteristic of modernity, the latter to be constituted by Benjamin's project itself (i.e. wakening from the dream world, from the world of phantasmagorias).

In this context, and amongst the many dimensions of Benjamin's explorations of modernity, three may be highlighted. The first is his investigation of the transformation of experience and perception (including also the non-visual, tactile sense) in modernity itself. Second, his detailed discussion of the representations of modernity, their significance and their transformation (media in the broadest sense, including fashion, as well as architecture and streetscape media). Third, his exploration of what Simmel referred to earlier as 'the culture of things' and what Benjamin himself termed 'the extinct world of things'.

His approach to representations is itself a stimulating one. The world (including that of modernity) is a text or series of texts for us to read. However, these texts can be presented initially in dreams (their reading requires awakening), in picture-puzzles (their reading requires a solution) and in hieroglyphics (their reading requires deciphering). These largely unwritten texts confront us as images in the city, its architecture, its objects, etc. They are seldom coherent and systematic, since they present themselves to us as fragments, sometimes as ruins. Benjamin is concerned with the issue of how and when we are able to decipher the images that are presented to us: in other words, with the problem of 'the coming to legibility' of images.

A dimension of postmodernity, and one which plays a prominent role in Benjamin's exploration of modernity is the transformation of representations. There are two aspects of this transformation highlighted by many postmodern theorists: first, a perceived shift from discourse to figuration (signs, icons) and the proliferation of images, and second, the problematization of the relationship between signifier and referent (in which the signifier *is* the referent). Certainly, Benjamin's detailed investigations of representations (including the commodity itself) are of importance here; so, too, in his study of the relationship between allegory and commodity. In this context, we would have to ask whether Baudrillard's assertion that we now consume only the images of commodities (the illusion of the illusion) is not already prefigured in Benjamin's own analysis.[31]

At this point, we should emphasize once more that the sphere of representation *par excellence* is that of circulation and exchange. Our experience of this sphere as autonomous has three implications. First, the sphere of circulation and exchange is a self-referential system. Its elements refer to other elements of this system. It is, stated differently, one that is dominated by an internal referential system. Second, outside the economic sphere, we can see the significance of this in Postmodernism's emphasis upon textuality. If one difference between the projects of modernity and postmodernity is that, in some variants of Modernism, reality is a text, whereas in Postmodernism, the text is reality, then we should note Benjamin's methodological statement that: 'The phrase "the book of nature" indicates that we can read reality like a text. That will be the approach here to the reality of the 19th century. *We open the book of past events*'.[32]

Third, this self-referential system is one which does not immediately give us access to that which lies beneath the surface of phenomenal forms. If we assert that this sphere of surface manifestations, representations, and phenomenal form *is* reality, then there can be no critique of that which it *represents*. There can be no critique of 'socially necessary illusion', no critique of ideology. Benjamin's starting point, however, is 'the object riddled with error', '"the object in itself" is not "in truth"'.[33] None the less, his position here is more complex. It is not so much that there is a 'beneath' in his critique that is separate from representation; rather, what is important or significant in 'the products of false consciousness...merely peeps out from behind the clouds, the foliage, the shadows' (III, 223). At all events, knowledge of the truth is associated with transcendence of illusion without 'the evaporation...of the object', but having rendered 'oneself sceptical of the "now" in things' (V, 1034).

Finally, the experience of postmodernity is often asserted to be accompanied by the increased significance of the aesthetic mode of apprehension of reality. David Harvey, for instance, suggests that 'the confidence of an era can be assessed by the width of the gap between scientific and moral reasoning. In periods of confusion and uncertainty, the turn to aesthetics (of whatever form) becomes more pronounced'.[34] What Harvey has in mind here is not merely an interest in aesthetics, but an aestheticization of reality, the beautification of the world instead of its transformation. Benjamin intended that his prehistory of modernity should extend down to *Jugendstil*, to an artistic movement committed to beautification. However, we can return to a significant connection with the first dimension of postmodernity outlined above: the apparent domination of the sphere of circulation and exchange. This sphere, too, creates its aesthetic appearance/illusion (*Schein*). As Simmel noted, 'aesthetic judgement...connects with *the mere image of things*, with their appearance and form, *regardless of whether they are supported by an apprehendable reality*'.[35] The symmetry of circulation and exchange is such a process, creating the 'beautiful illusion' of the sublime.

Benjamin's dialectical images of modernity were intended to force us out of our dream world, our phantasmagoria. He was sceptical of the announcement of the absolutely new as anything other than an essential illusory dimension of modernity. If phantasmagorias are a key to Benjamin's prehistory of modernity, then the simulacrum is a key feature in Baudrillard's putative postmodern society. The *Oxford English Dictionary* suggests affinities between the two:

> *Phantasmagoria.* An exhibition of optical illusions produced chiefly by means of the magic lantern first given in London in 1802.
> A shifting series of phantasms or imaginary figures as seen in a dream or fevered condition, or as called up by the imagination, 1828.
> *Simulacrum.* A material image, made as a representation of some deity, person or thing.
> Something having merely the form or appearance of a certain thing 1805.
> A mere image, a specious imitation, or likeness, of something, 1833.[36]

If indeed the origins of phantasmagorias and simulacra coincide, then does this not suggest that a prehistory of postmodernity is overdue?

If we ask why it is that Benjamin's work seems so contemporary to us, and has done so for over a decade – and this is particularly true of the *Arcades Project* – then is this not because there are affinities between the past he constructed and our recent present? Are we reliving, in a new form, dimensions of experience similar to those in the Second Empire? Its economic foundation was a dramatic increase in capital in the circulation sphere (speculation, fictitious capital, land/property speculation) that has affinities with that which Harvey associates with forms of flexible accumulation today.[37] Has not the past decade in some Western societies seen a phenomenal increase in the domination of this sphere, of circulation, exchange and consumption?

Whatever the answer to these questions, Benjamin's *Arcades Project* forces us to rethink the origins of modernity and its experiential transformations, not in terms of a chronology, but as a continuous process of 'coming to legibility', as a process of emergence. It constitutes one of the most stimulating attempts to explore multidimensionally the site of the metropolis and modernity (including archaeological and topographical explorations), as well as cultural productions in modernity. Many facets of his investigations are relevant for the exploration of the advent of that which Benjamin's work did *not* annouce: postmodernity.

NOTES

1. W. Benjamin, *The Origins of German Tragic Drama*, trans. John Osborne (London, 1977), pp. 45 and 46. Abbreviated references to the German edition of Benjamin's works, *Gesammelte Schriften*, ed. R. Tiedemann and H. Schweppenhäuser, 7 vols (Frankfurt/Main, 1974–) are given in parentheses (volume and page number).
2. W. Benjamin, *The Origins of German Tragic Drama*, pp. 43 and 44.
3. W. Benjamin, *The Origins of German Tragic Drama*, pp. 223 and 224.
4. W. Benjamin, *Charles Baudelaire: A Lyric Poet in the Era of High Capitalism*, (London, 1973),p. 176.
5. C. Baudelaire, *The Painter of Modern Life and Other Essays*, trans. John Mayne (London, 1964), pp. 3 and 4.
6. K. Marx, *Grundrisse*, trans. Martin Nichlaus (Harmondsworth, 1973), p. 251.
7. W. Benjamin, 'Central Park', in *New German Critique*, 34, p. 46
8. F. Nietzsche, *Sämtliche Werke: Kritische Studienausgabe*, ed. G. Colli and M. Montinari, vol. 7 (Berlin, New York, 1980), p. 817.
9. Cited in C. Asendorf, *Batterien der Lebenskraft: Zur Geschichte der Dinge und ihrer Wahrnehmung im 19. Jahrhundert* (Giessen, 1984), p. 38.
10. S. Kracauer, *Ornament der Masse* (Frankfurt, 1963), p. 253.
11. Cf. F. Desidiri, '"Le vrai n'a pas de fenêtres...": Remarques sur l'optique et la dialectique dans le Passagen-Werk de Benjamin', in *Walter Benjamin et Paris*, ed. H. Wismann (Paris, 1986), pp. 201–215, and S. Buck-Morss, *The Dialectics of Seeing* (Cambridge, MA, 1990).
12. W. Benjamin, *One-Way Street*, trans. Edmund Jephcott and Kingsley Shorter (London, 1979), p. 159.
13. W. Benjamin, *One-Way Street*, p. 362.
14. M. Sagnol, 'La méthode archéologique de Walter Benjamin', *Les temps modernes*, 40, 444, pp. 143–65.
15. A. Stüssi, *Erinnerung an die Zukunft: Walter Benjamin's 'Berliner Kindheit um Neunzehnhundert'* (Göttingen, 1977), p. 25.
16. W. Benjamin, *Charles Baudelaire: A Lyric Poet in the Era of High Capitalism*, p. 104.
17. E. Bloch, *Heritage of Our Times*, trans. Neville and Stephen Plaice (Berkeley, Los Angeles, Oxford, 1991), pp. 334–7.
18. Cf. Buck-Morss, *The Dialectics of Seeing*.
19. M. Calinescu, *Five Faces of Modernity* (Durham, 1986), pp. 263–312.
20. C. Jencks, *The Language of Post-Modern Architecture* (London, 1984).

21. C. Jencks, *What is Post-Modernism?* (London, 1986).
22. F. Jameson, *Postmodernism or, The Cultural Logic of Late Capitalism* (London, 1991), p. 1.
23. J. Lyotard, *The Postmodern Condition: A Report on Knowledge* (Minneapolis, 1984), p. xxiii. My emphasis.
24. M. Berman, *All That Is Solid Melts Into Air* (London, 1983).
25. J. Habermas, 'Modernity – An Incomplete Project', in *Postmodern Culture,* ed. H. Foster (London, 1985), and J. Habermas, *The Philosophical Discourse of Modernity,* trans. Frederick Lawrence (Cambridge, MA, 1987).
26. W. Benjamin, *Charles Baudelaire: A Lyric Poet in the Era of High Capitalism,* p. 106.
27. Marx, *Grundrisse,* pp. 254–5.
28. W. Benjamin, 'Central Park', p. 34.
29. S. Lash, *The Sociology of Postmodernism* (London, 1990).
30. Cf. P. Bourdieu, *Distinction: A Social Critique of the Judgement of Taste* (London, 1984).
31. J. Baudrillard, *For a Critique of the Political Economy of the Sign* (St Louis, 1981).
32. G. Smith, *Benjamin: Philosophy, Aesthetics, History* (Chicago, London, 1989), p. 52.
33. W. Benjamin, *Charles Baudelaire: A Lyric Poet in the Era of High Capitalism,* trans. Harry Zohn (London, 1973) p. 103.
34. D. Harvey, *The Condition of Postmodernity* (Oxford, 1989), p. 327.
35. G. Simmel, *Kant: Sechzehn Vorlesungen* (Leipzig, 1918), p. 197.
36. *The Shorter Oxford English Dictionary on Historical Principles,* 3rd edn, 2 vols (Oxford, 1973).
37. Harvey, *The Condition of Postmodernity.*

–2–

Walter Benjamin's Imaginary Landscape

Bernd Hüppauf

I

A conceptual tension between town and country can be traced back as far as the beginnings of European literary and cultural history. At times, this tension has been experienced as an antagonism, the opposition between *peasant* and *burgher* appearing irreconcilable. 'Country and town have constituted two mutually hostile areas since the beginning of civilization', writes Sorel in a text well known to Benjamin, further intensifying the opposition emphasized by Marx and echoing a topos of literature and the history of ideas.[1] In the course of the nineteenth century, however, this abrupt, economically-based contrast becomes increasingly blurred. Urban structures penetrate the countryside through the mechanization and rationalization of agriculture. The land is increasingly colonized by the city, and this transformation in the economic sphere is matched by changes in the aesthetic sphere. For Walter Benjamin, the perception and representation of landscape no longer stand in complementary opposition to the fragmenting conduct of science and technology in relation to nature; rather, they tend towards an identical model.

Another opposition, one which has, at times, been even more sharply accentuated, stretches just as far back into history: from the time of Herodotus's accounts of the Scythians onwards, urban culture and nomadism appeared to stand in irreconcilable opposition to one another. Compared to life without house or possessions, the difference between the sedentary peasant and the sedentary town-dweller appeared insignificant. The landscape of the nomad was the wide expanse, without centre or points of reference, without profundity and without any bond other than that to the wandering herds. For the citizen of the town, the nomadic always appeared as a threat: with the power and speed of a natural force, the nomads descend upon the town, taking what they need, destroying what they do not understand, and leaving in their wake a scene of devastation. The early cities of Asia Minor, the cities of Greece, Rome, the cities of medieval Europe, all felt themselves threatened by the wandering nomadic *hordes*. The Great Wall of China gives suggestive expression to this feeling of elemental threat. In a short text published in 1917 and taken from the fragment 'During the Building of the Great Wall of China' (*Beim Bau der Chinesischen Mauer*), Franz Kafka constructs the primordial scene of the clash between nomads and town-dwellers, in which not only the nomads, but also the nomadic, appear as an existential threat.[2]

In Benjamin's work, one finds an aspect which he himself positively emphasizes in an anthology devoted to the concept of landscape: namely that 'certain points' in his own work 'combine to form intellectual landscapes'. In Benjamin's imaginary landscape, town, country and nomadism are still recognizable elements, but they combine to form a new unity, with the result that a landscape emerges in which abrupt oppositions come into contact, intersect and mesh with one another. In Benjamin's imaginary landscape can be found not only 'vivid and archetypical cities, provinces and forgotten corners of the earth',[3] but also the landscape of the World War I front and that of a Utopian nature. The elements of this landscape and their construction as a whole never lose their ambivalence in Benjamin's work; but it seems that it is precisely this ambivalence which lends to this landscape its specifically modern character and facilitates instances of conceptual and metaphoric, physical and intellectual movement which point beyond Benjamin's own present to combine modern and postmodern positions.

Benjamin's landscape is first and foremost an urban landscape. The topography of the metropolis constitutes his imaginary landscape, as seen in the manner in which he constructs out of the Berlin of the turn of the century the urban environment of an idealized childhood within an upper-class milieu. In one of the pieces in this multilayered text, entitled *Tiergarten*, he addresses a number of central motifs of the theme 'landscape and city': nature and culture, labyrinth and order, tamed nature in park and garden, and wilderness, the explosion of experience (by the 'mothers of all being'), time and its 'standstill'.[4] Later, in the *Arcades Project*, he uses a topography of meanings of Paris in an attempt to spatialize the century in which temporalization celebrated its true triumphs, and he assembles materials for the construction of a city landscape which is clearly meant to transcend its own temporal space and contain within itself the experiences of the twentieth century.[5]

The question of the way in which nature, and particularly nature as landscape, belongs to the urbanized world of Benjamin's modernity leads to the observation that the image of landscape depicted by his texts is not only marked by the general, indissoluble relationship which creates nature as the result of human labour. One also comes across a specific development in which *city* and *nature as landscape* forfeit their opposition and are brought together within a comprehensive quality of the aesthetic and of technological modernity. Benjamin does not regard country and landscape exclusively with the eye of the city-dweller; in a remarkable way, town and country are structurally linked with one another. In an initially bewildering text in *One-Way Street*, Benjamin speaks of a 'mingling' and 'contamination' of the city, and of the country invading the city.

> Just as all things, in an inexorable process of mingling and contamination, are losing their intrinsic character while ambiguity displaces authenticity, so too the city. Great cities – whose incomparably sustaining and reassuring power encloses those at work within them in the peace of a fortress and lifts from them, with the view of the horizon, awareness of the ever-vigilant elemental forces – are revealed to be breached at all points by the invading countryside. Not by the landscape, but by what in untrammelled nature is most bitter: ploughed land, highways, night sky that the veil of vibrant redness no longer conceals. The insecurity of even the busy areas puts the city-dweller in the opaque and truly dreadful situation in which he must assimilate, along with the rigours of the abandoned open country, the monstrosities of urban architectonics.[6]

In this text, which, even for the unusual style of *One-Way Street,* spans an extraordinarily broad associative range, Benjamin speaks in four long and elaborately constructed sentences of the great cities of his epoch. He links them with a *power* which has a sustaining and reassuring effect and thereby encloses *those at work* in *the peace of a fortress*. This choice of words is already ambivalent. It associates the modern metropolis with a medieval fortification and, if one interprets this literally, with the tower of this fortification, which can stand for protection and the last resort of the defenders, as well as for a prison and hopelessness. Enclosed in such a peace of a fortress, the city-dweller is robbed of the *view of the horizon*. At the same time, however, the text links this elementary restriction of perception and orientation with the *sustaining and reassuring* power of the city for those at work, since in the peace of the fortress, the consciousness of the *ever-vigilant elemental forces* is also taken from them: urban productivity as a consequence of security, which at the same time means the loss of expanse, openness and orientation in space. In the subordinate clause, loss and relief, constriction and liberation are combined in a complex fashion. This complex thought is framed by the main clause: 'Great cities...are revealed to be breached at all points by the invading countryside.' The verb 'reveal' (*zeigen sich*) presupposes change, since it severs the 'appearance' of the cities from their 'essence'. It can be concluded that the city can also be thought in another way. Benjamin retains the idea of an *essence* of the city, one which is lost, however, in the city's present manifestation: its *authenticity* disappears to the extent that the closed unity of the peace of a fortress disintegrates, and the city thus forfeits its expression of essence through *mingling* and *contamination*; it declines in an *inexorable process*. This process replaces the sustaining and reassuring power, which once constituted the essence of the city, with the ambiguous.

The ambiguity arises as a result of the countryside invading the city, and that which in untrammelled nature is *most bitter* being transferred into the city. The city-dweller no longer experiences his urban environment in terms of protection and order. Rather, he is forced to assimilate this environment as if he, unprotected by the city, is now, even within the city itself, delivered over to menacing nature. In the context of the invasion of the space of the city by the *rigours of the abandoned open country*, the city's architecture becomes a *monstrous invention* in the eyes of the city-dweller. The experience of the city becomes one of horror. The concern in this dramatic process is expressly not with *landscape*; rather, Benjamin calls that which invades the city *untrammelled nature*. The close connection between the experience of an 'opaque and truly dreadful situation' of the city and 'untrammelled nature' leads to the question of the genesis and decline of the aesthetic perception of landscape.

As the development of the aesthetic gaze was tied to the loss of the premodern trust in the world, while at the same time liberating self-determined subjectivity, so now Benjamin sees in the inversion of this dual relationship in the early twentieth century a process that is just as ambivalent. The peace of a fortress characterizing the city makes possible the life of 'those at work', but only under the condition of constriction and of the loss of horizon. Security within the walls of the city goes hand in hand with the shield they provide against the 'elemental forces', which one could also call, to paraphrase another philosopher of the time, *the forgetting of nature (Naturvergessenheit)*. The image of the city which Benjamin depicts in this short text is not unlike that depicted by other authors writing at this time: for example, Spengler, Lessing and Klages. It refers back to earlier observations by Tönnies (1887) and Simmel (1903). The conjunction of constructive and destructive elements and the ambivalence of the evaluation of this intersection presupposes a break in the history of ideas. In Benjamin's city landscape, elements of two separate discourses are combined in a montage to produce a new image of the city that is linked with *country* and *landscape*.[7]

An extensive discussion has repeatedly emphasized that the modern landscape is not perceived by the senses in any simple way, but rather must be understood as the product of a complex process of historical development within which the senses, which themselves are subject to historical change, first create the landscape. The possibility of experiencing the natural environment in an aesthetic sense as landscape requires the attainment of a certain degree of independence and distance with regard to nature. Furthermore, well into the modern era, untamed, wild nature was perceived as ugly and terrifying. Only with the cultivation of a unified image of landscape did the perception of wild nature change; only then was it included in the aesthetic view.[8] A fundamental change in thought and visual perception was necessary before 'fear and horror' in the face of uncultivated nature could give way to the modern experience of fascination and the sensation of beauty. The gradual change from fear and incomprehension to the incorporation of the wild into the image of creation is a condition for the experience of nature in an aesthetic sense becoming possible. Only then does landscape become the paradigm for the experience of nature within modernity.

II

This development, as Joachim Ritter has shown, is closely connected with the formation of modern subjectivity.[9] At the end of the nineteenth century, the discourse of nature and landscape enters a phase of manifest crisis. The internalized, subjective perspective, the formation of which Ritter describes, disintegrates and no longer creates the precondition for an affective contemplation; rather, this function is now absorbed by the perspective of scientific abstraction and technical instruments. The order in the aesthetic image of landscape loses its innocence, and the power aspect of subjectivity sheds its disguises. And finally, the idea of coherent, internally structured space, within which modern landscape is constituted, proves to be culturally conditioned and relative, such that the concept of a landscape in which nature as a whole could be experienced in subjective freedom fades. In Benjamin's texts, this crisis is expressed as the inversion of the genesis of landscape, the end of subjectivity, and as the search for a re-evaluation of order and force.

In his doctoral dissertation, Benjamin already confronts the problem of the disappearance of essential nature from the physical world as a consequence of its aesthetic appropriation. In the context of Romanticism, he distinguishes between an 'authentic nature', which constitutes the content of the artwork, and the 'apparent visible' nature; these, according to Benjamin, must be strictly distinguished from one another in conceptual terms:

> in that the problem of a deeper essential identity of the 'authentic' visible nature in the artwork and of the (perhaps invisible, merely regardable [*anschaubar*], pre-phenomenal [*urphänomenal*]) nature present in the appearances of visible nature would then present itself. And this problem would possibly and

paradoxically be solved in such a way that only in art and not in the nature of the world would the authentic, regardable, pre-phenomenal nature be vividly visible, while being present but hidden (obscured by the appearance) in the nature of the world.[10]

This paradox is solved, as Benjamin shows in his later work, through the fact that the image of a nature viewed as authentically experienced, and thereby the concept of representation itself, is increasingly undermined. On the other hand, Benjamin also attempts to retain the concept of a lost, authentic nature, to which he links his Utopian landscape of liberated humanity. Town and country in this respect follow identical tendencies and become increasingly indistinguishable.

The disintegration of the rationalist image of space and its experience of landscape at the beginning of the twentieth century was accompanied by the simultaneous development of a new fascination with the concept of the nomad and nomadic thought. It is not merely coincidental that, at this time, knowledge in the fields of archeology and early history regarding the beginnings of the city and the nomads underwent rapid development. The uncertain concept of the nomad gained new contours in the academic disciplines and, for reasons which had little to do with the concept itself, was subject to re-evaluation within cultural discourse.[11] This change made possible the development of an imaginative field upon which wish-images, fears and dreams could unfold.

The image of the nomads is historically controversial. However, there is a basic stock of themes which have been preserved from the beginnings of their representation in history, ethnology and literature up until the present. Among these are the relationship of the nomads to war and external force, to space and to the natural environment, as well as the lack of stratification and the egalitarian constitution of nomadic societies. All three of these thematic areas are combined in the question of the nomadic relationship to the order of urban civilization. While this complex of questions remained more or less constant within the diverse discourses concerning nomads and the nomadic, their internal weighting and evaluation changed in decisive ways. In particular, the relationship of the nomadic to force and violence underwent a change in which can be read the principles of construction behind the image of the nomad in history, an image which was always based on the perspective of the city. The end of the literary convention of warlike nomads constitutes a decisive break. A sceptical attitude in regard to urban civilization is reflected in an altered evaluation of destruction and war, an attitude in which the fear of the nomadic disappears. The new image of the nomads developing from the early part of the twentieth century onwards owed as much as a cultural construction to the disintegration of the evolutionary historical models of the nineteenth century as it did to the deficiencies in experience of the urbanized lifeworld. In the discourse on the nomadic can be read a fundamental change in the modern mentality.

The nomads and the nomadic, without their own history from early Greek history up until the progress-orientated nineteenth century, constantly appear in the histories of urban civilizations as a threat, are dismissed and debased as 'the other'. Only after Nietzsche and Freud, had ethnologists and historians of religion initiated a revival of the memory of the origins of culture in violence and bloody sacrifice; and only after renewed emphasis, in opposition to the harmonizing conventions of the nineteenth century, had been put on the ongoing effects of these origins, which modern civilization conceals from itself at great cost, could the nomads be seen in a different light. Once the warlike, violent and cruel character of Graeco-Christian civilization was uncovered, the negative image of the nomad could be understood as a projection. To the extent that the veil with which civilization covers its own cruelty is lifted, the need for an image of the nomadic enemy was no longer perceived, and the image of an enemy armed with all the destructive features which are to be conjured away from one's own life experience-praxis faded. The otherness of the nomad becomes attractive to the extent that the practice of war, violence and destruction is recognized as one's own. The gaze now becomes free to regard other, hitherto neglected, features of nomadic mentality and life-praxis.

At the same time, the idea asserts itself that the nomadic does not pre-date the urban, but rather emerged concurrently with it and existed as its complementary form in contrast to the 'wild'. Accounts of journeys among nomads become popular. The nomadic appears in the midst of the city. The defence of the city, as Kafka's story vividly states, has long been neglected in favour of *work*, and the imperial palace which has attracted the nomads does nothing to drive them out of the city again. They do not work and, with all their disorderly filth, their lack of communication, rules and law, nevertheless have become part of the life of the city. They disturb and impede the 'businesses', but the businessmen are not in a position to ward them off or drive them away, and thus they support the nomads with food and everything they need. Kafka's archetype of the nomad is determined by elements of the violent and the warlike. While the city is the place of work and cleanliness, of trade, money, language, palace and garden, houses and stocks of goods, the nomads camp beneath the open sky, sharpen their weapons, spread filth, are cruel and speechless, know no rules and pursue the pure pleasure principle unrestricted by cultural codes. They and their horses eat meat in large quantities and become intoxicated with the warm blood and bellowing of an ox torn apart while alive. They do not use force, states the text, for they *are* the violent force: 'In the face of their attack, one steps aside and leaves them everything'. However, the text only apparently adopts the striking aspect of the urban discourse on the nomadic, its warlike violent character; for the withdrawal of a negative evaluation of nomadic violence fundamentally distinguishes it from the structure and function of the traditional discourse on nomads. In Kafka's case, the violence of the nomad is no longer based on the concealment of one's own violence and is no longer the projection of the cruelty of one's own culture onto that of the stranger. It is only a short step from this new evaluation of the nomads in a non-moral sense to the inversion of the model of evaluation: the destruction of rules and traditions, the injuring of custom and morals produces liberation.

The image of the nomad constituted an object for the projection of modern fears regarding the end of Western civilization; Spengler's 'intellectual nomad' is thus the product of an absolute lack of attachment in a technical civilization of the world as city condemned to decline.[12] However, there was also room for a mood of emergence and a Nietzschean sense of liberation. A modern need for liberation from repressive order and the constraints of civilization was able to discover in the nomadic the model of a form of life marked by a lack of attachment and a complete freedom to roam in physical as well as mental space. The warlike moment in the nomadic thus loses its menacing character and becomes, in the sense of Nietzsche's war metaphor, the necessary condition for the overcoming of decadence. Benjamin's pathos of renewal owes much to this new concept of the nomad.[13]

In the fantasies of the steppe, of the undisguised horizon and of the expansion of movement without sense of direction, was expressed the desire for a relationship to the world to which access had been buried by urban culture, a relationship that nevertheless appeared to be closer to one's own experiential history than the world of rigid, primitive cultures of hunters and gatherers. In the stylized construction of the nomadic in literary and cultural discourse, which increasingly became uncoupled from that of ethnology, was hidden the desire for access to cultural and aesthetic practices whose *last glimmer*, as Benjamin wrote, remained present in the world of modernity and could therefore be made visible and open to experience once again in order to comprehend one's own world and to change it from within.

The new image of the nomad was utilized most recently by Deleuze and Guattari for their analysis of capitalism and the psychological structure of modernity.[14] Their point of departure is the association of nomads with force, whereby they draw on the Nietzschean tradition of the viewpoint outside morality. The 'war machine' which they link to the nomad is not to be confused with disciplined, marching armies. It represents their opposite and follows other rules. It gives rise to the image of an elementary lack of discipline among warriors, who question all hierarchy, are volatile, unreliable and deceitful, and who have no fixed sense of honour. This war machine it is not instrumentalized by the state; it remains extraterritorial and works towards the constant undermining of the state's system of regulations. Nomadic thought, of which Nietzsche is their most preferred example, takes direct effect, without the mediation of authorities and institutions and is the motor of the modern counter-culture. Deleuze/Guattari develop, as the most important element of the nomadic, the concept of a space which the nomadic requires for its unfolding and which it simultaneously produces: not *striated* (cf. the French *striation*) and smooth, not already segmented by state, science or tradition. In their philosophical-literary image of the nomad, the nomadic 'war machine' battles with the state and the systems of science and culture which are based on two universals: namely, a restricted *whole* encompassed by a stable horizon and the *subject* which concentrates all being upon itself and transforms it into a 'being-for-us'. Between these two poles, truth and reality are ordered in a politically, scientifically and culturally structured mental space and governed by an epistemology with universal claims. Against the transcendental subject and the totality, the nomad sets the concrete unit of tribe-race and moves within a non-striated, horizonless milieu-space of steppe or desert.

The nomadic war machine is engaged in a permanent struggle for de-territorialization and de-codification. Its force is not that of the single act of destruction, of killing in the manner of the hunter killing his victim. In contrast to the attitude of the hunter, that of the warrior assumes a lack of differentiation or a convertibility of weapons and tools. The force of the war machine is lasting; it is not orientated to a single objective to be reached only once, but is rather the element of a social constellation. The war machine is part of an 'economy of force', and therefore an incessant process; it could only be established under the spatial-economic conditions of nomadic existence, not within societies of hunters or sedentary city-dwellers. Speed as a function of riding, of the open expanse and of the body as materialized movement, but without having as its goal the spoils of the hunt or the return to the house within the city, distinguishes the nomadic war machine from the army that the city establishes and disciplines as a means to achieve its goals. The task of the war machine is not the elimination of an enemy; war is not, in the conventional sense, its objective. With *war machine*, the text designates a feature of the nomadic or an invention of the nomads in relation to space; the smooth, non-striated space is its element: in this space it exists, develops its strength and deploys the people. Its aim is enabling the steppe or the desert, as non-segmented, non-subject-centred and controlled spaces, to grow. War is linked to this operation only in so far as states and cities as centres of power resist this restriction of their sphere of power. The war is the 'supplement' of the war machine, but is neither the condition of its possibility nor its goal. For Deleuze, it is in the *invention* of the war machine that the *essence* of the nomadic lies.[15] Its goal is revealed as lying in the destruction of the landscape of culture, and the opening of an unstructured and free space.

The boundless space of an imagined steppe and the strength of the nomadic which develops within it and subverts all regulation can be understood as the motor of the aesthetic innovations by authors of the experimenting modern. These are assimilated by Benjamin's concepts of the *barbaric* and *dispersal* (*Zerstreuung*). Benjamin's term *dispersal* is not only to be read in the sense of a mental constitution, but also in a spatial sense, following the model of the Bible: the single language and the Tower of Babel reaching to the sky contrast with the multiplicity of languages and the dispersal of the peoples into all lands, the assembly of the Jews around the temple with their dispersal throughout the world. The destruction of the centres is followed by diversity and a nomadic way of life. Following the destruction of the temple begins the boundless wandering of the Jews through the world, which opens out to them as space without the possibility for them to take possession of it.

The subversion of borders within the imagined space is a consequence of nomadic thought. If the Surrealists destroy the frontier between waking and sleep, as Benjamin states, and the threshold between narration and dream construction, between myth and technology in film becomes 'well-trodden' by a flood of images on a huge scale, so here an imaginary landscape of nomadic wandering opens out. Thresholds and borders become the object of attack; transgression becomes the goal. The fluency of 'image and language gains priority' over the ordering and meaning-positing intention, comments Benjamin regarding a quote from Breton: 'After you, beloved language.' The 'sense' (*Sinn*), the delimitation of one text from others and its identity concerns Benjamin just as little as it does the Surrealists, and his image of the modern novel and the film has just as little to do with literature. The concern here is 'literally with experience, not with theories, still less with fantasms'[16] observes Benjamin of Surrealism, which explodes the boundaries of the literary through de-codification. Benjamin calls for a reading of literature and film which interprets them as a site of destruction itself, as perpetrators in the continuation of war in post-war discourses and, at the same time, as an object of this process and a consequence of de-codification.

While the discovery of the nomadic can be understood as a consequence of the crisis of civilization and the search for an intellectual and aesthetic model for the revision and enlargement of the world of experience of the early twentieth century, its evaluation nevertheless remained ambivalent. The nomadic represented both a seduction and a permanent provocation:

a threat to urban civilization, the fear of a dissolution of cultural codifications and the hope of liberation through such decodification. Benjamin links this hope with the concept of a 'new, positive...barbarianism'.[17] Its experiential poverty offered the possibility to 'start from the beginning; to begin from the new; to get by with little; to construct from little'.[18]

In several notes to the *Arcades Project*, Benjamin combines these contradictory elements. Under the heading 'On the Hunter-Type of the *Flâneur*' (*Zum Jägertypus des Flâneurs*), he notes two quotations concerning nomadism taken from Spengler's *The Decline of the West* and in this context establishes a connection between early human history and the *flâneur* of the nineteenth century:

> The specifically modern reveals itself in Baudelaire again and again as the specifically archaic. In the *flâneur*, who is carried by his idleness through an imaginary city of arcades, the poet is confronted with the dandy...However, within the *flâneur* is a long-forgotten creature whose wistful gaze strikes to the heart of the poet. It is the 'son of the wilderness', the human being which was once betrothed to leisure by a generous nature...It pleases Baudelaire to find a reference in Chateaubriand to Indian dandies, a witness to the former heyday of these tribes.[19]

This note directly links the archaic and the nomadic. By mingling the images of the hunter and the nomad, he creates a problematic and contradictory construction which is based solely on its opposition to modernity. The contrast to the fundamental convictions of the nineteenth century could not be more drastically expressed. Benjamin's Baudelaire quotation expresses this altered understanding of one's own epoch in relation to the early period of history and to the anthropological sphere. He fuses the images of the archaic and the nomadic, altered through this contrast to the developmental thought of the nineteenth century, into a unit of whose internal contradictoriness he evidently remains unaware. The appeal to the archaic cannot be linked to the nomadic without a loss of substance in both concepts. This lack of conceptual clarity conditions Benjamin's connection between nomadic thought and, on the one hand, the explosive force of technological modernity and, on the other, the *flâneur* of the nineteenth century. The connection between *flâneur* and Indian does not escape the tendency to render it in idyllic terms which blur the contrast between the concept of the nomadic and the nineteenth century.[20] According to Benjamin, the traces of the dandy can be read in the nomadic. That which the modern poet expresses in his *works* is embodied by the *flâneur* in the lived *life* of dandyism, and both appear as urban versions of the nomad of the steppes, who is at the same time understood as son of the wilderness and Indian. Benjamin had noted from the French translation of Spengler the sentence: 'Le civilisé, *nomade intellectuel*, redevient pur microcosme, absolument sans patrie et spirituellement libre, comme le chasseur et le pasteur l'étaient corporellement.' Through this parallel, the re-evaluation of the nomadic appears in its harmonic variant. Detached from Spengler's aggressive-negative evaluation, Benjamin understands a modern, intellectual lack of attachment as the complementary form of a prehistorical freedom in a spatial-physical sense. He interprets the prehistoric nomad as a type of pre-urban life-form and sees it as resurrected in the *flâneur* at the historical zenith of the city. The text associates him with the heroic, which in the era of *décadence* is revived in a disguise which renders it virtually unrecognizable, namely, in the idleness of dandyism: 'Dandyism is the last glimmer of the heroic in the era of decadence.'[21]

While idleness, as Benjamin writes, is, on the one hand, *deeply marked* by the traces of the capitalist economic order, he sees it, on the other, as the revival of the time of a generous nature which granted the human being the freedom of the natural condition *and* that of the nomad prior to the genesis of modern civilization and capitalism. The formulation conceals the fact that here two different forms of freedom are drawn together: the freedom from societal coercion, named in the image of the child of nature, and a freedom in relation to nature, which is named in the image of the nomad, and at other points in Benjamin's work is linked with the return of the engineer to the simplicity of construction. The positive term of the 'new barbarians' aims to conceptually unite these two freedoms. However, such an extension of the conceptual field of the 'barbarian' not only overstretches etymology but also blurs decisive differences between the idealized natural condition and the societal counter-notion of the nomadic, between 'hunter' and 'herdsman', the incompatibility of which is conjured away through the desire to construct a homogeneous antithesis to modernity. In the freedom of the 'child of nature' just as in the quite differently conceptualized freedom of the unrestrained wandering of the nomads, the text sees the precondition for a heroic life and builds a bridge from there to artistic production within bourgeois society.

If one considers the explosive force which Benjamin grants to other points in the field of artistic production, then the position occupied by the nomadic in the context of the *flâneur* and the dandy in the *Arcades Project* expresses an astoundingly harmonizing conception which swallows the traditional connection of the barbarian with violence and counter-cultural explosive force:

We seemed to be hopelessly encircled by our pubs, our city streets, our offices and furnished rooms, our railroad stations and factories. Then came the film and blew up this prison world with the dynamite of tenths of a second, so that we now casually undertake adventurous journeys amongst its widely scattered ruins. Space is extended due to the close-up, movement due to the slow-motion replay.[22]

Due to the explosive force of film, the experience of space and time here gain a nomadic dimension, and from the forcefulness of language with which this aesthetic transformation is treated speaks the image of the warlike nomadic. Its dissolving and order-destroying effects, however, are not experienced out of a combination of dandyism and heroism, but rather in concepts such as *montage* and *dispersal* which Benjamin wrested from the culturally conservative thought of Spengler.[23] The connection which Benjamin establishes between nomadic thought and the devaluation of historical experience is obvious. The non-historical character of nomadism corresponds to the tendency to a self-undermining of history within modernity. Just as nomadic, non-striated space does not allow for experiences which can become stories and history, so too, according to this conception, this space dwindles in the present as a condition of the possibility of historical experience. In moments of freedom of the nomadic, a tendency to a postmodern overcoming of the system of the modern is revealed. However, at the same time Benjamin also strives to link the suggestive imaginative field of the continuous movement of the nomad through space, as well as his unfixed position within the historical process outside urban culture, with the image of the *flâneur*, and thus to gain a level of meaning for the interpretation of the nineteenth century and the city of modernity which lends this interpretation an anthropological depth. The link with the nineteenth century, the dandy and the *flâneur*, however, robs nomadic thought of its decisive strength and installs the concept of the nomad in an ordered pattern, precisely against which – in Benjamin's case, too – it rebels.

III

In so far as the development of subjectivity – a condition for the emergence of the aesthetic image of landscape – is tied to urban modernity, a crisis of civilization must become the integral moment of the disintegration of landscape. The untrammelled nature into which the landscape disintegrates is that of war. With the disintegration of landscape, the 'experience' of war became, as Benjamin succinctly states, 'overdue'. The failure of the interaction of subjectivity and landscape manifests itself 'most dreadfully' in the fact that the break by which the modern human being hoped to be released from cosmological ties into freedom leads into catastrophe. The landscape which emerges at the end of this attempt is the landscape of destruction of World War I.[24] This landscape can be read, together with the metropolis, as the other paradigm of modernity. The war breaches the cultural landscape with a raw violence of undreamt-of proportions, and does away with its subject-centred order. From the viewpoint of the time, the war explodes the landscape back into a state of wilderness which is at the same time steppe and the landscape of modern technology. The fields, paths, forests, villages, property borders, the points of the topographical order and centres disappear. The destruction of the war using modern technology created the open and directionless expanse of the nomadic landscape:

> Masses of people, gases, electrical forces were thrown into the open field. High frequency electricity ran through the landscape, new stars rose in the sky, the air and the depths of the sea roared with propellers, and everywhere one dug ditches for the victims in one's native soil. This great courting of the cosmos was for the first time fulfilled in planetary measure, namely, in the spirit of technology.[25]

Here then is the new 'untrammelled nature' beyond the landscape and subject-centred order. The 'order of the relationship' between human and nature, states Benjamin, was disturbed by a technology which was applied in pursuit of the domination of space. The inversion of this order, which explosively revealed itself in World War I after three hundred years of furtive development, swept away, together with the illusion of a self-determined subject, the perceived beauty of landscape and gave rise to a nomadic landscape of a new type. It is this new 'untrammelled nature', produced by technology, which invades the cities and once again brings the people the experience of horror which they had forgotten following the taming of nature in the interaction of science and the aesthetic viewpoint.

Benjamin's evaluation of this landscape falls into two parts. In a review essay, he accuses a collection of essays on war edited by Ernst Jünger of glorification and describes the attempt to suppress the horror of this landscape as fascistic. The landscape of destruction, according to Benjamin, is, for Jünger, nothing less than the life-element of the *heroic soldier type*. 'Every soldier type is reality, is a surviving witness of the World War, and it was actually the landscape of the front, his true homeland, which was defended in the post-war period.'[26] While this critique interprets the landscape politically and emphasizes, as does the text of *One-Way Street*, the menacing aspect of its continued existence in the city of the post-war period, in other parts of his work, Benjamin pursues its significance for the imaginary world and inquires as to its origin in metaphysics. In the landscape of the front he discovers the point of culmination of the dissolution of the nineteenth century in two different respects: German idealism, which had produced universal history in order to subject it to the compulsion to conform to the system of its conceptual constructions, had found its eclipse on the battlefield of World War I, and for the *flâneur*, the lived philosophy of the age of bourgeois subjectivism, the system of streets and trenches of the front, had brought the irrevocable end.

In the system of the landscape of the front, the space for subjectivity and experience, and with it the mentality of the *flâneur* as a European attitude regarding movement in space, disappeared. While the *flâneur* read in the open book of urban signs, and thereby, intentionless and searching for interaction with the built and lived environment, moved like a wanderer in the landscape through the city as through a sphere consisting of history and society with meanings which spoke to him, the soldier found himself in an environment without meaningful depth and without the possibility of communication with his world. He had to hearken to it intently, but it did not assimilate him, reducing his existence to the physical and its own – even from the perspective of the trench occupant – unlimited, pure flatness. The *flâneur* experienced the intensification of the affective ties to his world in that he plunged into the city, conferred a meaningful depth upon it and moved within it as in his own home. For the *flâneur*, moving under the open sky, the city nevertheless became an enclosed space which invited one to inhabit, to develop personal characteristics and to live out individual preferences. For the *flâneur*, wrote Benjamin, the city became a 'landscape': 'Or more precisely: for him the city disperses into its dialectical poles. It opens itself to him as landscape, it encloses him as chamber.'[27] This intensity of relationships explains the fact that the elements of the city speak to the *flâneur*: he has long chosen them in the same manner, or charged them with meanings and memories, as he does the pictures and items of furniture in his home. In a critique from 1929, Benjamin looks back upon this *flâneur* with melancholy. He mourns the loss of the 'philosophy of the *flâneur*' from the Paris of the nineteenth century, and observes in present-day Berlin how the *flâneur* has distanced himself from the philosophical stroller and developed the traces of the 'werewolf roaming restlessly in the social wilderness'.[28] While he emphasizes here a sense of loss and links the menacing image of the human as predator with the end of the *flâneur*, there are other places in Benjamin's work which place the positively characterized achievements of this invasion in the foreground; the *restlessly roaming*, the nomadic 'dispersal' becomes the emergence into a new era.[29]

The landscape of the front produced a radical contrast to the meaningful network of relationships of the bourgeois subject within this cultural landscape in which the *flâneur* thrives. It developed conditions for the radical endangerment of life, and while it disseminated the appearance of heroism, 'it shaped...the apocalyptical countenance of nature'.[30] It was the realization of modern technology: constituted out of elements of the city, of concrete and steel, a place of high speed, of telecommunications and of encoded messages, of the internal combustion engine in trucks and aeroplanes, of shafts dug in the earth. It attempted at all costs, writes Benjamin, 'to solve in mythical and immediate terms the mystery of an idealistically understood nature within technology'.

In a bitterly ironic tone, he comments on the landscape of the front:

> In the face of the landscape which has been made totally mobile, the German feeling for nature has taken an unexpected upturn. The peace experts, who have so sensitively settled the landscape, have been evacuated and, in so far as one could see over the edge of the trench, everything around had become the terrain of German idealism itself, every shell crater a problem, every wire entanglement an antinomy, every barb a definition, every explosion a claim, and the sky above the cosmic inner surface of the steel helmet by day, by night the ethical law over you.[31]

The complex connection between technology, the systemic thought of German idealism and the principle of the life-denying domination of nature is intimated here merely metaphorically and in parallels. The critique of civilization formulated by Nietzsche and his successors – Klages is the only one named in the review essay – were well known to Benjamin; and his own position owed a number of its fundamental insights to them – despite his distance from the political dimensions of the reception of Nietzsche at the time.[32] These sentences, too, must surely be read with reference to Nietzsche, whose attack on logocentrism influenced Benjamin's argumentation more than his critique of Jünger's image of war initially leads one to suspect. In a cryptic reference to Nietzsche, Benjamin speaks of the 'slave revolt of technology',[33] in which he sees a danger comparable to that which Nietzsche sees in the 'slave revolt of morality' (*On the Genealogy of Morals*), and he directs Nietzsche's anti-national and anti-state perspective against the assumed authority of the 'war engineers of the ruling class'. For Nietzsche, the 'terrain of German idealism' was no idyllic landscape, but rather a field upon which battle was waged with language for an order which aimed to enclose the totality of the world and subject it to the domination of abstract thought. The compulsion of the systems and concepts which threatened to become a danger to life itself were subjected to his own declaration of war, and, in the geneological laying bare of the illusionary character of the order which modernity had given itself, his aim was to blow this order open himself. While Benjamin rediscovers the 'terrain of German idealism' in the landscape of the front, his opinion is ambivalent: he quite clearly shares Nietzsche's declaration of war on the systemic thought of idealism and establishes a connection between the constraining character, which is concealed from this thought itself, and the violence of the war of the bourgeoisie. The end of this philosophy in the landscape of the front was 'overdue'. However, he is also forced to observe that this destruction did not bring liberation with it; he reads the works on war he has reviewed as proof of the continuing effect of a decrepit idealism in the disguise of a dark, lethal, steel-grey heroism. In Benjamin's view, the technological landscape of the front had exhausted its possibilities of destruction without, however, translating its inherent power into liberation: it brought nature 'to silence and was nevertheless the power which could have given it language'.[34]

The literature of the years around 1930 made clear that the landscape of the front was a place of continual de-codification: within it, written and unwritten codes, according to which civil society organized itself, were annulled. Both right-wing and left-wing war literature concerns itself with this destruction of rules which regulate the relations of humans with one another, their relationship to life and death, to force, property and to themselves. From the trivialities of everyday life – such as the rites of greeting or of eating – to the fundamental problems of law and metaphysics, the killing of prisoners or religion and force, the war literature reflects a field of de-codification. The war created a space in which this system of rules became a foreign body, one which was soon no longer legible. At the same time, however, this de-codification was accompanied by a rigid force which worked to define and assert new codes. The central focus here was not the system of military rules which organized the war of the nations; these were maintained with growing state-military power but also, from the spontaneous truce of Christmas 1914 across no man's land to the growing number of desertions to the revolt of Kiel, constantly avoided. In the landscape of war, however, other, unwritten codes developed, which structured action within the immense topographical and symbolic expanses of the war. Strategic and logistic planning by experts at headquarters, which had no direct relationship to 'life' on the front, and which were known and understood by only a few, delivered a construction plan for the structure and movement of the *front* system and for the movements within it. But neither structure nor movements ultimately followed such plans. They developed their own dynamic and became independent to the point where the plans stood in open conflict with the world of experience, where knowledge of them barely offered an orientation in the landscape of war, and where clear conflicts with the unwritten codes of the front appeared.

The front did not match the blueprints; and the blueprints, which should have taken the changes on the front into account, followed outmoded military codes. The failure of technologically and logistically conditioned developments was understood at an early stage to be a decisive reason for the fact that the war, contrary to all reason, stretched over years as a repetition of the ever-same. In this field of irrational duration, micro-spaces with their own intrinsic rules of behaviour developed but, on the other hand, rules also emerged which in all parts and on both sides of the front were identical. Seen through the eyes of those fighting, the landscape of war was in one sense as open and without order as was the landscape of the nomads seen through the eyes of urban civilization. Its only definite line was the front, which determined the direction of *in front* and *behind*,[35] and set limits on the range of the centres of planning and power. But even this line was unstable. There are numerous reports of soldiers getting lost 'on the way' to the front, of soldiers killed by their own artillery, of 'lost' soldiers without contact with the troops. The 'image of the enemy' was lost at an early stage, and with it the emotional orientation to the battlefield. Photos from the second half of the war show the contourless desert of the landscape of destruction with lost human bodies: 'A generation which had still gone to school by horsecar stood under the open sky in a landscape in which nothing remained unchanged except the clouds, and in the middle, within a forcefield of destructive currents and explosions, the tiny, frail human body.'[36] However, the gaze seeking the order necessary for survival concealed again and again this chaos and smoothed over the explosive effect of the landscape of war. The instruments of modern war technology themselves also worked to counter the perception of their subversion of order, which extended far beyond that of all previous wars. While they provided the means for de-individualization, emptying of experiential space and abstraction, they simultaneously created new codes of perception which projected rigid lines and divisions into contourless space and gave rise to a new landscape according to an urban model.

Structures emerged through which the experienced chaos was transformed not into experienced, but rather abstractly-structured repetitions of innumerable elements, in that a direction and connections were provided for the worm's-eye view which made possible a cognitive orientation of the ego in regard to its own uncomprehended experiences retrospectively and in anticipation of coming situations. A coherence which goes beyond the experience of the individual is produced as a consequence of the trained viewpoint, in which something is formed without the observer being able to constitute a cohesive picture. The political dimension of this aesthetic experience unfolded in the context of post-war reality. The destruction of familiar orders gave rise to an open and 'de-hierarchized' political landscape and, at the same time, to the imperative of a rigid, new systematization. In this contradictory situation, Benjamin's attempt aimed to save the nomadic thought of dispersal. Within the controlled spaces of domination in the cities, he looked for zones in which the life of the urban nomads could resist the old and now re-emerging compulsion to codify.

Under the threat of National Socialism, Benjamin oversimplified and did not do justice to his own evaluation of the nomadic when he coupled the question of the aesthetic closely with fascism: 'The masses have a right to change the property relations; fascism seeks to provide them with expression in terms of the conservation of these relations. Fascism consequently amounts to an aestheticization of political life.'[37] Here Benjamin subordinates the relationships between aesthetics and politics to a morally-based developmental model. From the opposition between a timeless aesthetic expression and the moral imperative of a change in property relations, there follows an identification of the amoral aesthetic with fascism. The category of the aesthetic, however, is – as Benjamin just as clearly elaborates – integrated via perception in the complex system of modernity within the constitution of society in such a way that it is not subjected to confrontation with a historical-philosophical ideal. The confrontation of aesthetization as a counter-historical fascistic ideology and a socialist policy of utilizing the liberating power of art forces the concept of the nomad out of the image of modernity in favour of that of the engineer.

To the extent that Benjamin's thought conceals the emergence of the nomad through the concept of an idealized natural state and equates the nomadic within the over-stretched concept of a new barbarism with the wild and with lost nature, he removes from the nomad its specific meaning. It is increasingly the barbarity of the amoral 'designer' (*Konstrukteure*) from which he expects the accomplishment of the 'new'. In the period of experiential poverty, the artists had a 'beginning from the the start' (*Vonvornbeginnen*) in mind, he wrote in an oft-cited passage,

> when they orientated themselves to the mathematicians and, constructed the world out of stereometric forms, as the cubists did, or when they, like Klee, followed engineers. For Klee's figures are, as it were, designed on the drawing-board and obey – as a good car in its bodywork obeys above all the necessities of the motor – their interior in the expression on their faces. The interior more than inwardness: that makes them barbaric.[38]

Through such emphasis on the *interior,* the concept of the nomadic becomes lost. The expectation becomes wholly associated with an explosive force inherent in the functional activity of construction. Violent force constitutes only one element among others in the modern image of the nomadic and, as Deleuze observes, can be equated neither with the goal-orientated killing of the hunter nor with the tendency of war to absolute destruction. Benjamin's thought incorporates the process-orientated character of the destructive, but also develops an inclination to establish the element of violence in absolute terms and to link it to a unique moment in history. In that his concept of the barbaric neglects the continual dissolution of boundaries in the physical as in the symbolic space of nomadic thought, it appeals to a natural state which is situated prior to the genesis of the city and its simultaneous opposition, the nomadic, and which must be retained for the Utopia. In the interior of the engineer's construction, which corresponds to the prehistorical depth of the barbaric under the conditions of the modern world, Benjamin seeks an authentic present, one which does not only contain within it the force to explode that which exists, but also the 'key to happiness'.[39] The critique of the warlike dimension of Futurism as aesthetic justification for capitalism is merely a moral position, in so far as the nomadic ideal is expelled from that of the barbarian and replaced with that of the wild, which Benjamin calls the barbarian. In his 'Manifesto of Futurism' (1909), Marinetti calls for taking hammers and pick-axes and tearing down the venerable cities, and this call is based on the proximity of the engineer and the primitive in a way similar to Benjamin's own view. As a result, the question as to the position from which Benjamin criticizes this programme is not easy to answer. In as far as the nomadic landscape is swallowed by the metaphysical depth of an authentic nature, the open space necessary for the unfolding of destructiveness is lost, so that it becomes a force which aims to possess or tends to be turned into absolute violence indistinguishable from traditional warfare. Benjamin's imaginary landscape clearly lies between the open expanse of the nomadic steppe and the caverns of magical incantations to nature, between the world of the wild, which he also calls barbarian, and that of the barbarians, to which he prefers the engineer of experiential poverty.

NOTES

1. G. Sorel, *Über die Gewalt* (Innsbruck, 1928), p. 150.
2. F. Kafka, 'Ein altes Blatt', in *Sämtliche Erzählungen*, ed. P. Raabe (Frankfurt/Main, 1976), pp. 129–31.
3. W. Benjamin, 'Landschaft und Reisen', in *Gesammelte Schriften*, ed. R. Tiedemann and H. Schweppenhäuser, 7 vols (Frankfurt/Main, 1974–), III, 92–3. All quotations from Benjamin refer to this edition. Abbreviated references in parentheses identify volume and page number.
4. *Berliner Kindheit um Neunzehnhundert* (VI, 237–9). This piece opens the text as it appears in the *Gesammelte Schriften*, whereas the revised edition of 1938 chooses another order. Sigrid Weigel underlines the transitional status of the text for Benjamin's writing with regard to the contrast between a 'life-history model' and a paradigmatic

'topography of images of memory' (cf. Chapter 5 by Sigrid Weigel in the present volume).

5. Regarding the reconstruction of the *Arcades Project*, cf. S. Buck-Morss, *The Dialectics of Seeing: Walter Benjamin and the Arcades Project* (Cambridge, MA, 1989).

6. W. Benjamin, *Einbahnstrasse* (IV, 100).

7. Of the newer titles among the continually growing literature on the theme of the city, see especially *Medium Metropole, Berlin, Paris, New York*, ed. F. Knilli and M. Nerlich (Heidelberg, 1986), and *Die Unwirklichkeit der Städte*, ed. K. Scherpe (Reinbek, 1988), with an extensive bibliography.

8. Cf. C. Begemann, *Furcht und Angst im Prozess der Aufklärung* (Frankfurt/Main, 1987), especially pp. 97–164; cf. also R.P. Sieferle, 'Entstehung und Zerstörung von Landschaft', in *Landschaft*, ed. M. Smuda (Frankfurt/Main, 1986), pp. 238–65.

9. J. Ritter, 'Landschaft, Zur Funktion des Ästhetischen im modernen Gesellschaft', in J.Ritter, *Subjektivität* (Frankfurt/Main, 1974), pp. 141–63. Cf. also K. Stierle, 'Die Entdeckung der Landschaft in Literatur und Malerei der italienischen Renaissance', in *Vom Wandel des neuzeitlichen Naturbegriffs*, ed. H.D. Weber (Konstanz, 1989), pp. 33–52.

10. W. Benjamin, *Der Begriff der Kunstkritik in der deutschen Romantik* (I, 113).

11. For an example of this early re-evaluation, see E. H. Minns, *Scythians and Greeks* (Cambridge, 1913). Later attempts are collected in *Pastoral Production and Society: Proceedings of the International Meeting on Nomadic Pastoralism, Paris 1–3 December 1976*, ed. L'Equipe écologie et anthropologie des Sociétés Pastorales (Cambridge, New York, 1979). Cf. also K. Benterrak, S. Muecke and P. Roe, *Reading the Country: Introduction to Nomadology* (Fremantle, 1985).

12. O. Spengler, *Der Untergang des Abendlandes* (Munich, 1922), vol. 2, pp. 118, 121.

13. In his essay on the 'destructive character', Wohlfarth refers to the 'Apollonian image of the destroyer': he refers to the 'liberation of the bourgeois subject from the drudgery of an unsuccessful emancipation and the development of a post-bourgeois character through the reversion to a pre-bourgeois model' as one of the objectives of Benjamin's examination of the concept of character. Cf. I. Wohlfarth, 'Der "Destruktive Character": Benjamin zwischen den Fronten', in *Walter Benjamin im Kontext*, ed. B. Lindner (Frankfurt/Main, 1978), pp. 69–70.

14. G. Deleuze and F. Guattari, 'Traité de nomadologie: La machine de guerre', in *Mille Plateaux* (Paris, 1980), pp. 434–522.

15. It is not only the retaining of an 'essence' of the nomadic that is problematic in this construction; for example, metaphors such as 'war machine' and 'non-striated space' are synthesized but used for the argumentation as if they were analytical concepts.

16. W. Benjamin, 'Der Sürrealismus' (II, 297).

17. B. Lindner, 'Technische Reproduzierbarkeit und Kulturindustrie: Benjamins "Positives Barbarentum" im Kontext', in *Walter Benjamin im Kontext*, pp. 180–223.

18. W. Benjamin, 'Erfahrung und Armut' (II, 215).

19. W. Benjamin, *Das Passagenwerk* (V, 969).

20. Characteristics of urban life in the twentieth century are also attributed to the *flâneur*, with an emphasis on the ecstatic and panic-stricken character of *flânerie*. Cf. D. Voss, 'Die Rückseite der Flanerie: Versuch über ein Schlüsselphänomen der Moderne', in *Die Unwirklichkeit der Stadte*, pp. 37–60. Another critic places the *flâneur* right next to the collector, who hunts for little collectibles, cf. M. Opitz, 'Lesen und Flanieren, über das Lesen von Städten, vom Flanieren in Büchern', in *Aber ein Sturm weht vom Paradiese her: Texte zu Walter Benjamin* (Leipzig, 1992), pp. 162–81.

21. W. Benjamin, *Das Passagenwerk* (V, 970, 969).

22. W. Benjamin, *Das Kunstwerk im Zeitalter seiner technischen Reproduzierbarkeit* (I, 499–500).

23. Cf. Spengler: 'The intellectual tension knows only the form of recuperation specific to the world metropole: the easing of tension, the "dispersal"', in *Der Untergang des Abendlandes*, p. 122.

24. Cf. B. Hüppauf, 'Räume der Destruktion und Konstruktion von Raum: Landschaft, Sehen, Raum und der Erste Weltkrieg', in *Krieg und Literatur*, III, 5/6 (1991), pp. 105–23.

25. W. Benjamin, *Einbahnstrasse* (IV, 147).

26. W. Benjamin, 'Theorien des deutschen Faschismus' (III, 246–7).

27. W. Benjamin, 'Die Wiederkehr des Flaneurs' (III, 195).

28. W. Benjamin, 'Die Wiederkehr des Flaneurs' (III, 198).

29. Franz Biberkopf's roaming through Berlin is an example of the replacement of the *flâneur* by the urban nomad. His existence is 'an ocean in the sense of the epic', writes Benjamin in a review (III, 230–7) and develops on the open surfaces of epic and ocean the concept of an overcoming of the 'crisis of the novel'.

30. W. Benjamin, 'Theorien des deutschen Faschismus' (III, 247).

31. W. Benjamin, 'Theorien des deutschen Faschismus' (III, 247).

32. Cf. H. Pfotenhauer, 'Benjamin und Nietzsche', in *Walter Benjamin im Kontext*, p. 115. Cf. also R. Reschke, 'Barbaren, Kult und Katastrophen: Nietzsche bei Benjamin', in *Aber ein Sturm weht vom Paradiese her: Texte zu Walter Benjamin*, pp. 303–39.

33. W. Benjamin, 'Theorien des deutschen Faschismus' (III, 238).

34. W. Benjamin, 'Theorien des deutschen Faschismus' (III, 247).

35. Cf. K. Lewin, 'Kriegslandschaft', in *Zeitschrift für angewandte Psychologie*, ed. W. Stern, O. Lipmann (Leipzig, 1916), pp. 440–7.

36. W. Benjamin, 'Erfahrung und Armut' (II, 214). It could be added that not even the clouds remained unchanged, since they were more frequently clouds of shrapnel and gas than of water vapour.

37. W. Benjamin, *Das Kunstwerk im Zeitalter seiner technischen Reproduzierbarkeit* (I, 467). Hillach points to a relationship to Rosa Luxemburg's theory of capitalism: cf. A. Hillach, '"Ästhetisierung des politischen Lebens": Benjamins faschismustheoretischer Ansatz', *Walter Benjamin im Kontext*, pp. 127–67.

38. W. Benjamin, 'Erfahrung und Armut' (II, 215).

39. W. Benjamin, 'Theorien des deutschen Faschismus' (III, 250).

Translated by Joe O'Donnell (Berlin)

–3–

On Aura and an Ecological Aesthetics of Nature

David Roberts

I

In *The Work of Art in the Age of Mechanical Reproduction*, Benjamin illustrates the aura of the work of art by reference to the aura of natural objects. It is a reminder that an aesthetics of nature underlies the aesthetics of art, a connection which is particularly important for Adorno's *Aesthetic Theory*. At the same time, however, if we substitute nature for the work of art and pose the question: 'Nature in the Age of Mechanical Reproduction?', then, I think, a change of perspective becomes apparent which indicates the distance between the interests of Critical Theory and contemporary ecological concerns. A leading advocate of an ecological aesthetics of nature, Gernot Böhme, has underlined this distance by arguing that Adorno's negative Utopia of reconciled nature represents the last and extreme expression of the alienation from nature inherent in the tradition of German aesthetics since Hegel.

In the first part of my essay, I will briefly present Böhme's programme for an ecological aesthetics and follow it with some comments which take up motifs from Benjamin's essay on *The Work of Art in the Age of Mechanical Reproduction*. Böhme suggests that post-Hegelian aesthetics contains certain potentials which are relevant for an ecological aesthetics of nature. In the second part of my paper, I want to examine these potentials in the work of Benjamin and Adorno – aura, mimesis, natural beauty – in order to ask whether the project of an aesthetics of nature represents, in relation to Critical Theory's legacy of reconciliation, a 'rescuing critique' comparable and complementary to Habermas's theory of communicative reason.

II

In 'Aesthetics of Nature: A Perspective?', the essay which opens the volume *For an Ecological Aesthetics of Nature*, Böhme sets out to define his own position in relation to German aesthetics since Hegel.[1] Adorno is the endpoint of this tradition, which placed the work of art at the centre of attention and thus excluded nature and natural beauty from the realm of aesthetics. The decisive figure here is Hegel, who breaks with the premodern conception of art as mimesis, the imitation of nature, for which natural beauty is the model of artistic beauty and in which artistic production is thought of as the continuation of nature or as the work of nature itself. For Hegel, natural beauty is only a lower, imperfect stage of beauty, since it lacks consciousness or spirit. Nature is spirit in the stage of alienation; natural beauty is not beautiful in itself, but only for us when it is raised to the level of artistic presentation. Hegel's definition of beauty is the sensuous appearance of the idea, the union of the sensuous and the spiritual.

Adorno rejects what he calls 'idealistic arrogance against all that is not spirit in nature', since precisely that which is nature and not spirit/mind/ consciousness is the very substance of beauty: that is, the other of reason, conceptual or instrumental thought. Adorno's definition of natural beauty – 'the trace of the non-identical in things under the spell of universal identity ' – thus points a way out from the hubris of modernity: the mythical spell cast by the domination of nature which is the key to his and Horkheimer's dialectic of enlightenment. But we can also add that Adorno remains caught in his own dialectic of enlightenment because he, too, can only conceive of nature as the other of instrumental reason, the functional administered world. For all his protest, he remains the Modernist *par excellence*, who celebrates the irreversible force of modernity which alone defines what is authentically progressive in modern art. Even if he writes a negative, self-cancelling myth of progress, he remains tragically tied to the idea of progress. His protest can thus be seen as complementary to the turning away from, rejection or repression of nature in the dominant line of modern art from Baudelaire to Cubism, Futurism, Dada, Surrealism, Russian Constructionism and beyond.

For Böhme, Adorno's negative Utopia of a reconciled nature represents the last and most extreme expression of alienation from nature. Art and aesthetic theory in the modern age are no less characterized by alienation from nature than modern science. If we are to find a new relationship to nature and rethink the relationship between art and nature, then a reorientation is required which breaks with the reduction of aesthetics to a theory of the work of art and grasps it instead, in Böhme's words, as a way of experiencing reality. In other words, a new aesthetic education of man is called for, which goes back to the original meaning of 'aesthetic' – perception through the senses. Its task is the rehabilitation and development of the senses which will sensibilize us to environments and atmospheres, and overcome the split between subject and object, mind and body, self and nature by helping us to grasp that we are ourselves a part of threatened nature. Adorno's nature as other was a projection of his suffering in relation to *society*, the present interest in an aesthetics of nature comes, for Böhme, from our suffering in relation to *nature*. The essence of the environmental problem lies in the fact that we have now begun to experience the effects in and on our own bodies of what we have done to nature. An aesthetics of nature is thus necessarily an ecological aesthetics. Its negative complement in contemporary art is the crisis of representation which takes the form of the representation of disappearing nature. Or to put it in another way, if modern art was the progressive destruction of the representation of nature, contemporary (or postmodern) art is the representation of the destruction of nature.

An ecological aesthetics can draw on a certain potential contained in the classical tradition. Böhme singles out three aspects.

(1) Adorno's concept of *mimesis* as the alternative to appropriation: that is, the recognition of the other in its own right, the preservation of the concrete and the individual. It is thus indebted to the traditional doctrine of the imitation of nature. The decisive aspect now is not just respect for nature but what Böhme calls the sympathetic dimension, the capacity for identifying experience which realizes our kinship with nature.

(2) The idea of nature as subject (Herbert Marcuse and Ernst Bloch), which rejects the modern scientific treatment of nature as cognitive object and mere material for practical manipulation. Nature is experienced as something which speaks to us, affects and engages us.

(3) Ernst Bloch's concept of an alliance with nature, which Böhme finds best exemplified in the theory and practice of English landscape gardening. The landscape garden overcomes the categorical difference between art and nature by demonstrating their partnership and co-productivity. It remains a model to be studied of a union in which nature aids art, and the artist aids the creation of future nature.

Böhme thus situates his project of an aesthetics of nature in relation to the crisis of the environment and representation. Both crises register the critical question of the relation of modern man to nature, and both can be tackled, Böhme suggests, by breaking out of the modern split between subject and object, mind and nature, abandoning, on the one hand, the exclusive reduction of art to the work of art and, on the other, opening up aesthetic experience to the environment.

David Roberts

The present situation of aesthetics Böhme sees as corresponding to that of the Romantic period. Then the hope was for the reconciliation of subject and object through art. Now the hope is for the reconciliation of man and nature against the background of the alienation from nature of both art and science since the Enlightenment definition of man as rational being.

If the end of the modern age (Böhme avoids the word 'postmodern') demands a change in human self-understanding, this change must involve the re-integration of nature (the body). Böhme defines the body as the primary manner of being-in-the-world and the basis of self-consciousness: that is, what used to be called human sensuousness, and which is now needed against the modern self-disciplining of the body. This makes aesthetics (development of the senses) central to anthropology today: specifically, the awareness and response to environments needs to be developed into the conscious shaping of nature. The term Böhme employs here for this project is that of Marx: the humanization of nature (and, of course, the naturalization of man), nature grasped as the extended body of man which directly affects his well-being. I should add, to avoid misunderstandings, that Böhme includes under 'environment' first and second nature. The city must be thought of as an ecological complex of man-shaped nature.

Rather than directly commenting on Böhme's programme, I would like to add some complementary observations on an aesthetics of nature. The Marxian project of the humanization of nature is ambivalent, to say the least, since it is entangled with the whole project of the domination of nature. The results now look more like devastation than humanization. In retrospect, the humanization of nature seems to be tied to the cultivated nature, the agriculture of premodern societies: that is, to the historical landscapes now threatened by industrial agriculture. (Australia, of course, lacks such historical peasant-based landscapes and is the product of modern agriculture.) I would thus place a humanized or cultivated nature between wild nature and industrialized nature.

Wild nature is natural beauty under the aspect of the *sublime*. Humanized nature is the transformation of natural beauty into the *pastoral* mode, for which the garden offers the perennial image of harmony between man and nature. Industrialized nature is the destruction of natural beauty. It is characterized by the monotony of monoculture and the loss of all natural and human historical contexts. It thus defies aesthetic experience, it is an aesthetic wasteland.

Wild nature and industrialized nature stand at opposite poles of man's relationship to nature, but they both exclude the human dimension. We do not recognize ourselves in either, or recognize ourself only negatively. The sense of the sublime induced by the contemplation of wild nature is that of the contrast between the majesty of nature and the spectator's insignificance, which awakens feelings of awe and veneration. Wild nature is both untouched by and indifferent to man. The sublime can manifest itself as silent grandeur but also as awesome natural catastrophes. Storms or volcanic eruptions can produce grandiose atmospheric effects, such as splendid sunsets. The aesthetic experience of the sublime can easily become an aesthetics of destruction. We recall that, for Nietzsche, the world is only justified as an aesthetic phenomenon. The burning oil wells of Kuwait, the atomic mushroom cloud, a city in ruins or flames – the sublime and the apocalyptic go together.

If the sublime expresses the domination of man by the elemental forces of nature, industrialized agriculture objectifies man's domination of nature and its transformation into the wastelands of mechanical reproduction. The reference to Walter Benjamin is deliberate. Benjamin celebrated the sense of the same released by mass production, and that, I suppose, would be the anti-aesthetic 'experience' appropriate to the destruction of natural beauty. We can agree, however, with Benjamin's hostility to the sublime represented by the fascist aestheticization of politics, without sharing his revolutionary illusions about the emancipatory effects of the destruction of aura.

It is useful to recall that Benjamin's definition of aura is illustrated in terms of natural beauty: the aura of a work of art refers to 'its presence in time and space, its unique existence at the place it happens to be'. Benjamin continues:

> The concept of aura which was proposed...with reference to historical objects may usefully be illustrated with reference to the aura of natural ones. We define the aura of the latter as the unique phenomenon of distance, however close it may be. If, while resting on a summer afternoon, you follow with your eyes a mountain range on the horizon or a branch which casts its shadow over you, you experience the aura of those mountains, of that branch.[2]

A further elucidation is required. In 'On Some Motifs of Baudelaire', Benjamin writes:

> Experience of the aura...rests on the transposition of a response to human relationships, to the relationships between inanimate or natural objects and man. The person we look at, looks at us in turn. To perceive the aura of an object we look at means to invest it with the ability to look at us in turn.[3]

Aura, I suggest, is the aesthetic experience which humanizes nature: that is, the aesthetic response to humanized nature (natural beauty) as opposed to the sense of the sublime in relation to wild nature or the sense of the same in relation to industrialized nature. It rests on a reciprocity between man and nature, the recognition of the one human and natural context or lifeworld. Aura could thus constitute the central element of a new aesthetic education of man proposed by Böhme.

III

The experience of aura is the experience of a mimetic or reciprocal relationship, illustrated, on the one hand, by reference to the aura of natural objects and, on the other, by reference to human relationships. Benjamin's focus, however, is not nature, but the work of art. If we ask about nature rather than the work of art in the age of mechanical reproduction, then the destruction of aura does not offer the promise of profane illumination. Rather, the destruction of natural beauty in painting, which falls victim to photographic reproductions, which reduce beautiful nature to commercial kitsch. Aura – 'that essence', as the dictionary tells me, 'which is claimed to emanate from all living things' – is destroyed by the photographic reduction of natural beauty to the merely visible, deprived of the atmosphere of its unique presence. The photographic image, we may say, is *nature morte*.

Clearly, the loss of the aura of the work of art, celebrated by Benjamin, offers an ambivalent enlightenment. If reproduction liberates the work of art from the spell of magic and cult, by the same token it severs the mimetic link between man and nature inherent in aura. The dialectic of enlightenment is once more enacted: 'The unique phenomenon of distance, however close it may be', which defines the aura of natural objects, becomes, as it were, the emblem of the infinite closeness and distance of the impossible object of desire – reconciliation with nature – so central to Critical Theory from Benjamin through to Habermas. This infinite closeness and distance is the very 'essence' of the negative Utopia of an aesthetics of nature, around which Adorno's work circles in a prolonged meditation on Benjaminian motifs. This endless circling can only be broken by Benjamin's short-circuiting leap out of the homogeneous time of natural history. Adorno's circling is endless not only because the dialectic of enlightenment holds us fast in the realm of natural history, the realm of the eternal return of the same, but also because the dialectic registers at the same time the doubling of our relation to nature into the infinitely distant and the infinitely close. It is the infinite distance of a false enlightenment, driven by radical anxiety, whose very striving to deliver man from domination by nature delivers him over to the mythical spell of fate. But there is also the infinite closeness of true enlightenment, which is the memory of nature in the subject, the spontaneous mimetic impulses of our inner nature which momentarily dissolve the iron cage of self-preserving identity. This doubling (of enlightenment and of nature) is inherent in Adorno's and Benjamin's reading of the split between subject and object as the history of the Fall. The origin of negative dialectics is natural history: it is the theology set in motion by the Fall, which splits nature into fallen and redeemed nature. Fallen nature is the world theatre of Benjamin's *Trauerspiel*, of Lukács's second nature in *The Theory of the Novel*, of Adorno's totally reified world. Its other is redeemed nature, the nature that never was and that only the natural beauty of the work of art can fleetingly evoke. Aura, mimesis, natural beauty – these traces of the unique and the non-identical – are the constant reminders that an aesthetics of nature underlies Adorno's aesthetic theory, but it is a theological aesthetics of nature, which springs from his and Benjamin's ambivalent – negative and redemptive – relation to and conception of nature.

This can be illustrated by Adorno's treatment of natural beauty in his *Aesthetic Theory*,[4] a concept which has disappeared from aesthetics since Kant and is reintroduced by Adorno in protest against its displacement and usurpation by the subject. The exclusion of natural beauty represents, for Adorno, the dark shadow of idealist aesthetics, the denial that nature and art refer to each other, that natural beauty is essential to the theory of art (AT, 98) – and by this Adorno means modern art, the art of the last two hundred years. If art was traditionally defined as the imitation of nature, Adorno proposes that modern art be understood as the imitation of natural beauty. Natural beauty thus has a double reference: to the beauty of nature and to the beauty of art, while the concept itself (like natural history), partaking as it does of both nature and art, is expressive of the mimetic (subject/object) relationship itself. The beauty of nature is closely tied to the beauty of art, since the aesthetic experience they call forth is, in Kantian terms, disinterested. Freed from the interest of material exploitation or of scientific knowledge, nature can appear as natural beauty. The suspension of the interest in domination awakens the memory of a domination-free state of nature – which probably never existed, Adorno hastens to add, since the surrender to the beauty of nature also carries with it the danger of regression. Natural beauty masks the terror of nature's mythical spell (AT, 104–5). The Medusa head of the sublime lurks behind the beauty of nature. Within the dialectic of enlightenment we discern the dialectic of Romanticism's ambivalent fascination with nature. When Adorno says of art that 'origin is the goal' (AT, 104), this Romantic motif (borrowed from Karl Kraus) means the redemption of nature, *not* the return to nature, and the path to the redemption of nature is through the natural beauty of art. It is thus hardly surprising that, for Adorno, the natural beauty of art excludes the imitation of the beauty of nature. Natural beauty is undepictable, as kitsch shows. The only authentic depictions of nature are the landscape paintings of the past which present nature as *nature morte*: that is, as natural history, as the allegorical cipher of historical transience (AT, 106). As

Adorno puts it, the biblical taboo on images (a favourite topos of the theory of the sublime from the eighteenth century through to Freud's study of Michelangelo's *Moses*) is both theological and aesthetic in intention. In turn, we can add that the natural beauty of art is both aesthetic and theological. Aesthetically, modern art approaches natural beauty through a process of spiritualization which is not to be understood as alienation from nature (AT, 121), but rather as the process of the subjectification of art through which its aesthetic objectivity is realized: 'Aesthetic objectivity, the reflex of nature-for-itself, is the pure execution of the subjective element of teleological unity; only thus do the works become similar to nature' (AT, 120). The work of art as second nature is thus not the imitation of first nature, but the anticipation of a nature-for-itself which does not exist, the unknown something which goes through and beyond the subject (AT, 121). That is to say, in aesthetic objectivity, subjective intention is transmuted into the non-intentional, into that which is beyond intention and approaches non-human nature, but non-human nature raised to expression. Modern art (the fusion of subjectification and objectification) is thus, for Adorno, theologically the only figure in which something like the language of creation can appear (AT, 121).

Thus, if for Früchtl nature is Adorno's model of truth,[5] we must add that this truth can appear only in art's redemption of nature. The authentic work of art is the allegorical figure of anticipated reconciliation: 'Nature's beauty consists in appearing to say more than she is. Now the idea behind art is to wrest this "plus" from its contingent setting in nature, appropriating nature's appearance and making it determinate, which means among other things, negating its unreality.'[6] This surplus of natural beauty is the aura of nature, which art seeks to master and possess through the self-transcending closure of aesthetic objectivity. And so, in art's faithfulness to itself – that is, its aesthetic objectivity – it accomplishes what nature seeks in vain· the work of art opens its eyes (AT, 104). Contrary to Hegel, Adorno insists that the beauty of nature is close to the truth, but that it hides itself in the moment of nearest proximity. The dignity of nature springs from the not yet existing, a dignity which has been passed on to hermetic art (AT, 111).

Just as Adorno takes Kant's concept of natural beauty and transforms it into his own concept of art, so he appropriates Kant's analysis of the sublime in nature in order to characterize the sublimation of nature achieved through the spiritualization of hermetic art (AT, 293). To the subject's experience of the sublime in nature, analysed by Kant, corresponds the cathartic shock through which the truth content of the work of art manifests itself: that is, the breakthrough of objectivity into subjective consciousness (AT, 363). This dialectic of subjectivity and objectivity in the work and in reception partakes of the sublime in a double sense. For the recipient, the prison of subjectivity is momentarily dissolved, allowing oppressed and repressed nature to speak. The modern work of art, in turn, is sublime because it strives to communicate the incommunicable (AT, 292), or if you prefer, in Lyotard's formulation, to present the unpresentable. In other words, modern art is sublime or it is nothing. Its paradoxical justification is its impossible struggle to communicate the sublime, which it can only realize negatively by laying bare the contradictions between spirit and material, contradictions which must destroy the (beautiful) semblance of art. The legacy of the sublime is thus undiminished negativity (AT, 296), through which reconciliation alone can find expression. And this reconciliation – defined here by Adorno as the emancipation of nature from its unfreedom (*Naturwüchsigkeit*) and from the dominating sovereignty of the subject – is the return to nature, and this return is sublime (AT, 293).

I can now reformulate my earlier statement about natural beauty in the following form: the sublime both points and bars the way to the return to nature. Adorno's aesthetic theory is not only a theory of the sublime, it is also a sublime theory, driven to circle endlessly around the paradox of the communication of the incommunicable. In the process, nature is sublimated to the point of disappearance, leaving only its aura, its spiritual essence behind, like the smile of the Cheshire cat.

IV

Adorno's sublime theory of the hermetic work of art stands at the opposite pole to Benjamin's hopes of the profane illumination to be set free by the destruction of aura in mass art. Habermas attempts to resolve the contradiction in Benjamin's attitude towards aura (both affirmation and negation) in terms of a 'rescuing critique'.[7] In his famous essay on Benjamin, 'rescuing critique' has a double import. On the one hand, it is meant to characterize the central impulse of Benjamin's thought, on the other, it signals Habermas's own rescuing reformulation of the idea of reconciliation in Critical Theory: that is, the linking of human emancipation to the resurrection of nature, which Habermas sees as common to Marx, Adorno, Benjamin, Horkheimer, Marcuse and Bloch.

Habermas argues that the loss of aura liberates what is contained in the mimetic experience of aura: the metamorphosis of the object into the partner of the subject. The unique phenomenon of distance, however near, is the signature of reciprocal happiness. It is the profane form of the mystical experience of the presence of God, veiled in the auratic work of art, unveiled, made public, in de-ritualized art. We could think of profane illumination as the paradox of enchanted disenchantment, or as the allegorical mystery of the everyday world which Benjamin discovered in

Surrealism. The history of art is read by Habermas as the history of mankind's efforts to rescue man's original mimetic capacity – the unbroken correspondence between the human organism and surrounding nature – from its original dependence on and subjection to nature. The function of art is to preserve mimesis while dissolving the spell of myth. The loss of auratic correspondences in the modern world thus explains the opposed but complementary responses of Adorno's hermeticism and Benjamin's mass art. The one point in the direction of nature, the other, as read by Habermas, in the direction of the lifeworld.

Habermas's own project of 'rescuing critique' seeks to overcome the impasse represented by what he sees as Benjamin's vain attempt to combine mysticism and enlightenment and by Adorno's irrational clinging to the idea of universal reconciliation: that is, what I have called the mystical-theological reading of the subject/object split as the history of the Fall, which underlies Adorno's Freudian understanding of the birth of consciousness as the repression of inner 'nature'.[8] The split between fallen and redeemed nature corresponds to the split between objectifying, dominating instrumental rationality and its other, mimesis. It is precisely this splitting of reason, this doubling of enlightenment, which Habermas seeks to heal by breaking with the alienation inherent in the philosophy of consciousness. In the *Theory of Communicative Action*, he writes that the rational core of mimesis can be regained only by abandoning the paradigm of philosophy of consciousness – the subject representing and working on objects – in favour of the paradigm of philosophy of language, in which cognitive instrumental rationality is grasped as part of a more comprehensive communicative rationality.[9] In short, Habermas sets out to rescue the profane truth of mimesis by substituting intersubjective understanding for universal reconciliation. The idea of reconciliation is transformed into the regulative idea of a non-coercive socialization, in which the lifeworld takes the place of nature, via the mediating instance of art: 'Modern art harbours a utopia that becomes a reality to the degrees that the mimetic power sublimated in the work of art finds resonance in the mimetic relations of a balanced and undisturbed intersubjectivity of everyday life.'[10]

As Habermas had already made clear in 1969, Adorno 'hesitated to moderate the idea of reconciliation to that of autonomy and responsibility', because it 'would not entail the demand that nature opens its eyes, that in the condition of reconciliation we talk with animals, plants and rocks'.[11] Communicative reason does not include dialogue with nature, but it does enable us to see that the theology of universal reconciliation remains the other of the reductive ontology of Western objectivizing rationalism, which has made the world alien and humans homeless (deprived of a sense of place in an environment of endlessly obsolescent mass-produced things).[12]

It brings out more clearly that the concept of enlightenment is shot through for Benjamin and Adorno with all the ambivalence of emancipation from and redemption of nature. The dialectic of enlightenment is in reality the intertwining of enlightenment and Romanticism, which art reproduces and bears witness to. If the function of art is to preserve mimesis through redeeming the promise of nature by breaking its mythical spell, then the work of art is the other of natural history in the double sense that it is the negative truth of nature and of history: that is, it is the image – the momentary auratic apparition – of the truth of a redeemed natural history.

V

Habermas's 'rescuing critique' is a step forward in that it shows how the intertwining of enlightenment and Romanticism in Critical Theory is inextricably tied up with the subject/object paradigm. It is a step backwards in that his 'rescuing critique' preserves the concept of mimesis only by separating enlightenment and Romanticism. Habermas is the enlightenment heir of Critical Theory. The other possibility of mimesis – its Romantic legacy – lies in the renewal of an aesthetics of nature, whose condition likewise is the break with the subject/object paradigm. Both Habermas and Böhme, as we have seen, propose a new aesthetic education of man. For Habermas, 'the mimetic relations of a balanced and undisturbed everyday life' offer the realization of the Utopian promise of modern art. For Böhme, the recovery and cultivation of our aesthetic sensibilities, rooted in our bodily being-in-the-world, offers the realization of the Utopian promise of Romantic art. Each seeks to rescue the profane illumination released by the decay of aura by going beyond the frame of art. In so doing, their distinct but complementary versions of the sublation of art bring into focus the two dimensions – the intersubjective and the natural – which Benjamin employs in order to explicate the aura of the work of art: 'Experience of the aura...rests on the transposition of a response to human relationships, to the relationships between...natural objects and man.'

In conclusion, I would like to make two points: (1) Habermas and Böhme represent alternative but complementary 'rescuing critiques' of the sublime political-aesthetic paradigm of redemption in modernity. Their break with the sublime takes the form of the reappropriation respectively of enlightenment's common sense and of Romanticism's natural sensibility. (2) Etymologically speaking, ecology is the injunction to put our house in order. To do this, we need both sense and sensibility. Ecological aesthetics needs communicative reason if it is to change our domination of nature in the direction of a new alliance between man and nature.

NOTES

1. G. Böhme, *Für eine ökologische Naturästhetik* (Frankfurt/Main, 1989).
2. W. Benjamin, *Illuminations, Essays and Reflections,* ed. (with an introduction by) H. Arendt, trans. H. Zohn (New York, 1969), pp. 220–1.
3. W. Benjamin, *Illuminations,* p. 188.
4. Abbreviated references in the text (AT, page number) are to T. W. Adorno, *Ästhetische Theorie* (Frankfurt/Main, 1974).
5. J. Früchtl, 'Natur als Projektion und Adornos Modell von Wahrheit', *Philosophisches Jahrbuch,* 96, pp. 271–381.
6. T. W. Adorno, *Aesthetic Theory,* trans. C. Lenhardt, ed. G. Adorno and R. Tiedemann (London, 1984), p. 116.
7. 'Consciousness-Raising or Rescuing Critique', in J. Habermas, *Philosophical-Political Profiles* (Cambridge, MA, 1983), pp. 29–63.
8. Cf. D. Ingram, 'Habermas on Aesthetics and Rationality: Completing the Project of Enlightenment', *New German Critique,* 53 (1991), p. 92.
9. J. Habermas, *Theorie des kommunikativen Handelns,* (Frankfurt/Main, 1981), I, p. 523.
10. 'Questions and Counter-Questions', *Praxis International,* 4 (1984), p. 237.
11. J. Habermas, 'Theodor Adorno: The Primal History of Subjectivity – Self-Affirmation Gone Wild', in *Philosophical-Political Profiles,* pp. 108, 107.
12. Cf. A. Heller, 'World, Things, Life and Home', *Thesis Eleven,* 33 (1992), pp. 69–84.

4

A 'Hermaphroditic Position': Benjamin, Postmodernism and the Frenzy of Gender

John Docker

I The Ambivalence of Modernism

In a famous phrase, Marx once referred to the frenzy of capital at work in the world. What I would like to do in this essay is explore Benjamin's attitudes to mass culture and modernity in relation to the frenzy of gender at work in Modernism, in notions of feminine and masculine, maternal and paternal, concerns that continue in new forms and intensities within that bundle of contradictory theories and pronouncements we yet wish to call Postmodernism. In this quest, I will be particularly drawing on hints and clues in Witte's intellectual biography of Benjamin and Susan Buck-Morss's speculative study of Benjamin's vast unfinished work on the early nineteenth-century Paris arcades. I will also be analysing Benjamin's texts on Baudelaire, posthumously-collected essays and fragments that grew out of the *Arcades Project.*

'Benjamin' is a name that immediately signifies how much we have to face the history of Modernism as almost bafflingly diverse, contradictory, and ambivalent. In the early twentieth century, 'Modernism' could mean the modern movement or 'International Style' in architecture. Le Corbusier's architectural Modernism, along with avant-garde movements like the Cubist or Constructivist or Futurist, extolled the possibilities of the machine age, of new technology, engineering and cities. Le Corbusier argued in his 1920s manifestos that architecture should reject the ornamental, decorative and symbolic efflorescence that consumed the surfaces of late nineteenth-century building and interiors. Such surface effects were merely female and frivolous, to be opposed by an austere, calm, serene male reason. For Le Corbusier, the twentieth-century engineer was a cultural hero, and modern processes of mass production and standardization of materials – in bridges, Atlantic liners, railways, airplanes, racing cars, North American wheat silos and skyscrapers were to be welcomed as technologically permitting that Utopian architecture which would soar above a world nearly destroyed by nineteenth-century notions and spirit of urban design.[1]

In sharp contrast was high literary Modernism, a term I will use here to include both radical-conservative literary and cultural theory as exemplified in the Leavisite movement in the UK, and the pessimistic Marxism of the Frankfurt School, as in Adorno and Horkheimer.[2]

II High Modernism

For F. R. Leavis in his Modernist manifesto, *Mass Civilisation and Minority Culture* (1930), everything that Le Corbusier celebrated was felt to be dangerous to the continued existence of true cultural standards. In particular, 'America' signified the fate of Europe, or at least England, if the march of mass production and standardization could not be halted. 'America' represented the mass production and standardization occurring in mass culture, in the press, advertising, publicity, Hollywood film, and broadcasting. Only a 'very small minority' was still holding out against the demiurge of Americanization, the death of the finest spirit that must follow literary and cultural 'levelling down'. Community, tradition, continuity, unity with the rhythms of nature, and proper cultural leadership by an acknowledged elite have given way to the urbanized industrial era, the triumph of 'the machine'. In the twentieth century, we are so smothered by new and worthless books and other mass culture 'distractions' that 'severe thought' is hardly possible any longer. For Leavis, as for so many other high literary Modernists – as Andreas Huyssen has pointed out in his essay 'Mass Culture as Woman: Modernism's Other'[3] – there was always hovering a trope of mass culture as female, as a kind of bewitching, smothering succubus overwhelming concentration and contemplation. Against such distraction, Leavis advocated a 'serious critical organ' (*Scrutiny*) that would restore borders, landmarks, boundaries between true as against mass culture. Standards of discrimination had, before it was too late, to be set for others to follow.[4]

The empirical evidence for F. R. Leavis's apocalyptic assertions was supposedly provided in Q. D. Leavis's *Fiction and the Reading Public* (1932), where she sees herself as a kind of cultural anthropologist, carrying out participant observation on mass culture subjects: for example, by occasionally visiting circulating libraries and newsagents to observe how they acquire their reading matter. The results of this research are, Q. D. Leavis reports, profoundly depressing. The mass of people in England were being coarsened not so much by their social conditions as by their reading and viewing, in particular the romance, thriller and detective books they borrowed, many American, with women being the main offenders in putting their hands out for such 'worn and greasy novels'. The sensibility of the mass of people had now become second-rate, gross, fatally crude, cheap and vulgar. They were distracted by melodramatic and sensational literature which overemphasized the visual and pictorial at the expense of senses assumed to be more subtle, like those that are engaged in reading serious literature. Literary Modernism constructed a hierarchy of the senses corresponding to a hierarchy of sensibility, ruled by reason, severe thought and critical distance, which in turn corresponded to a hierarchy of literary forms. The heights were inhabited by genres foregrounding the tragic, the pessimistic, the bleak, while melodrama, romance and detective fiction lay at the base, permanent cellar-dwellers in aesthetic history.[5]

Because people now live not in villages and small town communities, but in cities, where they lead lives of desolate isolation, amusement – of the dance-hall, cinema, popular theatre – has to compensate for the 'poverty of their emotional lives'. How does Q. D. Leavis know that millions and millions of people across the UK lead lives of emotional poverty? Her only evidence, as far as I can detect, is that she observed that popular readers in libraries don't ask questions about the books they have borrowed. Q. D. Leavis deduces from her visit to a circulating library that mass culture readers are 'passive' in their acceptance of such reading, which is also like a 'drug habit', inducing 'wish-fulfilment', 'self-indulgence' and 'vicarious living', leading to mass 'conformity' and the 'herd' mentality.[6]

I don't think it's too fanciful to say that all subsequent literary modernist analyses of mass culture are but footnotes to *Mass Civilisation and Minority Culture* and *Fiction and the Reading Public*. Adorno and Horkheimer's (in)famous essay on 'The Culture Industry: Enlightenment as Mass Deception' in *Dialectic of Enlightenment* can be seen as following maps and signposts already established and put into general circulation by the Leavises. In the Frankfurt School there might be no nostalgia for a myth of pre-industrial communities in touch with the dubious rhythms of nature, but the demiurge is predictably 'America', where the mass of people are held to exist in grimy, spiritless cities. Industrialism has created an 'iron system', the mass production and standardization of all things, including mass culture, from thriller, detective and adventure movies to songs, radio soap operas, and the 'idiotic women's serial'. The might of industrial society has become lodged in people's minds, for mass culture has but a single purpose: 'obedience to the social hierarchy'. The mass have become passive, their imagination stunted: 'Real life is becoming indistinguishable from the movies', Hollywood film forces its 'victims to equate it directly with reality'. The mass spectator can only react 'automatically'. Advertising and publicity are manipulating people in a kind of 'psycho-technology', which is invading the very language and gestures of the audience, publicly in the cinema as amongst the 'girls in the audience', but also in their private lives, affecting the 'most intimate reactions of human beings', so that the 'way in which a girl accepts and keeps the obligatory date', or the 'inflection on the telephone' or in the 'most intimate situation', in short, the 'whole inner life', is now moulded by the culture industry.[7]

Remembering the ethnography performed by Q. D. Leavis in a circulating library, it's difficult to see what kind of ethnography Adorno and Horkheimer have engaged in in order to arrive at such knowledge. Adorno and Horkheimer simply assert, with a kind of magical positivism, what 'girls in the audience' are feeling. They somehow know the 'whole inner life' of these young women, how they talk on the telephone, how they accept and keep a date, what their psychic state is in the 'most intimate situation'.

Adorno and Horkheimer know the truth, as in the 'true kind of relationship' people should have but can't in America. They know that art is always opposed in a binary way to mass culture, and that it must involve tragedy, pain, the ascetic, the austere.[8] They know what mass culture invariably is, though their textual acquaintance with it seems disablingly slim, and they know the 'whole inner state' of mass audiences and Americans and humanity generally.

In the *Culture Industry* essay, Adorno and Horkheimer were producing positions that, in the rise and spread of post-war media and cultural studies, would become highly influential, if not convention and orthodoxy, at least until the 1980s and the challenge of Postmodernist theories more sympathetic to popular culture.[9]

III Benjamin on Mass Culture and Modernity

Benjamin doesn't so much oppose this high Modernist tradition as stroll purposely through and around it, sceptical, observant, challenged, certainly in, but never fully of. In *The Work of Art in the Age of Mechanical Reproduction* – the essay that Adorno and Horkheimer were replying to[10] – Benjamin returns a positive verdict on the relationship between popular film, audience response and psychoanalysis. Film, he feels, does for optical and acoustical perception what Freud's *Psychopathology of Everyday Life* did for perception of hidden depths in ordinary conversation, the camera introducing us to 'unconscious optics as does psychoanalysis to unconscious impulses'. It can thus bring about for film audiences a 'deepening of apperception'. Popular audiences are not, as the high Modernist tradition would have it, merely unconscious, and hence uncritical in their response to film, since, Benjamin argues, 'the critical and the receptive attitudes of the public coincide'. The pleasures, the so-called 'distractions' of cinema, don't prevent audiences from thinking and reflecting. And such audiences are also highly active in the way they enjoy film, as against the forbidding auratic atmosphere of the salon, for in the cinema they can organize their own conditions of reception, in 'simultaneous collective experience'. This is why, Benjamin says, popular audiences will not respond to painting or to avant-garde movements, even when 'politically progressive', as in Picasso or the Surrealists, but will attend enthusiastically to a Charlie Chaplin film or a 'grotesque' movie. In *The Work of Art in the Age of Mechanical Reproduction*, Benjamin defends audiences which high Modernism, as Patrice Petro points out, perceived as merely female, the 'girls in the audience' in Adorno and Horkheimer's disdainful commentary. In his reference to popular audiences preferring 'grotesque' movies, Benjamin is also implicitly defending popular interest in melodramatic and sensational genres.[11]

Benjamin, nevertheless, as Petro notes, is drawn to the modern city as a figure of fascination and dread, attraction and threat, alluring, absorbing, threatening, demonic, endangering contemplation and critical distance.[12] Benjamin, that is, was not at all immune to the Modernist syndrome identified by Andreas Huyssen: identifying mass culture and modernity as unnervingly female. Benjamin is also not at all immune to Adorno and Horkheimer and mainstream Frankfurt School theory, particularly his alarm at the apparent deathly infiltration of the market and commodity form into every relationship: cultural, psychic, sexual.

These alarms and ambivalences are explored in *Charles Baudelaire: A Lyric Poet in the Era of High Capitalism*. Baudelaire's poetry is related to Paris as the representative metropolis of the nineteenth century, that city which, above all others, is the focal point of modernity's politics, economy, and the phantasmagoria of its fantasy life. The text connects Baudelaire to divers milieux and tableaux of explanation, not least the demoralizing effect in France of the commercialization of literature and culture generally from the end of the third decade. With the new cultural section, the *feuilleton*, in the newspapers providing a market for *belles-lettres*, serious writers now have to exhibit their work surrounded by expanding advertisements, serial novels, and news items. Photography also quickly became commercialized. The first photographers belonged to the avant-garde, as did their clientele, revealing the new medium's potential for montage, the 'agitational utilization of photography'. From the middle of the nineteenth century, however, with a special place reserved for it at the World Exhibition of 1855, photography served the market, with the constant demand for sales creating the new medium as ever-modish, determining its subsequent history. At the same time, photography itself, offering limitless quantities of figures, landscapes and events in place of a picture for a single customer, enormously increased the sphere of the market-society.[13]

The Baudelaire book is at times, many times, positively Adornoesque, as well as drawing on Marx's trope of the commodity form as central to life under capitalism, requiring a kind of religious submission to objects of abstract value, idols, a cult, a theology. The world exhibitions which became a feature of the nineteenth century were, says Benjamin in this mood and mode, 'places of pilgrimage to the fetish Commodity', glorifying exchange-value rather than appealing to use-value, creating a phantasmagoria into which people entered in order to be 'distracted'. People 'yielded' to the 'manipulations' of the 'entertainment industry' while 'enjoying their alienation from themselves and others.' In the 'enthronement' of the commodity and the 'glitter of distraction' there did exist and persist a promise of Utopia, a deep desire for past images of classlessness and abundance, a land of Cockaigne, a primal wish-symbol, as in Fourier's imaginings. But in the ever-spreading market, society such phantasmagoric, Utopian desires were held out in the cynical form of the commodity.[14]

In the World Exhibition of 1867, Paris was radiantly confirmed as the capital of luxury and fashion. The 'nature' of fashion was revealed in the way the 'fetish Commodity wished to be worshipped', for fashion 'prostitutes the living body to the inorganic world'. Fashion represents the rights of the 'corpse'. The 'cult of the commodity' indeed recruits to its service a fetishism which 'succumbs' to the 'sex-appeal of the inorganic'.[15] We are not very far here from the discourse and moralistic language of Q. D. Leavis's *Fiction and the Reading Public*.

Even the cultural figures Benjamin otherwise admires, the *flâneur* and the writer, cannot altogether escape; they yield and succumb. The *flâneur* saw the city through whose crowds he strolled now as a landscape, now a room, and both features went into the construction of the department store, which succeeded the early nineteenth-century arcades that had concentrated on luxury items. The department store made use of *flânerie* itself to sell goods: 'The department store was the *flâneur*'s final coup.' With the appearance of the *flâneur*, the intelligentsia came into the market-place, in order, they thought, to observe it, but 'in reality' to find a buyer. Writers like Baudelaire felt part of a rebellious bohemia, but the poet, too, had to market himself; even his eccentricity became a selling point, a commodity. Baudelaire compared the situation of the modern man of letters to that of the whore. The prostitute becomes a key figure of and for the age. Like the arcades of old, which are 'both house and stars', the prostitute offers a dream image, but she is also 'seller and commodity in one'. Baudelaire, Benjamin reminds us, achieved his only sexual relationship with a prostitute.[16]

In the Baudelaire book, then, Benjamin frequently appears as conventional high Modernist, in bleak images of mass culture and the city, often delivered in a language of essence, truth, encapsulation, inscribing a centre to a phenomenon, knowing it up and down and around and across, pinning it to the page. He will talk of the 'true situation', 'above all', 'at the bottom', 'in actuality', 'in a nutshell', 'the essence', 'its nature', 'in reality', 'the quintessence', the 'real aim'. He will unify and totalize, in particular when relating culture to consciousness. Benjamin argues that the images of past and present that mingle in the 'collective consciousness' are transfiguring images by which the collective seeks to 'transcend' the present. The collective looks back not to the recent past with which it seeks to break, but beyond, to Utopian images of a primal past lodged in the 'collective unconscious'. These are the images, however, which become imbricated with the commodity, as with fashion and its tireless drive for novelty, engendering illusions in the 'collective unconscious', illusions that become the 'quintessence of false consciousness'. In this epoch, the law of dialectic, the possibility of social transformation, is consequently at a standstill.[17]

False consciousness: that trope, common to Frankfurt School Marxism and high literary Modernism alike, of the mass in modern society, in a state of illusion, unlike the theorist, the critic, the writer, magisterially surveying history, aware of humanity's true cultural and aesthetic needs, gazing, mapping, pointing, warning, guiding, prescribing, panoptic. False consciousness: that disastrous move.

In the Baudelaire book, then, Benjamin would appear to be aligning himself with a history of discourse where the modern city and its culture can be invariably characterized as abyss, as death by commodity form, Utopian hope and desire transmuted into illusion and fetish, modernity's glitter, but the chuckle, the death grin, of the ever-victorious, ever-enveloping, ever-destroying market.

Yet the text also allows doubts and qualifications and difference to appear and swirl about and haunt this discourse: Adornoesque meets arabesque. In particular, there are moments when the argument not so much tries to encapsulate Baudelaire, his personality and poetry, his life and times, in an iron system of concepts, as permit analysis to drift, into surmise, surprise, perplexity, mystery, uncertainty, confusion. The argument stages stabs at essentializing explanation, then moves off again into doubt, that Baudelaire, the text's supposed representative cultural figure of the nineteenth century, has been explained, that he or any other cultural figure and historical period is explicable. The text works at uncovering Baudelaire for dissection, description and analysis, yet comes across mask after mask; the clear outlines of an essential, illuminated Baudelaire beckon, appear graspable, then fade into enigma and rebus.

Who was Baudelaire? What were his masks? Baudelaire conceived of the writer under capitalism as whore and rightful companion of whores; as Benjamin puts it, Baudelaire 'nonchalantly includes this creature in the brotherhood of the *boheme*'. But Baudelaire also patterned his image of the artist and of writing after other figures. The writer was like a fencer, his pen stabbing, jabbing, parrying, in a fantastic duel with paper and words. At another point, Benjamin talks of Baudelaire's use of language, in particular the way similes disturb the verse like intruders. He quotes some examples, as in: 'Nous volons au passage un plaisir clandestin/Que nous pressons bien fort come une vieille orange' (We hastily steal a clandestine pleasure/Which we squeeze very hard like an old orange) – similes that reminded me of another strand of the history of modern literature, Raymond Chandler's witty, hard-boiled detective fiction. Baudelaire, says Benjamin, would mix an elevated, lyric vocabulary with 'confusing' allegory, with words of ordinary provenance and of urban origin, introduced suddenly, without prior preparation, in a mode of brusque coincidence – a reconnoitring and besieging of a subject that Benjamin likens to the *Putsch*, and has him comparing Baudelaire to the conspirator Blanqui.[18]

Baudelaire felt affinity with figures important in the formation and history of Modernism, cultural figures on the margins, outsiders, predestined for doom. The artist, the writer, was a hero, for it 'takes a heroic constitution to live Modernism'. Indeed, Modernism for Baudelaire existed under the sign of suicide, where suicide was not resignation, but heroic passion (a view, says Benjamin, that looks forward to Nietzsche). Poets derive their heroic subject matter from the refuse of the streets, and so are comparable to the ragpicker, with both poet and rag-picker at work while the good citizens of the city sleep. The poet feels kinship with the 'irregular existences led in the basements of a big city by criminals and kept women'. The *apache*, the Parisian tough, who abjures virtue and laws, terminating the social contract forever, is also heroic. Because, in general, Baudelaire didn't possess any convictions, he could assume ever new forms for himself, fencer and Blanquist putschist, *apache* and rag-picker, *flâneur* and dandy. But the writer can only *act* heroes: 'Heroic modernism turns out to be a tragedy in which the hero's part is available.' Yet, says Benjamin, behind the masks, Baudelaire preserved his incognito.[19]

Benjamin is intrigued by the alterity, the idiosyncrasies, of Baudelaire. Passages of Baudelaire's writing can be 'particularly strange', with baroque illuminations whose connections the poet shrewdly obscures. Baudelaire's dreams involved images that were 'profound, secret, and paradoxical'. Baudelaire was drawn not only to the whore but to other female images and figures. In his poetry, images of Paris intermingle with images of Woman and Death, and he was fascinated by the *femme passante* in mourning. He was also attracted to the literary figure of the lesbian, derived from antiquity but also a heroine, in his eyes, of Modernism, because involved in a passion that earned social ostracism, his own ideal. (Baudelaire wrote on one occasion to his mother: 'I want to raise the whole human race against me. The delight this would give me would console me for everything.') The lesbian also seemed to appeal to a Baudelairean erotic ideal, the 'woman who bespeaks hardness and mannishness'. Such admiration may also relate to Baudelaire's profound antipathy to pregnancy. Yet, Benjamin notes, while Baudelaire was drawn to the lesbian as literary figure, he had no sympathy for lesbianism in actual daily life. Such contrary extremes were characteristic, allegorical. His every attitude was subject to 'abrupt, shock-like change'. At the same time there was an accompanying 'lack of conviction, insight, and steadiness'. Energy mixed with nonchalance and indolence (as in the dandy).[20]

Benjamin was also intrigued by Baudelaire's 'devastating irony' and 'macabre humour', as in the image Baudelaire 'presented in the February days – brandishing a rifle on some Paris street corner and shouting "Down with General Aupick!" (his own stepfather)'. Such humour could also take an unpleasant form, prefiguring fascist writing, as in a diary entry: 'A fine conspiracy could be organized for the purpose of exterminating the Jewish race.'[21]

In *Charles Baudelaire*, a coherent image of Baudelaire, and thereby of the Modernism he is held to represent, slips away. The very notion of representation, that cultural figures and texts might represent an age or period – a key concept and endeavour for Marxism as for any sociology of art, for cultural studies in general, then and now – comes under question. Here we find allegory as Benjamin conceived and deployed it, not as clear unified meanings but the reverse, destruction of all deceptive totality, mesmerizing multiplicity, series and clusters and constellations without continuum, death within fragmented life, Baroque emblem, Gothic theory.[22]

IV Modernism and Postmodernism

Benjamin was interested not only in allegory as fragmentation but in carnivalesque inversion, the comedy and poetics of the grotesque, as we can see in 'Naples', the essay he wrote (in 1925) with the Latvian Communist Asja Lacis. 'Naples' works on a contrast between Northern and Southern Europe, particularly in relation to architecture and street life. In the North, the house is the cell of a city's architecture, civilized, private, ordered, a gloomy box. In Naples, however, building and social and domestic life are porous, they interpenetrate, in courtyard, arcade, gateway, stairway, window, balcony, roof, becoming a 'theatre of new, unforeseen constellations'. People orient themselves not by house numbers but by shops, wells and churches; churches hide themselves in baroque ways, where initiates can occupy themselves in devotion or despair. 'The stamp of the definitive is avoided': all is porosity, in a passion for improvization, and buildings, like the street, are used as a popular stage, a great panorama, a fantastical variety show. In the street, everything joyful is mobile, from the uproar of popular festivals to the circulation of music, toys, ice cream. Bazaars are like fairy-tale galleries. Because the Neapolitans are a seafaring people, the fish market teems with starfish, crayfish, cuttlefish, often devoured raw with a little lemon. On the fourth or fifth floors of tenement blocks, cows are kept. Families merge into each other.

Unlike the confined, bourgeois, literary world of the Viennese cafe, the Neapolitan cafe is profligate with excessively hot coffee as well as sherbets, spumoni and ice cream, with people 'unable to sit down and stagnate in them', talking in a language of gestures where ears, nose, eyes, breast and shoulders are constantly activated. Whereas Northern sleep is protected, in Naples there is an interpenetration of day and night, noise and peace, street and home. Naples is like the African *kraal*, where each private attitude or act is permeated by streams of communal life. In the Naples essay, that which is constructed as Northern European – the aura of the intensely private and individual – is waylaid by the Southern European, and beyond Southern Europe, Africa: life as communal, enjoyment as simultaneously collective.[23]

It's not at all surprising that Benjamin can be seen as anticipating Poststructuralist theories of textuality as well as various motifs of Postmodernism. Benjamin stages quotation and interpretation in a way that easily brings to mind Bakhtin's notions of texts as polyphony, discourses speaking to each other in competing contesting contrasting voices. His writing is, we might say, heteroglossic, pulled by contrary movements, centripetal, centrifugal. The Adornoesque desire to deliver truths about modernity and mass culture in a language of essence mingles with an allegorical method that fissures and splinters the object of analysis. The definite mixes with the porous. Melancholia meets theatricality. A focus on final verdicts and definitive judgements is distracted by an eye for idiosyncratic features, macabre moments, grotesque humour. Representativeness encounters singularity. Modernist magisterialism is dethroned by fallen humanity. Such theatrical staging of argument brings to mind Barthes's evocation of the ideal text, in 'The Death of the Author', as a 'multi-dimensional space in which a variety of writings, none of them original, blend and clash', a 'tissue of quotations drawn from the innumerable centres of culture'. It reminds us of Lyotard talking of communication as language-games, as *agon*, jousting, duelling.[24]

In Benjamin's texts, there is staged a tension between principles and experience conceived as paternal and maternal. In his intellectual biography, Bernd Witte argues that Benjamin, in his writings on his childhood in a turn-of-the-century upper bourgeois Berlin Jewish family, reacted against his father as patriarch. His relations with his father were always very tense. Benjamin grew to identify paternal domination – and its capacity to inflict powerless suffering on those weaker in the family or in a lesser social position – with the bourgeois order, an order he would spend his life rejecting. The father is formal, martial, punishing, work-obsessed, achievement-oriented, attempting to dominate his son's consciousness with notions of time, duty and purpose; at school, the teacher is an extension of paternal domination. In contrast and opposition, the child is drawn to the mother as tender and consoling, especially when she comes to the bedside of the frequently ailing child to tell him stories. The mother is endowed with the storyteller's archaic, almost magical healing powers. The mother is an image of harmony, of body and text, womb and cave and word, harmony which strikes the adult as always no longer accessible, a lost plenitude, yet also Utopian promise, a suddenly transformed world, Messianic.[25]

As alternatives to patriarchal bourgeois domination, the child is drawn to other female images, feeling solidarity with the archaic, motherly figure of the old servant, or the maiden as nurse.[26] This attraction to female or feminized images appears frequently in literary modernism. We might think of the interest of *Ulysses* in Bloom as Jewish outsider, exploring and revealing his consciousness as the reverse of formal, martial and patriarchal. Ellman tells us that Joyce became interested in a theory announced in a contemporary text, Otto Weininger's *Sex and Character* (1903), that Jews are, by nature, womanly men, a phrase applied to Bloom in *Ulysses*; and Joyce also decided to give Bloom the middle name of a woman, Paula.[27] In his *Flaws in the Glass: A Self-Portrait* (1981), Patrick White revealed how much, as a child of wealthy respectable parents, he sought the nurturing company of his beloved nurse, Lizzie, his in-effect mother. With his outsider's sensitivity, White as a child found himself in empathy with the 'whores' living nearby in Sydney's Kings Cross. White, the developing writer, could enjoy the subtleties of a 'feminine sensibility' which masculine males lacked; he could be equally 'possessed by the spirit of man or woman'.[28] In White's novels, a maternal principle, of warmth, sympathy and receptivity, in male as well as female characters, is frequently valorized with characteristic insistence.

In *Of Grammatology*, Derrida suggests that Rousseau desired to pursue the image of the lost mother through his lover, whom he calls 'Mamma', but the mother, the origin promising regained wholeness and harmony, the certitude of totality, of presence, of stabililty of meaning, the logocentric, that which promises to resist the abyss of unconfinable meanings, can never be reached, except through creating images, substitutions, supplements, representations which beget more representations, the productivity, the ceaseless work, the deferment and difference, of discourse.[29]

Benjamin, the child as outsider, is drawn to the market women in Berlin, to the ancient hetairismic companionship of women, but comes to realize they promise warmth, closeness and abundance only in the destroying form of the commodity, of market capitalism.[30] Witte writes that Benjamin could conceive of Paris as Goddess, unapproachable, whom the writer yet attempts to approach through the limitless writing on Paris by poets honouring their beloved, the revered. The writer adds to this writing with *his* writing, but Paris remains ever-elusive, the city of mirrors reflecting back his own image. The writer tries to reach the unfathomable centre through evocations of the arcade, point of entry into the labyrinth. But the *Arcades Project* itself, unfinished fragments, is testament to the impossibility of reaching essence or totality, or even coherence.[31]

In *The Dialectics of Seeing: Walter Benjamin and the Arcades Project*, Susan Buck-Morss quotes a passage where Benjamin is musing about the fleeting sense of Utopia caught in fashion: 'That which the child (and the grown man in his faint memory) finds in the old folds of the dress into which he pressed himself when he held fast to the skirted lap of his mother – that must be contained by these pages.'[32]

The early nineteenth-century Parisian arcades – in their consumer fantasia, their shop signs and window displays, of curiosities, nick-nacks, bric-à-brac, hosiery and lingerie, dresses and coats, hats and accessories, exotic materials – beckoned as a female world, as a teasing, ambivalent reminder of the lost world of Benjamin's childhood, when he was introduced to and shown around Berlin by his mother.[33] He came to know the city as cave of commodities, feeling his mother humbled by her idolatrous worship as consumer. Such idolatry, such transmutation of revered mother into female as involved with dangerous pleasures, would also be found in the Parisian arcades, as they tempted passers-by with gastonomical perfections, intoxicating drinks, gaiety in the vaudeville theatres, and in the first-floor galleries, the sex sold by fashionably-dressed ladies of the night.[34]

The structural aspect of the Paris arcades, Buck-Morss tells us, suggested to Benjamin another history, for they were the first international style of modern architecture. Their kaleidoscopic, fortuitous juxtaposition of shop signs and window displays was a visible form of montage, a principle which would come to fruition in the Eiffel Tower. The arcades were precursors of the international expositions, the first world exposition held in London in 1851, its Crystal Palace similarly constructed out of iron and glass, industrial fairs which became mass entertainment, part of the new pleasure industry. Yet, while the arcades used iron and glass, they did so in a spirit of looking back; Benjamin felt that the arcades resembled Christian churches, while the first department stores, with their immense glassed-in roofs, seemed to be modelled after Oriental bazaars. Newly-processed iron was used for ornament, particularly in continuous balconies, even the Eiffel Tower having iron lace-like effects. It would be quite a long time before the wrought iron and steel first developed for railroads would be combined with glass in the construction of modern skyscrapers.[35]

The early nineteenth-century arcades, Buck-Morss says, were, in Benjamin's view, in a 'hermaphroditic position' in relation to the history of modern architecture. On the one hand, the interiors of the galleries were ornamental, replete with neoclassical columns, arches, and pediments. On the other, the glass and iron structuring would be taken up by twentieth-century architects like Le Corbusier, who admired the engineering involved in railroads, machines, and bridges. Benjamin admired the hangars and silos also admired by Le Corbusier in his 1920s manifestos.[36]

Le Corbusier, of course, despised the eclectic ornamentality and decorativeness of nineteenth-century building as merely female and superficial, like a feather on a woman's head.[37] We might, however, now apply Benjamin's perception that the early nineteenth-century arcades were 'hermaphroditic' to postmodern architecture, which, under the sign of Las Vegas – or at least Venturi, Scott Brown and Izenour's *Learning from Las Vegas* – developed an architectural language which both drew on Modernism and its language of space, structure and function, yet extravagantly, flamboyantly, excessively, revived eclecticism, a juxtaposition and kaleidoscope of styles and periods. *Learning from Las Vegas* also admired the Oriental, intimate, strolling aspect of the arcades that were built as part of the casinos, arcades that were warm, receptive, welcoming, inclusive, that were not, like the Modernism that Postmodern architecture questioned and challenged, hard, soaringly phallic, monumental, self-admiring.[38] I would argue that the Postmodern buildings of Sydney's Darling Harbour urban park are also 'hermaphroditic', a mixture of exhibition buildings, museums, aquarium, and festival market-place constructions, talking to Sydney as a historic port city, formed, Crystal Palace-like, of glass and metal, open, porous, popular, unforbidding.[39]

In *The Dialectics of Seeing*, Susan Buck-Morss rejects the appropriation of Walter Benjamin as Poststructuralist and Postmodernist. I don't think he is either: such appropriation could not respect the alterity of Benjamin, his singularity, his embeddedness in early twentieth-century Modernism. Benjamin would appear to have always followed Marx in opposing the commmodity form, the 'Hell that rages in the soul of the commodity'.[40] Here he is unlike the movement of Postmodernity we associate with an American trajectory, in Pop Art and *Learning from Las Vegas*, a

Postmodern aesthetic in historic compromise with the commodity form
and capitalist market society. Yet, yet – in the Baudelaire book – Benjamin
tells us that Marx's reference to the 'soul of the commodity' was a jest.[41]
And in *The Work of Art in the Age of Mechanical Reproduction*, he is
favourable indeed to mass-produced popular film.

In *The Dialectics of Seeing*, Buck-Morss is concerned to stress how
much the *Arcades Project* constitutes commodity society as gambling and
fashion, ruin and dust, as the fetishistic fragmentation of the living body,
as catastrophe, as futility, as the shock of the new and its incessant
repetition, as Hell, the very image which, she notes, so pleased Adorno
(initially) about the project.[42] In the strand of the Baudelaire book evoking
the urban crowd's isolation and uniformity, we might think of another
strand of Postmodernism, the cultural theory of Baudrillard,
apocalyptically bleak, seeing reality, reason, truth, representation and pre-
commodity community engulfed by an ecstatic, illusory phantasmagoria
of mass culture, information, and data, a lunar cold world of simulacra.
Postmodernism is itself a heterogeneous contradictory phenomenon, in
many ways repeating in new variations the unresolved and perhaps
unresolvable conflicting discourses of Modernism.

NOTES

1. Cf. Le Corbusier, *Towards a New Architecture* (London, 1965) and *The City of Tomorrow* (London, 1971).
2. Cf. J. Docker, *Postmodernism and Popular Culture: A Cultural History* (Cambridge, 1994).
3. A. Huyssen, *After the Great Divide: Modernism, Mass Culture and Postmodernism* (London, 1986), Chapter 3.
4. F. R. Leavis, 'Mass Civilisation and Minority Culture' (1930), reprinted in *For Continuity* (Cambridge, 1933), pp. 16, 19, 30–2.
5. Q. D. Leavis, *Fiction and the Reading Public* (London, 1932; reprinted New York, 1974), pp. 7, 23, 76, 129, 164.
6. Q. D. Leavis, *Fiction and the Reading Public*, pp. 6–7, 19, 25, 51–5, 57–8, 88, 182, 194.
7. T. W. Adorno and M. Horkheimer, *Dialectic of Enlightenment* (London, 1979), pp. 120–7, 130–1, 138, 145, 152, 161–7.
8. Adorno and Horkheimer, *Dialectic of Enlightenment*, pp. 141, 152–4, 165.
9. Cf. J. Bruck and J. Docker, 'Puritanic Rationalism: John Berger's *Ways of Seeing* and Media and Culture Studies', *Theory, Culture and Society*, 8, 4 (1991).
10. Huyssen, *After the Great Divide*, pp. 152–3.
11. W. Benjamin, *Illuminations* (New York, 1969); Patrice Petro, *Joyless Streets: Women and Melodramatic Representation in Weimar Germany* (Princeton, NJ, 1989), p. 49.
12. Petro, *Joyless Streets*, pp. 57–63.
13. W. Benjamin, *Charles Baudelaire: A Lyric Poet in the Era of High Capitalism* (London, 1989), pp. 27, 29, 162–3.
14. W. Benjamin, *Charles Baudelaire*, pp.159–60, 165.
15. W. Benjamin, *Charles Baudelaire*, p. 166.
16. W. Benjamin, *Charles Baudelaire*, pp. 34, 170–1.

17. W. Benjamin, *Charles Baudelaire*, pp. 34, 69, 81, 88, 91, 159, 166, 170–2, 174.
18. W. Benjamin, *Charles Baudelaire*, pp. 34, 68, 70, 97–101.
19. W. Benjamin, *Charles Baudelaire*, pp. 67, 74–5, 78–81, 96–8.
20. W. Benjamin, *Charles Baudelaire*, pp. 14-15, 75, 77, 90-96, 171.
21. W. Benjamin, *Charles Baudelaire*, pp. 13-14.
22. W. Benjamin, *Charles Baudelaire*, pp. 95–6; B. Witte, *Walter Benjamin: An Intellectual Biography* (Detroit, 1991), pp. 63–4, 76–8, 81–2, 91, 182. Cf. also M. Cohen, *Profane Illumination: Walter Benjamin and the Paris of Surrealist Revolution* (Berkeley, CA, 1993).
23. W. Benjamin, *Reflections* (New York, 1986).
24. R. Barthes, *Image-Music-Text* (Glasgow, 1979); J. Lyotard, *The Postmodern Condition: A Report on Knowledge* (Manchester, 1987).
25. Witte, *Walter Benjamin: An Intellectual Biography*, pp. 14–7, 131, 140–1, 143–7. Cf. also Petro, *Joyless Streets*, p. 62.
26. Witte, *Walter Benjamin: An Intellectual Biography*, pp. 144–5.
27. R. Ellman, *James Joyce* (Oxford, 1982), pp. 342, 373, 395, 450–1, 463–4, 515. See also S. L. Gilman, *Freud, Race, and Gender* (Princeton, NJ, 1993), pp. 77–9, 142.
28. P. White, *Flaws in the Glass: A Self-Portrait* (London, 1981), pp. 20, 34–5, 113, 81, 153.
29. J. Derrida, *Of Grammatology* (Baltimore, London, 1980), pp. 159, 179, 152–3, 156–7, 163.
30. Witte, *Walter Benjamin: An Intellectual Biography*, p. 146.
31. Witte, *Walter Benjamin: An Intellectual Biography*, pp. 181–2.
32. S. Buck-Morss, *The Dialectics of Seeing: Walter Benjamin and the Arcades Project* (Cambridge, MA, 1991), p. 276.
33. Reading these pages in *The Dialectics of Seeing*, I was reminded of Christina Stead's *The Man Who Loved Children*, that great comic novel exploring a disastrous relationship in a decaying-genteel house, where the lon-suffering Henny retreats to the mysterious female interior world of her bedroom. The children love coursing into her room, its dusky smell, with its combination of dust, powder, scent and body odours that stirred their blood, 'deep, deep'. Sometimes the mother allows the children to snuggle into the shawls, old gowns, dirty clothes ready for the wash, and blankets thrown over her easy chair. Sometimes they could look into what they call her treasure drawers, in which spill and toss all sorts of laces, ribbons, gloves, flowers, jabots, belts, collars, hairpins, powders, buttons, imitation jewels, shoelaces, pots of rouge, bits of mascara. They would plunge their hands into the drawers, with sparkling eyes and rapt faces, until their fingers would strike something they didn't recognize, and their faces would grow serious, surprised. Henny's room always remains a mystery, 'a refuge of delight, a cave of Aladdin'. Cf. Christina Stead, *The Man Who Loved Children* (1940; reprinted Harmondsworth, 1985), pp. 68–73.
34. Buck-Morss, *The Dialectics of Seeing*, pp. 83, 284, 286.
35. Buck-Morss, *The Dialectics of Seeing*, pp. 39, 74, 83, 85–6, 111, 131.
36. Buck-Morss, *The Dialectics of Seeing*, pp. 126–31, 149.
37. Le Corbusier, *Towards a New Architecture*, pp. 32–3, 37, 214.
38. R. Venturi, D. S. Brown and S. Izenour, *Learning from Las Vegas* (Cambridge, MA, 1988).
39. Cf. my *Postmodernism and Popular Culture: A Cultural History*, Chapters 7 and 8.
40. Buck-Morss, *The Dialectics of Seeing*, pp. 54, 186, 222.
41. W. Benjamin, *Charles Baudelaire*, p. 55.
42. Buck-Morss, *The Dialectics of Seeing*, pp. 57, 96, 101, 106, 121, 176, 191, 211, 280.

II
Gender/Utopia

5

Reading/Writing the Feminine City: Calvino, Hessel, Benjamin

Sigrid Weigel

I The Disappearance of the Woman in the Feminine City [1]

In the series of fifty-five images of cities – framed and interrupted by conversations between the legendary emperor of the Mongolian dynasty, Kubla Khan, and his Venetian envoy, Marco Polo which are strung together to make up Italo Calvino's book, *Le città invisibli* (1972), there is, among others, the story of the genesis of a city. This city is built on the place where different men, in pursuit of a common dream, encounter one another in order to construct, while they fail to realize the object of their desire, rooms and walls out of which the city emerges. They daily go to work in the streets of the city after having long forgotten their dream. This story of the genesis of the city of Zobeida[2] refers to a relationship between images of femininity and of cities, one which is significant for the literature of the city. The city is constituted here by way of the attempt to confer permanence on the wish expressed in the dream: whereby the dreamer becomes a founder of a city, the work of the unconscious becomes the work of the subject in the process of civilization, in which the work of forgetting is implicit. The city is thus constituted as a site marked by the absence of the woman, in whose place an alliance of men congregates, held together by the lack of the feminine. The image of the woman in which the allure for the man is compressed points in this scenery to where the woman is not.

It is for this reason that the inhabitants of the city are described as uncomprehending in regard to the desires of those arriving in the city. In the attempt to capture their vision in walls, the men have imprisoned themselves and now regard the city as a trap. However, in its *topography*, 'the streets, which circle around themselves like a knot', the dreams of the city founders from which the city has arisen have left their traces which resemble or seek to imitate the paths of pursuit, the paths of the pursued image of a woman which has been lost from sight. Furthermore, the fact that the city bears the *name* of a woman sheds light on still another element of the original desire for the feminine; the magic of its naming, its creation in language,[3] recalls the underlying desire retained in the symbolic creation.

All fifty-five of the invisible cities in Calvino's book have names which can also serve as women's names: from Diomira, Dorotea, Anastasia to Leandra, Melanie, Adelma to Pentesilea, Teodora and Berenice. Furthermore, the composition of the text at no point allows the suspicion to arise that it is dealing with real cities, with the result that the femininity of the cities is clearly referred to their imaginary character. However, the invisibility and unreality of the cities described is not understood as the antithesis of real cities, or even urban reality. Rather, with his invisible cities, Calvino thematizes the real power of the imaginary and the place and image of the city as a paradigm of symbolic production: the city as scene of writing. Through the series of city images, the impossibility of narrating the cities expressed in the conversations between Kubla Khan and Marco Polo is referred to fundamental structures in the history of the symbolic.

Calvino's frame story is concerned with the attempt of the Tartar emperor to take possession of his empire by having his envoy report to him on the cities. It is not only the conversation between the two, one that employs different languages as well as silent gestures and silent commentary, which proves to be difficult, but also the relationship of the conversation to its object and the speakers. The theme shifts from the attempt to discuss individual cities to a reflection upon patterns, forms, models, upon the invisible order and the laws which determine the cities and their histories, whereby the goal of conquest and possession is deferred into the infinite: that is, the unattainable. Here, something is repeated and reflected in the story *about* the cities which is registered in the city images themselves. For example, depictions are described as distortions, signs as traces of another, the visible as an image of something invisible, language as deception, sceneries as repetitions, as the return of the repressed. The impossible linguistic representation of the city is in this way referred back to the language *of* the city.

Calvino's motif of imaginary cities radicalizes a moment implicit throughout the history of city representation: namely, the fact that the image of a city is more a figure of thought than a portrayal, that in the image of a city, whether expressed in myth, in the text or in the city's architecture, the patterns of order and thought of a society or culture express themselves. The city as paradigmatic site of the work of civilization – as a site which shields itself from external nature and in which the repressed returns in an altered form – can be comprehended as the concrete symbol of a culture. In the fifty-five stories of *Invisible Cities*, Calvino, in his reconstruction of numerous city myths, renders visible the pattern of symbolic structures which are written into them.

The story of the genesis of the city of Zobeida thus refers to myths of foundation,[4] albeit in a modern version, in which the recollection of the mythical primordial scene of the city's founding is only visible in rudimentary constellation. The walls, for example, recall the function of the city walls in ancient myths of city foundation as a protective barrier around the newly-established order. This order dissociates itself from the wild, untamed nature outside, from that space in which the hero proves himself as dragon-slayer in order to then be rewarded inside the city as a citizen with the woman as spouse and mother of his children. For the feminine, the city walls symbolize a splitting of the feminine into the untamed, feminine nature without, which is manifested in the image of the dragon, the hydra, the chimera and other such images, and the domesticated woman and her petrified, ossified form of existence trapped within the walls of the city; the city walls thereby mark the limits of the place of the woman within the social sphere as one who has been buried alive. The designation of the city with the name Zobeida recalls, on the other hand, the allegorization of cities as feminine personifications, which fluctuate between the extremes of the 'Whore of Babylon' and the 'New Jerusalem', and which frequently appear in secularized myths in the form of a virgin to be conquered, a seductive mistress or a reassuring, protective mother.[5] However, the genesis of the city of Zobeida can be established within *modernity*, in so far as its history, on the one hand, already presupposes the invisibility of the feminine as mute support of the system which is not itself manifest.[6] On the other hand, the history of the city proceeds from the desire for the feminine, a desire which is repressed into the unconscious.

As the streets of the city are described here as a stage for the longed-for repetition of a dream scene, so the city becomes the scene of a writing of the unconscious: the translation into the symbolic is realized via the absence of the woman. Its hero has transformed himself from the hero of antiquity into the subject of the writing, into the author. *His* symbolic production, which takes the place of the absent woman, now appears as 'feminine'. In his own sensation of captivity, however, he has forgotten its premise: the petrification and exclusion of the feminine. The elements of this story thus refer to three historical levels in the relationship between the images of the city and of femininity: to the mythical level of city foundation, with its splitting of the feminine; to the allegorization of the city as woman, and to the dream image, associated with the feminine, of a city within modernity.

With this story, Calvino has reproduced, within a remodelling of city mythology which can be read as a structural portrait of the writing of cities, the function and the place of the feminine within this writing. Whether the reproduction also has the effect of circumventing this function will ultimately depend on the perspective and work of reading. For the history of city representation, it would then constitute the 'last possible writing of an epoch',[7] which is to be considered as the concretization of the modes of expression of the subject. However, Calvino does not herald a new epoch – for example, in the sense of the 'postmodern'; rather, he destroys, similarly to Benjamin before him, a particular idea of the future established within the continuum of time, both with regard to its *Utopian* or its *apocalyptic* version. While Kubla Khan finds in his atlas the 'regions still not discovered or founded', and those cities 'which are threatened by nightmares and bewitchments', Marco Polo answers him, in their last conversation, with an allusion to the fleetingness of Utopia in illumination, in fragments or in signals outside the continuum of space and time. He takes a position counter to a progressive model of history, without endorsing notions of apocalypse under whose fixed stare on the prospect of annihilation the existing oppositions and differences within the social move out of view – that is, into oblivion. Hell, according to Marco Polo, is constituted in our daily living together. In this sense, too, the city appears in Calvino's work as a place of unrealized desire.

II *Flânerie* and the City as Scene of Writing

In his book *Spazieren in Berlin* (1929), Franz Hessel describes *flânerie*, or strolling, as a 'promenade without fixed goal', and as setting out 'on the undreamt-of adventure of the eye', during which 'new proximities and distances' emerge, as a particular form of reading: '*Flânerie* is a form of reading the street whereby human faces, displays, shop windows, cafe terraces, streetcars, automobiles, trees become so many equally weighted letters which together yield the words, sentences and pages of a book that is always new. In order to stroll properly, one cannot have anything too definite planned.'[8] Such remarks *about flânerie* or strolling, however, are found in Hessel's work only in scattered form; his book is more the text of a *flâneur*. Nevertheless, his 'book that is always new' is at the same time like a writing of the second degree, one which emerges out of the reading of the streets. For 'the *flâneur*' is always already a literary concept or a writing concept. The figure of the *flâneur* is less the representative than the medium of a writing, in so far as he devotes himself to the reading of the city-writing in order to imitate it as the subject of his own writing on paper. For this he is responsible as author, but he is not its *auctor/* autonomous creator. Grasping the aimless roaming about as a movement which does not follow a phallic economy, but is rather associated with the feminine, and constitutes the grounds upon which 'feminine' features are sometimes ascribed to *flâneurs*. On the other hand, the *flâneur* is always also an observer, and women are a popular object of his gaze or his curiosity.[9]

In his essay on Surrealism (1929), Benjamin depicts the *flâneur* as a type of the 'profanely illuminated'. This depiction is found in a text which contains in compressed form his theory of the magic of language as well as his philosophy of history as looking towards that which has been, a text which he himself describes as an 'opaque screen before the Arcades Project'.[10] The 'city of Paris itself' is here described as 'the most dreamed' of object of the material world: 'And no face is surrealistic to the same degree as the true face of a city' (II, 300). Drawing on the function of the unconscious for surrealist practice, Benjamin names as the leitmotif of his city writings the dream structure of the cityscape, by which is meant not the dreamscape of a city, but rather that which is dreamed in the image of the city – that is, the form of the city analogous to the forms of expression of the unconscious: the city as labyrinth, as topography, as web, the streets of Paris as a 'net of veins of the imagination' (V, 1208), the city, then, as the scene of a writing which can only be deciphered by a reading in the 'double sense of the word, in both its profane and its magical meaning' (II, 209). This is a reading which understands how to decipher the language of things by abandoning itself to those tidings which are presented within the visible figurations as fleeting or dialectical images. Of the types found among the profanely illuminated, which Benjamin refers to in his essay on Surrealism – the reader, the thinker, the one who waits, and the *flâneur* – the *flâneur* becomes such an important figure because his activity includes all the other forms of profane illumination.

In his well-known review of Hessel's book, Benjamin, alluding to the hieroglyphic form of the language of dreams, speaks of the 'Egyptian dream book of he who is awake' (III, 198), unlike Kracauer, who speaks in his own *flâneur* text of 'daydreaming'.[11] Benjamin is concerned with a constellation in which he who is awake abandons himself to the images and structures of the dream's work. The paradigm for this in his *Arcades Project* is the threshold of awakening, which is outlined already in the 'Initial Notes' as a 'unique experience of the dialectic', and in the early drafts as an 'exemplary case of the act of remembering' (V, 1006, 1057), a case from which the dialectical method characterizing his conception of history is derived: 'To work through (*durchmachen*) that which has been with the intensity of a dream, in order to experience the present as the waking world to which the dream refers!...Every epoch has this side which is turned towards dreams, its child side' (V, 1006). Just as the 'now of recognition' corresponds to this constellation as a structure of time, so too, in a topographical respect, the transition, the threshold, the passage can be understood in ritualistic terms as a *rite de passage*.[12] In the gaze directed back to the past, it is the dream that extends into the waking world and the reference of that which has been to the time of the present (*Jetztzeit*) which is so significant here for Benjamin and which distinguishes his writing from a mere depiction of a doubling of that which has been or that which is dreamed. He makes this clear in a distinction between his own work and the urban mythology of Surrealism, between his work and Aragon's *Le paysan de Paris*, which, with its description of the Passage de l'Opéra in Paris, played no small part in prompting his *Arcades Project*: while Aragon stands firmly in the realms of the dream, Benjamin is concerned with the awakening, with the 'resolution of the "mythology" into the historical space' (V, 571).

The topography of the city is thereby read, as it were, as a third writing which emerges from the analogy of images and structures in myths and in the unconscious: the script-image of the city as a third writing in which the correspondences between cultural history and the history of the subject are represented. In the many years during which Benjamin worked on the *Arcades Project*, from the early drafts in 1927 until his death in 1940, a number of individual projects crystallized out of this large-scale plan. As far as the fundamental constellation is concerned, the awakening of the subject in his *Berlin Childhood Around 1900* can be most clearly distinguished from the different attempts he made to read Paris as an image of the nineteenth century with regard to the awakening of the collective. Nevertheless, it is always the *city* which constitutes the place of awakening and also the scene of the writing which is to be deciphered.

III The Path to the Mothers

Oddly enough, in his review of Hessel's work, at the beginning of which he distinguishes between two groups of city portrayals, Benjamin speaks not of these two images of the city, but of the journey into the distance and the journey into the past, to which his Berlin book can be attributed, as can his Paris project. Benjamin had himself already described several long-distance journeys, producing city images of Naples (1924), Moscow (1927), Weimar (1928) and San Gimignano (1929).[13] The Hessel review, however, marks a definitive shift to an interest in the city in the sense of a journey into the past. This shift is combined with a shift in perspective in regard to feminine images of the city. While the city images already referred to in Benjamin's work contain no femininity myths, he had nevertheless referred in journalistic essays to the well-known images of the city as goddess or beloved.

'Paris as Goddess' is the title of a review published in 1928 in which he reads the Paris novel of the Romanian author Marthe Bibesco as a 'bibliographical allegory': Paris as a goddess in the midst of 'an incalculable quantity of books of a thousand forms' with which it is paid homage and in which it is reflected. In reference to historical allegories of the conquered city, Benjamin interprets this city novel by a woman as: 'a counter-image to a popular subject of the old masters. How often do they not show us the victorious commander when he receives with representative gesture the keys to a conquered city? Here a conquered heart hands over its keys with an equally grand gesture to the city goddess' (III, 142).[14] Benjamin ironically addresses the difficulty for a woman of establishing a position as an author within an image-history which allocates places in a quite explicit gender-specific fashion. He cites a chapter title of the novel, 'One does not marry a city' (*On n'épouse pas une ville*), and adds to this: 'namely Paris, to which she ultimately weds herself in the form of an airforce lieutenant'. Equating the heroine with the author of the novel, Benjamin sees in its action a (role-)reversed redemption of the image of marriage denied in the title. Rather than fall back on this or comparable images of femininity, Benjamin, in his own city writings, describes the place of the feminine in the writing of the city and finds those places in the cityscape which are connected with feminine forms.

In the Hessel review, in which the city book appears as the writing of memory, the 'Path to the Mothers' – which could be seen as a an epigraph to *Berlin Childhood* – is thematized. Although Hessel does not actually speak of childhood, Benjamin's review reads like an initial draft for his own Berlin book:

> *Spazieren in Berlin* is an echo of what the city tells the child from early age onwards. It is a thoroughly epic book, a memorizing while strolling, a book for which memory was not the source but rather the Muse. The Muse moves along the streets and each of them slopes downwards. She leads the way down, if not to the mother, then nevertheless into a past which can be all the more entrancing because it is not only the author's own, private past. (III, 194)

The fact that the path of memory to the mothers is described here as sloping downward makes clear that the text is not concerned with the mother as person, that the path to the mothers describes, rather, a viewpoint directed to the hidden, the invisible. This direction is also indicated by those stony figures which Hessel had described as representatives of 'second-hand myth', or as *plebs deorum*, and which Benjamin now judges as 'those knowledgeable of the threshold' (*Schwellenkundige*) or as 'guardians of the *rites de passage*'.

In the recollection entitled 'Tiergarten' in *Berlin Childhood Around 1900*, Benjamin again takes up aspects of his Hessel review. Hessel himself

– in an allusion to Aragon's *Le paysan de Paris* – is described and at the same time disguised here as the 'peasant of Berlin'. He leads the first-person narrator to the mothers of the garden; with his help, the caryatids and others 'knowledgeable of the threshold' of the Tiergarten villas are 'taken by their word' (IV, 238).[15] If the Tiergarten here takes the form of an area of numerous points of transition between nature and culture, between city and wilderness, between a magical language of nature and the signs of the symbolic world, so Benjamin finds in the city those places in which the memory of what has been excluded from the city appears. These become visible by means of a cultivated art of losing one's way in the city, which thereby comes to be equated with a labyrinth. Within the mode of this art of losing one's way, the path through the city becomes a *reading*, and the cityscape becomes a writing, in which different places occupied by the feminine can be distinguished. Thus, the subterranean regions, transcribed with the mothers, are to be understood as pre-symbolic, while the caryatids and others 'knowledgeable of the threshold' represent allegories or petrified embodiments of a memory of wilderness or myth *within* the symbolic, or, formulated another way, replacements of the pre-symbolic which have become images within the order of the metropolis. These mark or inhabit the points of transition.

In the section 'Loggias', placed at the beginning of the final version of *Berlin Childhood*, Benjamin then compares the images and allegories 'which dominate my thinking' (IV, 294) with the caryatids on the loggias of the courtyards in the west of Berlin. As threshold between inside and outside, as a place of 'the uninhabitable' and 'seclusion', in which 'time becomes obsolete', the loggia is one of the variants of the arcades belonging to childhood within the topography of the city. It is dominated by the caryatids, allegories given material form in stone. Noticeable here is the fact that, of those 'knowledgeable of the threshold' found in Hessel, the 'caryatids and Atlases, the cherubs and *pomonae*', it is the feminine forms which are given particular attention. This method corresponds with the fact that already, in his Hessel review, Benjamin (within one – grammatically incorrect – sentence) had moved from the enumeration of the above-mentioned 'threshold gods' (pl. masc.) to the feminine form of 'guardians of the *rites de passage*'. He thus shifts the focus from Hessel's 'second-hand myths' to the significance of such forms within writing, and thereby illustrates the fact that allegorical representations in our culture predominently utilize the feminine (em-)body(ments).[16] In *Berlin Childhood Around 1900*, the caryatids face other stone forms which cannot be counted among 'those knowledgeable of the threshold', forms which do not belong to the *plebs deorum*, but which have to be considered, as in the case of Friedrich Wilhelm and Queen Luise in the Tiergarten, representative figures or, as in the case of the 'radiant Victoria' on top of the Victory Column, as allegories of domination and political power.

However, before Benjamin could reproduce the symbolic function of such figures in his text, he had to bid farewell to an autobiographical style which still marked the preliminary draft of *Berlin Childhood*, the 'Berlin Chronicle' which he sketched in 1932 on Ibiza.[17] In the 'Berlin Chronicle', a *life-history* model of autobiographical representation still competes with the topographical concept already established here as the representation of the subject's memory,[18] with the reference to memory as one of a location (VI, 486) and with the image of losing one's way in a labyrinth, which refers to the city as it does to writing – concretely to the blotting paper of the school exercise book (VI, 469). Yet the image of the labyrinth is also employed as a diagrammatic scheme, in the form of family trees, of acquaintances with different people (VI, 491). In the revised version of *Berlin Childhood*, this autobiographical concept – the depiction of a life-history as a figuration of human relationships – steps back behind a topography of images and traces of memory, and with it, the biographical, singular aspects behind the paradigmatic constellations of a bourgeois childhood at the turn of the century: those *'images...*in which the experience of the metropolis are precipitated in a child of the bourgeois class', as Benjamin puts it in the foreword to the revised version of *Berlin Childhood*.[19]

Along with the method of representation, however, the characters also undergo a change in status. Where concrete persons such as the mother, the grandmother, the girlfriend, the (female) teacher or the market women appear, their significance within the text is imperceptibly moved into the symbolic. Just as, for Benjamin, the sign aspect of language also has a flashing magical significance, so too the figures in this childhood text are given a symbolic significance. As personnel inhabiting the scene of memory, they take their place alongside other images and forms. Works of art, imaginary and mythical forms, goddesses of stone and fantasy, are given equal weight alongside concrete persons from the childhood of the first-person narrator. It is hardly necessary to emphasize that the focus here is above all on feminine figures.

Thus the Ariadne in the section 'Tiergarten' refers as much to the Ariadne who leads the heroes through the labyrinth as it does to one of the youth's early loves, to whose name – Luise von Landau – a magical memory trace is attached, as described in the section 'Two Riddle Images' (*Zwei Rätselbilder*). Thus the aunt, who resides in the oriel of the house at the 'corner of Steglitzer and Genthiner' streets, appears as the guardian of a memory in which the names of what has been, of the villages and clans, are stored. And the 'only cosmopolitan' (*weltbürgerlich*) among the 'palatial homes' (*hochherrschaftlich*) which the youth has come to know, the home of the grandmother, is described as the 'motherland', in regard to the feeling of security which it conveys, as well as in a colonialist sense as a secure point of departure for the numerous journeys of the grandmother to places which appear to the boy like colonies of her own home or place of residence. The grandmother's taking of possession of these 'colonies' is symbolized in the picture postcards which she sends from places visited, particularly in the relationship displayed between the cards' image and writing: 'And the large, pleasant handwriting which played at the foot of the images or formed clouds in their sky, showed them to be so completely inhabited by my grandmother that they became colonies of the Blumeshof.'[20]

The section 'Market Hall' can be read as a counter-image to this, in which the market hall becomes a mythical image of fertility and overflowing sensuality. The description of the portly bodies and ponderous movements of the market women amidst the fruits and foods flows into the image of the fertile, devoted womb offering itself, such that the juxtaposition of voluptuous female bodies and foodstuffs displayed as wares is emphasized as an imaginary image for the connection between fertility and sensuality. From here, it is not far to the whores assigned to the streets, to that place from where the promise comes of being able to withdraw from the rule of the mother, and for this reason, the streets are also described as 'procuring' (*kupplerisch*). In contrast to such *images*, the nanny is recalled through her *voice*, due to the fact that this takes on significance as a disturbance in the situation of gradual awakening when 'the winter morning familiarized me with the things in my room'.[21]

But it is the figure of the mother in the text which exhibits the most multifaceted significance. She repeatedly moves into the image (of memory) in relation to closeness or distance, power or powerlessness. Obviously, the concern is not only with the 'mother' in regard to the personal mother; the word is also used to describe mythical places. The spheres assigned to the mother are given another mysterious significance as well: for example, in the description of the corner of the parental bedroom in which the mother's morning coat hung behind a curtain as a 'dark nook': 'The darkness behind the curtain door was unfathomable: in the corner was the infamous pendant of translucent paradise that opened itself to me with my mother's toilette closet...Such was the old, secret weaving spell that once had possessed its place in the spinning wheel, divided up now into heaven and hell.'[22] Similarly described is the 'sewing box' of the mother, which divides into a well-ordered 'upper region' and a 'dark underground, the jumble'. From the box, 'infamous temptations' for the childish desire for discovery and destruction come, namely the temptation to break with one's finger through the pieces of ornamented paper which are stuck to the new cotton reels and which cover the hollow space beneath, and then to feel the hole. In other scenes, such childish desires for conquest take on the form of an initiation rite, as is the case when, for example, the 'butterfly hunt' is described as a change from the mimetic adaptation (to the movements of the escaping animal) to a catching hold of human existence, or when, in the section 'Pfaueninsel and Glienicke', the symbolic taking possession of new territories by the youth is recalled, and the failure of such conquests is described as the loss of a 'second fatherland'.

In characterizing Benjamin's *modus operandi* as a whole, it becomes clear that, instead of drawing analogies between woman and city in a text which follows the images and traces of memory in the topography of the city, he reproduces the signature of the feminine within this topography: a semiotic of feminine places within the writing, presented in a series of childish, primal scenes in the city from which arises the visual and sign function of images of women.

The precision with which Benjamin deals with this material is revealed by comparing the final version of the text with its earlier variants. In revising the text, he leaves aside images in which the feminine functions merely as metaphor and thereby gives rise to a sexualization of the object of description. An example is the metaphorical rendering of the railway station, Anhalter Bahnhof, as a 'maternal cavern of the railway' (IV, 1; 246), or the scene in the pantry, in which nibbling at food is described through a metaphor of sex, and reference made to a renewed virginity of the food following the tasting (IV, 250). The further omission of those scenes which thematize the streets, the whores and the labyrinth of the city opening to the sexual drive should not only be attributed to the situation of the Jewish writer in the context of fascism,[23] but also to the fact that these images were to be used in another city book of Benjamin's, the *Arcades Project*. In this work, which was to be dedicated to the awakening of the collective, the whores reappear as inhabitants of the city's arcades.

The whore is here understood as an allegory of modernity, due to the fact that the fetish character of the commodity is most manifestly recognizable in prostitution. The embodiment of beauty, desire and happiness in the image of the woman, this aura of the feminine, fades into mere appearance when it confronts the commodity character of the woman as prostitute. When the woman is described in this context as an allegory, then this is no longer in the sense of a functioning form of representation, but rather in the sense of a dissolution of such a representational function: for Benjamin assumes that the devaluation of the organic, which accompanied the traditional allegorical representation, is surpassed in the commodity, and above all in the figure of the whore, when 'in the prostitution of the large cities...the woman herself becomes the article of mass-production' (I, 668). Thus the woman, for Benjamin, is not an allegory of modernity because she embodies the modern, but because, in her, the devaluation of the living within the modern world of commodities scatters and destroys its very appearance. Where we are 'dealing with the prostitute as the commodity that most completely fulfils the allegorical perception...the scattering of the allegorical appearance...is invested in this fulfilment'.[24] In this respect, Benjamin can also write, in the outlines for the *Arcades Project*, 'that the images of woman and death penetrate a third, that of Paris' (V, 1233).[25] For the drawing of an analogy between woman and city is analysed as a function of the destruction of the organic: formerly through the allegory, within modernity through the commodity.

If one draws a comparison with Calvino's book, it becomes clear that both authors, Benjamin and Calvino, practice a deconstructive form of writing[26] in regard to myths of femininity, but that they can be distinguished from one another in that Calvino no longer claims to refer to the real when his 'invisible cities' move in the realm of the imaginary, while Benjamin includes the language of things in his expanded concept of writing (anticipating Derrida). He outlines an image of history by – to use his own formulation in the essay on Surrealism – seeking to decipher the visual and phyce of the city.

NOTES

1. This is an edited version of an article published originally in German in S. Weigel, *Topographie der Geschlechter: Kulturgeschichtliche Studien zur Literatur* (Reinbek, 1990).

2. This is the first story in the third chapter, under the heading, 'The Cities and the Wish 5', in I. Calvino, *Die Unsichtbaren Städte* (Munich, 1985). T. de Lauretis, in *Alice Doesn't: Feminism, Semiotics, Cinema* (Bloomington, IN 1984), has read Calvino's story of the city of Zobeida as a paradigm for the significance of the woman for the dominant semiotic concept. However, she is not concerned in her book with the gender-specific history of city representation and writing.

3. Concerning the magic of naming, cf. Benjamin's theory of the magic of language, above all in his essay 'Über die Sprache überhaupt und über die Sprache des Menschen', in W. Benjamin, *Gesammelte Schriften*, ed. R. Tiedemann and H. Schweppenhäuser, 7 vols (Frankfurt/Main, 1974–), II, 140–57. All quotations from Benjamin refer to this edition, unless otherwise noted. Abbreviated references identify volume and page number.

4. Cf. H. Kurnitzky, *Ödipus: Ein Held der westlichen Welt. Über die zerstörerischen Grundlagen der Zivilisation* (Berlin, 1978), and K. Heinrich, 'Das Floß der Medusa', in *Faszination des Mythos: Studien zu antiken und modernen Interpretationen*, ed. R. Schlesier (Basel, Frankfurt/Main, 1985).

5. Examples of such allegorization can be found in S. Weigel, '"Die Städte sind weiblich und nur dem Sieger hold": Zur Topographie der Geschlechter in Gründungsmythen und Städtedarstellungen', in S. Weigel, *Topographie der Geschlechter*.

6. See J. Kristeva, 'Die Produktivität der Frau: Interview von Elaine Boucqey', in 'Das Lächeln der Medusa', *Alternative*, 109, 1976, p. 167.

7. See J. Derrida, *Grammatologie* (Frankfurt/Main, 1974), p. 43.

8. F. Hessel, *Ein Flaneur in Berlin* (Berlin ,1984), p. 145.

9. In his reading of the things and people he classifies as equally-weighted letters, Hessel also names a series of female figures: from the 'long-legged girl' (p. 8), the 'small young

girl girl from Wertheim and Tietz' (p. 32), the typist and the 'post-war Berlin woman', which he characterizes as 'young avant-garde' (p. 37), to the 'Ladies Babylon and Renaissance' in the *Tanzpalast* (p. 50), the circus women in the Lunapark and the dancing girls from the revue, to the feminine part of the petrified representatives of a 'second-hand myth' (p. 155), as they are found in the stonework of house entrances, façades and public spaces which are seen as particularly important for Benjamin. – In his *flâneur* texts, Siegfried Kracauer speaks of the 'excesses' of the act of strolling about as more appealing than encounters with individual women, such that the seductiveness of the streets is substituted for that of women. This can be interpreted within the context of a writing concept of *flânerie*, and compared with what Kracauer describes as the pleasure of the *activity* of writing as 'useless activity', which likewise means more to him 'than a woman or one's friends'. Cf. his texts 'Erinnerung an eine Pariser Strasse' (1930) and 'Das Schreibmaschinchen' (1927), in S. Kracauer, *Straßen in Berlin und anderswo* (Berlin, 1987), pp. 7–11 and 82–6.

10. W. Benjamin, *Briefe*, vol. 2 (Frankfurt/Main, 1966), p. 489.
11. Kracauer, *Straßen in Berlin und anderswo*, p. 41.
12. On the concept of 'threshold' as the core of Benjamin's theory, cf. W. Menninghaus, *Schwellenkunde: Benjamins Passage des Mythos* (Frankfurt/Main, 1986).
13. Cf. here 'Benjamins Städtebilder', in P. Szondi, *Lektüren und Lektionen* (Frankfurt/Main, 1973), pp. 134–49.
14. Cf. here B. Witte 'Ein ungeschriebenes Buch lesen' in *Passagen: Walter Benjamins Urgeschichte des XIX. Jahrhunderts*, ed. N. Bolz and B. Witte (Munich, 1984), pp. 7–12. A year after the article 'Paris as Goddess', Benjamin once more takes up the theme under the title of 'Paris, the City of Mirrors' in order to write about the 'interaction of city and book'. The city as book, as pile of books, the mass of books as declarations of love to the city, the spaces of the city as indecipherable writing, the city as mirror and the image of Paris in the mirror of the Seine: the text has the effect of a memorizing of the different variants of this interaction (IV, 356–9).
15. On *Berlin Childhood*, cf. A. Stüssi, *Erinnerungen an die Zukunft: Walter Benjamins Berliner Kindheit um Neunzehnhundert* (Göttingen, 1977).
16. On the phenomena of feminine allegories, see Weigel, '"Die Städte sind weiblich und nur dem Sieger hold": Zur Topographie der Geschlechter in Gründungsmythen und Städtedarstellungen'.
17. This is not to say that Benjamin here subscribed to an illusionary immediacy, a 'writing of life': the author, who otherwise always avoided using the 'I', reports rather that 'this subject, which has for years been accustomed to remaining in the background, did not so easily allow itself to be asked to take frontstage' and of the 'caution of the subject which, represented by the "I", can demand not to be exploited' (VI, 476). Cf. his early reflections on the 'I' in the 'Tagebuch' in 'Metaphysik der Jugend' from 1913, in which he speaks of the 'accession to the throne of one who abdicates' (II, 101). M. Schneider discusses *Berlin Childhood* from the aspect of disguising in his study of autobiographical texts of the twentieth century; cf. *Die erkaltete Herzensschrift: Der autobiographische Text im 20. Jahrhundert* (Munich, 1986).
18. See the formulation 'Lebens-Bios-graphisch' (VI, 466).
19. W. Benjamin, *Berliner Kindheit um Neunzehnhundert* (Frankfurt/Main, 1987), p. 9.
20. *Berliner Kindheit um Neunzehnhundert*, p. 50.
21. *Berliner Kindheit um Neunzehnhundert*, p. 29.
22. *Berliner Kindheit um Neunzehnhundert*, pp. 62–3.
23. Individual sections of *Berlin Childhood* initially appeared in the *Frankfurter Zeitung* and in the *Vossische Zeitung* between December 1932 and August 1934, under a pseudonym after May 1933. Scholem had advised Benjamin not to publish the section 'Awakening of Sexuality' due to the (not only) at that time explosive connection between Judaism and sexuality. Further passages or themes which were omitted during the revision are those which were taken up in other projects of Benjamin's, such as, for example, reflections on photography, on linguistic theory and on shock.

24. W. Benjamin, *Briefe*, vol. 2, p. 752.
25. In Buci-Gluckmann's study of femininity as an allegory of modernity, the semiotic and metaphorical significance of the 'feminine' in Benjamin's writings comes off badly – due to the accentuation of the androgenous and the topian orientation of the reading. Cf. Ch. Buci-Glucksmann, *Walter Benjamin und die Utopie des Weiblichen* (Hamburg, 1984).
26. Destruction is registered in Benjamin's method of construction as the latter's precondition. Cf. his relevant entry in the *Arcades Project* (V, 587).

Translated by Joe O'Donnell (Berlin)

6

Sirens of Gaslight and Odalisques of the Oil Lamp: The Language of Desire in the *Arcades Project*

Margaret Mahony Stoljar

On 30 December 1929, Walter Benjamin wrote in his *Paris Diary*: 'No sooner does one arrive in the city than one is presented with a gift. It is idle to resolve not to write anything about it. The past day is built up as children re-build the table of presents on Christmas morning' (IV, 567).[1] So it is not surprising that what Benjamin does write about Paris often reads like the language of love. A year earlier, he had chosen an eloquent sub-title for the short essay, 'Paris, City in the Mirror': 'Declarations of love by poets and artists for the "capital city of the world"' (IV, 356). The examples mentioned there prompt Benjamin to call Paris the city of mirrors, going beyond the somewhat banal epithet of *Ville lumière* to foreshadow an important linguistic motif of the *Arcades Project*: female beauty as an object of pleasure for the male spectator. At one point, he notes an observation of Engels, comparing Paris with an odalisque (V, 291), and the prototypical image of seductive femininity in the odalisque will play a special role in his evocation of the lost character of the city.

The *Arcades Project* was to be Benjamin's Paris book; in a sense, it was to be his own declaration of love for the city he was to call 'the capital of the nineteenth century'. But to consider the eroticized language of the *Arcades Project* merely as the product of Benjamin's personal love for Paris would not only be to trivialize it but also to leave out of account the dimension of his work concerned with the philosophy of history. Benjamin's intention was far from being to write a description of contemporary Paris; rather, the city was to serve as the foundation for a history of the nineteenth century. It was to exemplify the particular quality of the appropriation of the past, a process that was to be made tangible through the framing of a series of fleeting moments which, because of their transience, would assume a special beauty. Benjamin's deconstruction of modernity, lent materiality in his conjuring up of the past, is steeped in his awareness of this process of appropriation and the central function of images of beauty in it. Consequently, it is a movement of desire which he seeks to articulate in erotic metaphors. In the arcades of Paris (*Passagen*), he found the kind of concretely surviving form of the past which was indispensable to his task; for this reason they become a basic trope of his argument.

The *Arcades Project*, which comprises more than a thousand printed pages, was only published in 1982. It is primarily Benjamin's private collection of excerpts, consisting of hundreds of extracts from works of history, philosophy, psychology, literature, technology and sociology, all connected with his central theme of modernity and its most striking exemplar, the city of Paris. The extracts, written in French or German, are interspersed with a series of original fragments that make up Benjamin's commentary and were to serve as the foundation of his own book. The manuscript was begun in 1927 and remained unfinished at the writer's death in 1940.

In the course of these years, Benjamin was working on the philosophy of history, primarily in the context of historical materialism in the style of the Frankfurt School. Given this approach, it was an essential task of the historian to shape the past in such a way that the process of history should appear concretely in it. The past was always to be so conceived that the present must necessarily be understood as proceeding from it.

The fact that Benjamin was prepared to acknowledge historical materialism as a philosophical method does not mean that he refused to take account of other, quite disparate or even opposed methodologies. While he was, in the first instance, concerned to explore all the forms in which the past continues to survive, in order to make the process of history more tangible, it was all the more important in his eyes to investigate also such non-material dimensions of this process as our perception of time and memory. As a result, insights deriving from psychoanalysis and from the idea of myth in the collective unconscious remained equally valid.

As an unpublished work, which exists only in a provisional form, the *Arcades Project* is a paradigmatic Postmodern text *avant la lettre*. The alphabetical ordering of the different sections of the manuscript, each concerned with a single overall topic, suggests a random structure which could be described as a counter-exposition. Yet, although the work is put together like a mosaic made up of quotations and fragments, it still reveals a kind of rhetorical impulse in its exploration of the relation between self and memory.

This essay sets out to call attention to some characteristics of the language which takes shape in the commentary of the *Arcades Project*, which, given that it remained a private text, can be regarded as specially authentic in this respect. In particular, it will focus on the fact that the idea of the penetration of the past by the historian is raised in figurative language employing the erotic and the feminine as key concepts. By creating for the language of memory a category of desire which is at the same time *feminized*, Benjamin cuts through the dynamic of his own text and effectively brings it to a halt. To the extent that woman as an object of desire is reified, she is deprived of a voice, she is silenced. Consequently, where categories of desire are feminized, the woman reader's ability to engage with the text is extinguished. Benjamin's feminization of remembering is integrally connected with his conception of the perceptibility of the past.

It has been remarked that the motives for Benjamin's exploration and representation of the past do not rest on nostalgia.[2] Rather, the past is to be investigated as process, as the substance of the dynamic of history. None the less it is strikingly apparent in the *Arcades Project* that the Paris of the past is presented as something desirable. It is not only a conceptual but also a psychological goal, for the material reality that it once was, which is gone but can be recalled imaginatively, held a particular fascination for Benjamin. The city was to serve the purposes of history as an enchanting image preserved in the spaces of memory.

In his *Theses on the Concept of History*, Benjamin sums up in epigrammatic form the principle upon which he sets out to write about the past. This comment demonstrates the plasticity of his thought and of the language that endows the *Arcades Project* with its particular character:

> The true image of the past whizzes by. Only as an image, which flares up just at the moment when it can be recognized, never to be seen again, can the past be captured...For it is an irrevocable image of the past that threatens to vanish at every moment of the present which does not recognize itself as encompassed in it. (I, 695)

In the *Arcades Project*, the perceptibility of the past as an image is explained epistemologically as its momentariness, as the 'now of the recognizable'. The momentariness of the recognizable image implies, for the broadly Marxist ways of thought espoused in part by Benjamin, a radically new conception of the historical appropriation of the past, whereby its dialectical movement is brought to a halt. The 'now of recognizability' is displayed in the halted dialectical image, where the past can uniquely be glimpsed in concrete form (V, 577, 590–1). Two related aspects of Benjamin's practice as a philosopher of history can be distinguished in the concretization of historical material: namely, the image as an opening to the process of history, and the necessary vanishing of the image. It will become apparent that these two ideas shape Benjamin's evocation of the past, both conceptually and in its metaphorical expression.

Benjamin conceived of the contemplation of a historical image not as a static activity, but as dialectical. In his exploration of the concept of the aura in the essay 'On Some Motifs in Baudelaire', he writes of the special quality of perceptibility which makes it possible for an object to draw the gaze of an observer to itself. Herein lies the essential aspect of the aura. But the dialectic of seeing also sets up movement in the opposite direction: 'The aura of a phenomenon means endowing it with the ability to direct its gaze' (I, 646–7). It is as if the fact of being looked at itself causes a process of animation or awakening, the beginning of a kind of existence which hitherto was only potential. In the process of historiography, whereby one can uncover a view of the past such that the dialectical relations between image and observer become active, this function of perceptibility as mutual animation plays an essential part. But in the *Arcades Project*, it is striking that the image of the past takes on feminine character, while the perceiving subject is unambiguously to be understood as male. This perspective will become more specific later in discussion of the figure of the *flâneur*.

The second essential aspect of Benjamin's epistemological method is the idea of the vanishing image. The puzzle of history consists in discovering the special image that can best demonstrate the character and the dynamic of an age. For the meaning of the image to be penetrated, one must catch sight of it at the precise moment when it can be recognized. The now of the recognizable makes it possible for us to take possession of the authentic being of the historical moment. But that which disappears at the moment when we wish to appropriate it takes on, of itself, the character of the desirable. That is why the search for this moment can only be articulated in the language of desire, because to take possession of the image resembles the conquest of a lover. Without explicitly illuminating the implications of his own train of thought, Benjamin regards the past as something desirable, and therefore as something beautiful.

Among the earliest notes to the *Arcades Project* is the following: 'It is high time to discover the beauties of the nineteenth century' (V, 995). Wherever he speaks of the cultural transition from the past to the present, one can detect in Benjamin's language a note of regret in the face of a general loss of authenticity. That which is vanishing acquires the aura of the beautiful. In the essay 'The Story-teller', Benjamin foresees the approaching end of the art of story-telling as a result of the dying of wisdom, that quality he describes as 'the epic side of truth' (II, 442). Even though he maintains that this process ought not to be regarded as decadent, but as 'a phenomenon that accompanies the forces of production of a given historical period', he still cannot help pointing to a 'new beauty in what is vanishing', a kind of beauty that can only be perceived in the fleeting moment when it is about to be extinguished forever. Captured at its vanishing point, the past rests momentarily within the sight of memory, like the imperceptibly disappearing frames of a film. What is now being activated is the psychic and aesthetic effect of the act of framing in the momentary halting of time. Each moment of framing, however rudimentary, offers something unique to the gaze: the auratic quality of a work of art represents an exemplary instance. In Benjamin's aesthetic, the beauty of that which is vanishing, made visible in the point of time which is brought to a halt as a single image, possesses this quality of uniqueness; it is something which is contemplated with delight. But such contemplation of beauty is not that pleasure free of all interest which, according to Kant, we experience in our perception of the beautiful. Instead, it is something active, part of the dialectical exchange between subject and world, individual and memory. This active appropriation of the world through seeing is at the heart of the *Arcades Project*. While Benjamin interprets our contemplation of the past as a process of appropriation by the actively-seeing subject, he formulates the pleasure of seeking, discovery and surrender in the language of desire. The historian becomes the lover of the past.

In order to be able to represent the experience of the nineteenth century in an authentic way, it was necessary to choose an appropriate motif possessing unambiguous cultural resonance, one which could function as an icon. It needed to represent the past in the form of an image, and at the same time to demonstrate the survival of the past in the here and now. In the space-time of Paris, which mysteriously continued to exist in his own day in the Seine, the *quais*, the streets and, above all, in the arcades, Benjamin found a means of writing its history. The Paris arcades became the necessary central figure whereby, in a complex and evocative series of images, the transformations of industrial capitalism in the nineteenth century and the nature of modernity could be interrogated.

The arcades represent a secret world which can be discovered by the observer who enjoys sufficient leisure and curiosity. Writing from the point of view of the 1920s and 1930s, Benjamin first traces the changing world of the passer-by of the early nineteenth century. From this, new perspectives open up on the Paris of Baudelaire, the turn of the century and Benjamin's own day. The fleeting scenes which the stroller sees passing as if on a cinema screen are like the single images of memory which take on recognizable form only for a moment. For Benjamin, they are the shape and substance of history.

Such glimpses of the past resemble the mysterious, half-conscious memory of a dream. There is an existential riddle in the fact that, at the moment of awakening, we recognize a dream but also lose it. Benjamin brings together the idea of waking from a dream and the transformation of consciousness through the insights of historical materialism. The dream re-animates the materiality of the past, which continues to exist both in the collective unconscious and imperfectly in reality, while waking represents Benjamin's goal of recognition (V, 608). Waking is the figurative representation of the self-consciousness of society, which, for the first time, becomes aware of the dialectic of history.

The direction of the *Arcades Project* is not so much towards characterizing the general process of appropriation as attempting to give tangible form to its content, the now of the recognizable in the momentary flaring of the Parisian past. The materiality of such moments as they are evoked in the images of the arcades is explored in distinctly eroticized language, the function of which is to characterize the activity of calling up the past as like the quest of a lover. Since, for Benjamin, the erotic belongs unequivocally to the semantic field of femininity, one can rather speak of a *feminization* of his language. As he describes the details of life in the arcades, Benjamin repeatedly evokes the crossing of thresholds and the penetration of doorways, the pleasure of expectation and of intimate meetings, the innocent seduction of displays in boutiques, and the charm of chance encounters. The softly-lit spaces within the arcades open so that the historian as passer-by and as lover may enjoy a glimpse of what is hidden, before it is lost forever.

Once a woman reader is conscious of such language, it becomes apparent to her that a gender-neutral reading of the text is not possible. There are certain kinds of discourse which, even if they are concerned with the erotic, do not produce such an effect. A text may deal with the intensity of emotional experience or the moves of erotic play, but as long as it is free of any subjective identification, the question of gender-specificity does not necessarily arise. Plato's *Symposium*, for example, does not require a gender-specific reading. Although the *Arcades Project* is not primarily concerned with sexuality, the consistent feminization of its themes makes it impossible to read it in a gender-neutral way.

Seeking to describe the character of the arcades, Benjamin turns to the figure of the *flâneur*, the (male) stroller in nineteenth-century Paris. It is he who can uncover the secrets of the arcades; the (male) eye of the *flâneur* moves across their feminized interior in the same way as the historian seeks the transient images of the past. It can easily be appreciated that the feminization of the arcades constructs a space for the (male) historian or reader, within which he can move with the same enjoyment and curiosity as does the *flâneur*, ready for those fleeting encounters that can be experienced in a dream. But as the woman reader notes the constant use of erotic figures, both as recurring image and as metaphor, she becomes ever more strongly aware of its questionable nature. What does it mean for her that the speaking voice in the text is unambivalently male, that the other of history is perceived as female? What happens when a woman reads in Benjami's thesis *On the Concept of History*, concerning the historical materialist: 'He leaves it to others to expend their energy with the whore called "Once upon a time" in the bordello of historicism. He remains master of his powers: man enough to explode the continuum of history' (I, 702). The sexual (and sexist) imagery which appears in Benjamin's last completed work with shocking force betrays a constant, seemingly unconscious mode of expression which the author uses in this exemplary passage to articulate the founding principle of his whole undertaking.

What does it mean for me that Benjamin, once described as 'the hero of all subversions',[3] should have been blind to the critical category of gender, while his own text urgently demands its application? The answer is that the dialectic indeed comes to a halt, not in the sense of a meeting of present and past, as Benjamin interpreted it, but in the sense that I, as reader, can no longer engage with it. In terms of his own idea of the aura, the perceptibility of the woman as object, her power of active response to the (male) subject as beholder, is thereby destroyed. If the past as woman remains passive, the dynamic of (female) appropriation by the present is brought to a halt. Benjamin's dialectical images indeed remain, as Roland Barthes once remarked of the image *tout court*, that from which I am excluded.[4] Three motifs from the world of the arcades will serve as examples to explain what the halting of history as woman means for the understanding of Benjamin's text. They are the seductive quality of what is vanishing, the penetration symbolism of the threshold, and the archetypal image of the odalisque.

The *Arcades Project* betrays that longing for spaces and sensations which today can be recalled only obscurely, but which earlier were hidden in a magical world that could be entered by the privileged city-dweller. In his essay 'Paris of the Second Empire in Baudelaire', Benjamin remarks of the sonnet 'A une passante': The delight of the city-dweller is love not only at first sight but also at the last glimpse' (I, 547–8).[5] As he strolls among the crowd in the street, the city-dweller responds erotically to the many faces that pass and the many discoveries that entice him. With Benjamin, as with Baudelaire, it is impossible to imagine the protagonist as other than male, a fact which is implicit in Benjamin's figurative language. The fleeting appearance of beauty in a face, a figure or an object which he sees once and never again arouses the desire of the city-dweller. He longs for the beauty that delights him; he desires it, perhaps not so much to possess it as to be taken up within it, as in a dream. He is like Orpheus, who turns to look at his beloved as she moves further and further out of his reach.

For Benjamin, the world of the arcades represents the period immediately before the triumph of industrial capitalism, which he depicted allegorically in the piercing of the arcades at the time when the great boulevards were built. During the 1850s and 1860s, many of the arcades were destroyed as part of a process that Benjamin calls the *Haussmannization* of the inner city, after the architect of the new plan. If the life of the arcades can be called up once more through a kind of history-writing in images, this process can reveal a last glimpse of the vanished pre-capitalist world. At the time when Benjamin arrived in Paris as an exile in the 1930s, the special beauty of this lost world, embodied in the arcades, could be imagined, as it can still today, like a beloved face disappearing in a crowd. This beauty has disappeared forever, for the dialectical turning point, the furthest point in the dialectic where history turns back upon itself, has both arrived and passed away with the onset of the industrial age. The arcades provide a perfect example of the dialectical image, since they can be contemplated both at the high point of their historical existence and at the first moment of their decline.

Benjamin sees the *flâneur* not merely as the historical figure of the pedestrian in the city, who in Baudelaire and many other writers becomes a key motif of the age. He assumes symbolic meaning in the *Arcades Project* by metaphorically reproducing the activity of the historian. His strolling through the city represents the historian's search for the vanishing image of the past. On the one hand, he is enticed by the dream of the past which evokes in him debilitating feelings of nostalgia; but he must resist the temptation of the beautiful dream. He is not only to perceive the beauty of the past, he must also place it in a frame, as it were, so that it can be recognized as *past*, as the moment when the present comes into being.

An unavoidable ambivalence in contemplating the past, which embodies not only what is desired but also what is dialectically tangible, is apparent in Benjamin's recurring image of the city as text. Working in the Bibliothèque Nationale on the *Arcades Project*, Benjamin describes the painted ceiling of the reading room which depicts a summer sky looking down 'from Arcadia' (V, 571, 1059). The comment points to his characterization of old Paris, and of the past as a whole, as having the quality of a lost enchantment. But in the present, Paris appears in the form of something able to be read, as a collection of texts among which one can move as in a large room: 'Paris is a great library through which the Seine flows' (IV, 356). As a source of fleeting appearances, the city evokes the historian's nostalgia; as reading material, it offers him the possibility of appropriating the historical moment as a dialectical image.

The allure of the arcades derives from the ambiguous promise of what is hidden. Its particular resonance lies in the paradoxical interiority of the arcades, where encounters normally experienced in private rooms can take place in a public place. The surviving arcades of Paris can be explored today in the quarters around the Bibliothèque Nationale and the Bourse. They are narrow passageways with glass-vaulted roofs, seldom more than two storeys high, so that their architecture is of little more than domestic proportions. They are lined with small shops filled with objects that reveal the domestic, and particularly the feminine, aspect of the life of the city: hats, gloves, jewellery, stockings, scarfs, *bibelots*, writing paper, stamps.

The markedly feminine character of the world of the arcades entices the *flaneur* with the promise of secret pleasures. To cross the threshold of the arcade means to leave the public space of the street in order to pass into the kind of private world which is otherwise found only in a domestic setting. As in a boudoir or a salon, the hustle outside in the street becomes remote, and the rhythm of social intercourse is slowed so that private conversations can have free rein (V, 612).[6] The text as a whole sketches a topography that is saturated with lavish images of femininity: 'A series of lithographs...showed women in a dim, curtained boudoir, luxuriously stretched on ottomans...the image of those salons where the gaze was lost in bunched door-curtains and swelling cushions' (V, 282–3). Through a series of motifs of an erotic or sexual character, one is constantly reminded of the acts of penetration and entrance.

While the *flâneur* in the street is drawn by the infinite attractions of the metropolis, in the arcade he expects the heightened pleasure of satisfaction. But he also finds renewed delight in promise and discovery inside, where the soft, mysterious glow of lamps or gaslight plays on the flagstones. Boutiques and cafes entice him with their delightful disorder: 'Everywhere stockings play guest roles, appearing now among the photographs, then in a dolls' hospital, and once on the side table of a bar, watched over by a young woman' (V, 995). The seductive invitation of the arcades is further multiplied by the sensuous magic of the mirrors that line them, so that the space within is wonderfully extended and filled with ambivalently whispering glances (V, 671–2). The mirror, like gaslight, becomes for Benjamin a figure which stamps the particular character of Paris during the early nineteenth century. The fleeting quality of mirror images symbolizes the puzzling transience of time and memory.

The city-dweller strolling through the streets is free to enter the arcades, a circumstance regarded by Benjamin as full of symbolic meaning. Crossing the threshold is an image of ritual choice, entrance into the realm of pleasure. Caught in the unceasing enticement of the city, where the magnetism of the next street corner or of the back of a woman walking in front of him [sic] becomes ever more irresistible, the *flâneur* knows that the rites of entrance are accessible to him (V, 525, 1053).[7] But if he decides to enter, he will be drawn into the spell of the threshold: he will be initiated thereby into a new phase of life. Strolling in the street consists of the constant deferral of pleasure for the sake of the disembodied thrill of seeking. But now the initiate is taken up into the arcade, it embraces and receives him.

Although the concept of the magic of the threshold in the *Arcades Project* can be variously interpreted, it is always linked with the idea of flight from the everyday (V, 617–8). A ritual of transition allows the pilgrim to enter a new life phase, but for Benjamin, crossing the threshold of the arcade also means to penetrate the past. The seduction of the arcades is like an invitation to leave the everyday world behind, to seek the magical realm of memory. This multifaceted realm can only be discovered in a shaded place which is hidden from harsh daylight. While the present can be perceived in the ordinary light of day, the past appears in twilight, as in a pastel drawing by Odilon Redon (V, 668, 672).

In the traditional adventure story, the pilgrim sets out from his home and goes through a gate in order to begin his quest in the outside world. But the pilgrim who wishes to escape from the everyday modern world must take the opposite path: he must go through the gate of memory to reach his goal in that protected space within the self whose symbolic image is the arcade. And on one occasion, Benjamin attempts a simple interpretation of the series of images which hitherto he has only placed beside one another without explanation: 'Whoever steps into the arcade is passing through the gate in the opposite direction. (Or he makes his way into the intra-uterine world)' (V, 522). This specifically Oedipal image, which is not met with elsewhere in the erotic language of the *Arcades Project*, is a key to the whole problematic of the arcades in the evocation of memory. It is also a key to the ambivalent eroticization of the past, which is both origin and beloved object. Finally, this image gives form to one of Benjamin's most profound themes in the idea of collective memory.

A more frequently-occurring motif in the *Arcades Project*, however, is the association of the arcades and the *flâneur* with all the paths of memory that lie beyond rationality: for example, in dreams, daydreaming or narcotics. Just as the stroller is enticed by fleeting, dream-like images, so also does the seeker of the past reach for images which constantly threaten to escape him. In the *Arcades Project*, it is the odalisque who best embodies the charm of the past. It is she who reigns over that magical interior which symbolizes at once the psychic origin of the self, the aesthetic pleasure of uncovering, and also sexual fulfilment.

Benjamin's iconography of the interior is crowned by the discovery there of the odalisque. Bathed in soft light, she represents a stylized emblem of feminine beauty and sexuality. The power of her attraction rests primarily on the fact that she offers an erotic invitation, but also, as an emblem, she possesses the quality of a transfiguring universality. As an idealized feminine icon, she embodies something of the ambiguity of the Madonna, who combines the allure of virginity with the archetypal image of motherhood. On the basis of Oedipal sexuality, the odalisque also points the way to the past. Like Faust, the *flâneur* descends into a secret realm to seek a common past as in myth: 'He saunters along the street; each street takes him downwards. It leads down, if not to the Mothers then at least into a past which can be the deeper when it is not his own private past' (V, 1052).

The odalisque is the iconic representation of that mysterious and hidden sexuality which ceaselessly attracts the stroller in the city. The power of the odalisque rests on the aura of promise and mystery which surrounds her; her many-layered and strangely innocent magic requires the ambivalent glow of a lamp or of gaslight. By her 'Oriental' gaze into the distance, her self-possessed posture as she stretches voluptuously on her couch, above all through her stylization as a familiar artistic motif, she appears to the spectator as a universal, as it were an impersonal object of desire (V, 282). As a dialectical image, she remains always out of reach.

The odalisque becomes a central motif of the *Arcades Project* because Benjamin uses the image in his exposition of the dialectical turning-point towards modernity. This fateful moment, where the world of the arcades is lost forever, is symbolically fixed by Benjamin in the first use of electric light in the arcades. He compares this moment with the earlier, less historically momentous change that occurred in 1817 in the Passage des Panoramas with the appearance of gaslight, focusing on this as a keyword in the *Arcades Project* (V, 656):

> The arcade is all that in our eyes. And it used to be none of all that. They, i.e. the arcades, radiated in the Paris of the Empire period like grottoes. Whoever stepped into the arcade in 1817 heard on one side the song of the sirens of gaslight, and on the other he was enticed by the odalisques of the oil lamp. (V, 1045)

The introduction of gaslight in itself was a forerunner of the industrial age, but the modest range and the discretion of the new technology was not powerful enough to destroy the character of the arcades or to render the odalisque lifeless by denying her the quality of perceptibility. Only with the arrival of electricity in the last decades of the nineteenth century did the arcades suffer violation. Then the odalisque was robbed of her aura and the faerie grottoes could no longer survive, for their seductive glow was extinguished in the harsh electric light. The enchantment of the arcades, which had been accessible to the contemporary city-dweller, is wholly transformed in the framework of modernity:

> With the flaring of the electric lights, the guileless illumination was extinguished in these passageways, which were suddenly harder to find, and, indulging in a black magic of gateways, gazed from blind windows into their own interiors. That was not a decline but a turning point. At one blow they were the hollow form from which the image of 'modernity' was cast. (V, 1045)

The mysterious spell of the threshold which promised so much no longer existed. What was a windowless, whole world ('The true has no windows': V, 661) feels itself inadequate and turns its eyes impotently inwards. Since the difference between outside and inside is cancelled out from now on, the essential interiority of the arcades loses its meaning. They are nothing but an empty shell, discarded at the triumphal arrival of modernity.

In those forms which appear after the dialectical turning point as well, the feminine in the life of Paris plays a key role for Benjamin. Since his dialectical images are not arranged on a chronological axis of development, these later forms contribute additional dimensions to the feminization of Benjamin's figurative language; but what cannot be found in these contexts is any sense of desire. It is not only Section O of the manuscript, which bears the heading 'Prostitution. Play', that deals with different aspects of public sexuality in the nineteenth century. The odalisque is transformed into the prostitute of Baudelaire's time and later, the courtesan can be recognized once more in the woman cyclist on the *fin-de-siècle* poster (V, 110, 112). The figure of the odalisque, saturated with the power of universal attraction, is supplanted by the whore, whose favours can be won only through the anarchical tricks of fortune: 'The same thing that gazes at the player from every number on the green cloth – fortune – winks at him here from the bodies of all women as the chimaera of sexuality' (V, 612). As soon as the image of the odalisque in the arcades is replaced by that of the whore, the past no longer smiles upon the historian. Instead of vanishing beauty, there appears in the harsh daylight the grotesque, ugly stereotypes of a derided femininity: 'The female fauna of the arcades: whores, grisettes, old witch-like saleswomen, peddlar-women' (V, 617).

Very many images of femininity which are mentioned in such contexts seem to provoke distaste or unease in the writer. These attitudes are clearly apparent in the linguistic register, which betrays a conception of sexuality as something morally reprehensible or perverse. Baudelaire's flowers of evil are the symbol of the whore (V, 348); the flower motifs of *art nouveau* are a transfiguration of sterility, the ideal beauty of the age is the frigid woman (V, 692, 294). Prostitution is depicted as a phenomenon of decadence and as a deleterious effect of the progress of capitalism: 'Prostitution sets up a market of female types' (V, 641). By means of the exchange value of prostitution, sexuality has become a commodity fetish of modernity (V, 637).

Fashion, too, is singled out in the *Arcades Project*, for, like prostitution, it represents the intersection of femininity and commerce. Fashion is related in a profound way to sexuality, since both have their existence in 'the landscapes of the body' (V, 118). While single examples of the erotic meaning of fashion are mentioned in a more or less detached way (the sexual symbolism of women's hats or of the crinoline: V, 131), it is portrayed in a mainly negative light. While sexuality is degraded to a commodity through prostitution, Benjamin finds in the materiality of fashion the compulsive need to locate the sexual in the inorganic world, thus reifying it even more transparently and irrevocably (V, 118). According to this idealized conception of sexuality, fashion appears as the opposite of (true) love: 'In every instance of fashion there is something of a bitter satire on love, in every one of them all sexual perversions are mercilessly laid out, each of them is filled with secret resistance to love' (V, 113). It is not only that sexuality can be sold but also its physicality that Benjamin seems to regard as depraved. The exploitation of sexuality in the mass consumption of the metropolis represents a new, perverse kind of commodity fetishism. Since the woman who is dressed and made up in the same way as many others appears as a mass product, marketability itself becomes attractive (V, 427).

The linguistic register of the *Arcades Project* embraces many erotic and sexual metaphors which, in the absence of the hidden charm of the odalisque, represent the challenge of a sexuality that is shamelessly displayed for sale. The woman reader must certainly acknowledge that the lavishly- described historical and topographical milieu, as well as the characteristic originality of Benjamin's observations, lends engaging force to his language. But from a feminist perspective, it appears alienating and disappointing despite all the virtuosity of thought and style. Doubtless Benjamin evokes a universal response in the male reader, so that his language of desire (or of distaste) is able to enhance the plasticity of an exposition that is already conceived in images. Thus, it allows the past to be articulated comprehensibly, while otherwise it can be recognized only in a schematic or abstract way. The multiple resonance of these images is an index of Benjamin's complex existential and intellectual positions: for instance, of the unresolved contradictions between historical materialism and the desire to incorporate other interpretations of the world deriving from the unconscious and from memory. It is this second approach that largely has the upper hand in the *Arcades Project,* since the mode of the commentary is figurative rather than expository.

Although they survived only in fragmented remains, the arcades nevertheless offered a way of shaping the past and participating in it; they became part of a dream landscape in which the ancestral world could be spiritually experienced. As if wishing to stress his materialist orientation, Benjamin compares the evocation of inherited memory with the participation of the embryo in the common life of its species. But the comment can be found in a paragraph which underlines the non-materialist dynamic of the work as a whole, whereby ideas otherwise conceived of as lying beyond rational thought are given figurative, genuinely poetic expression:

For who is able at a stroke to turn the lining of time inside out? And yet dream stories are nothing else. And one cannot speak of the arcades in any other way, they are architecture in which we re-live the life of our parents and grandparents as in dreams, as the embryo in the mother re-lives the life of the animals. Existence in these spaces flows without accent like events in dreams. (V, 1054)

As I read, I have no objection to the desire for this dream landscape that can be discerned throughout the *Arcades Project*. It is not Benjamin's use of the category of desire in the images of the arcades that disturbs me; it is rather his feminization of these categories to give form to historical evocation. For me, history, time and the past cannot be penetrated in the guise of the feminine.

NOTES

1. All quotations are my translations from the German edition: Walter Benjamin, *Gesammelte Schriften*, ed. R. Tiedemann and H. Schweppenhäuser, 7 vols (Frankfurt/ Main, 1972–). References in parentheses identify volume and page number.
2. See, for example, S. Buck-Morss, *The Dialectics of Seeing: Walter Benjamin and the Arcades Project* (Cambridge, MA, 1989), p. 145.
3. Dominique Bourel, *Le Monde*, 8 August 1986.
4. *Fragments d'un discours amoureux* (Paris, 1977), p. 157.
5. Also in 'On Some Motifs in Baudelaire' (I, 623).
6. Cf. 'On Some Motifs in Baudelaire' (I, 627, 649).
7. Benjamin allows himself a pun in the phrase *rites de passage* (V, 521–2).

Benjamin, Fourier, Barthes

Michael Hollington

I Two-way Streets

In November 1822, Charles Fourier uprooted himself from his French provincial background and came to live in Paris for the remaining fifteen years of his life. He moved to the capital in search of a patron who might provide financial backing for his Utopian scheme for the reorganization of society through the creation of co-operative 'phalansteries' based upon the principle of a harmonisation of human passions, as advocated in his theoretical writings from 1808 onwards. He lived out those years in a state of heightened expectation, in the belief that 'civilization' was about to come to an end – by 1824 – or that the North Pole was to be free of ice by 1828.[1] It is said that he returned to his lodgings each day at noon in the hope that the desired Maecenas might present him or herself; eventually one did, and in 1833 the first phalanstery was founded at Condé-sur-Vesgre, only to fold within a year. Fourier himself lived frugally on 900 francs a month, an inheritance from his mother; the meagre lifestyle such an income might afford is vividly rendered in Heine's portrait: 'How often I used to see him strolling under the arcades of the Palais Royal with both pockets of his old gray frock coat bulging so that out of one the neck of a bottle would protrude and out of the other a large loaf of bread.'[2]

'The majority of the Paris arcades originate in the decade and half after 1822' (V , 45): so runs the opening sentence of the exposé of the *Arcades Project* written in the spring of 1935, declaring a major focus on this period of Fourier's life in Benjamin's later work. In October 1933, he, too, had arrived in Paris to begin the last chapter of his own life, a seven-year exile during which the extreme precariousness of his own financial position and the apparent imminence of a much grimmer Armageddon for 'civilization' may have engendered a measure of self-identification, with Fourier functioning as a courage-teacher. One note reads: 'With Fourier one is reminded of Karl Kraus's saying: "I preach wine and drink water'", and another quotes Michelet on Fourier: 'What a singular contrast between such ostentatious materialism and a life that was spiritual, abstinent, disinterested!' (V, 792, 777) Haunting the arcades in penury at a second remove beneath the vaults of another marvel of nineteenth-century French construction in iron, the Bibliothèque Nationale, Benjamin quickly turned his attention to his *frère semblable*. In the month prior to his arrival, a few faithful disciples had celebrated the centenary of the first phalanstery, and one of them, Auguste Pinloche, had also marked the occasion with the publication of an introductory study of Fourier, together with selections from his work. The earliest notes in the 35-page Fourier section of the *Arcades Project* are extracts from it, and one of Benjamin's first contributions to the *Zeitschrift für Sozialforschung* in 1934 is an appreciative review of Pinloche's book (III, 428). In addition, there is that exposé section, 'Fourier or the Arcades', another review of 1937, and scattered references to Fourier throughout Benjamin's later writings, up to and including the *Theses on the Philosophy of History* – in all, a tangible, if fragmentary, body of work.

In the autumn of 1935, Benjamin got to know Pierre Klossowski, who was to become the French translator of *The Work of Art in the Age of Mechanical Reproduction*. Their first meeting occurred at one of the gatherings organised by Contre Attaque, the short-lived Surrealist political movement born of a temporary 'agglutination' between the circles surrounding Georges Bataille (who worked in the Bibliothèque Nationale, and with whom Benjamin was already in contact) and André Breton. Klossowski's portrait of Benjamin singles out as of particular importance the Fourierist aspects of his intellectual and temperamental cast at that time: 'He was awaiting that total liberation which would accompany the arrival of a universe of play in the terms of Fourier, for whom he had a boundless admiration. I don't know of anyone who in our times has lived so intimately in the Paris of Saint-Simon and Fourier.'[3] And his enthusiasms were infectious. As Bischof and Lenk have stressed, Benjamin not only reacted to French Surrealism; it in turn reacted to him, most obviously in its later stages of preoccupation with Fourier.[4] In November 1935, Georges Bataille announced a series of forthcoming pamphlets, amongst which are projected studies of three supposed precursors of the 'moral revolution' that Contre Attaque was working towards. On this occasion, the trinity of names is Sade, Fourier and Nietzsche, and Klossowski is named as the author of a pamphlet on Fourier which would show how an economy of abundance could be created by a liberation of human passions.[5]

Klossowski did not write that piece at that time, but henceforth Fourier became a feature of the Surrealist landscape. The publication in 1947 of André Breton's *Ode to Charles Fourier* or of Queneau's 'Dialectique hégélienne et séries de Fourier' in 1963 mark the intervening years before 1970, when Klossowski finally produced his 'Sade et Fourier' in a number of the magazine *Topique* specially devoted to Fourier. In the same month, Roland Barthes's essay 'Vivre avec Fourier' appeared in *Critique*, the magazine that Bataille had founded; it was incorporated the following year into his book, *Sade, Fourier, Loyola*. There are multiple lines of connection between Barthes and the Surrealists, some of whom had known Benjamin: it was Nadeau who helped launch his career, and Bataille who suggested the importance of Balzac's *Sarrasine* to him. He had known Klossowski at least since the late 1940s, when, with an appropriately Fourierist feeling for the reign of Harmony, he had been a regular visitor to the apartment in the rue Canivet to play piano duets with Madame Klossowski.[6]

II Between Marx and Fourier

This phrase, which attempts to locate the co-ordinates of a cardinal late Benjamin axis, is the title of a short piece that Klossowski wrote in 1969 for a page on Benjamin in *Le Monde*. It was picked up later by (amongst others) Chryssoula Kambas in her important book on Benjamin in exile, and by Bernd Witte, who suggests that Benjamin's dismayed reaction to the Moscow trials led him to turn more and more from Marx to Fourier.[7]

Unlike others before and since, Benjamin, applying Alois Riegl's non-evaluative concept of the *Kunstwollen* in the sphere of political thought, believed neither in evolutionary models of nineteenth-century socialism nor in binary distinctions between its 'scientific' and 'pre-scientific' incarnations: he believed in 'brushing against the grain' to redeem allegory from its obliteration by symbol, or Utopian writing from its subordination to the classics of communism. As with Baroque tragedy in the 1920s he was indeed interested in 'origins', and Fourier – responding with intense delight to the first arcade (the Galerie des Bois in the Palais Royal) as early as 1789 on his first visit to Paris, and beginning to elaborate his project from the very earliest years of the new century – clearly seemed to qualify as a nineteenth-century pioneer (both Benjamin and Barthes note how he calls himself an 'inventor'). He was an important two-way vessel of transition, looking back from the period of the Empire to the Enlightenment and small-scale capitalist production at the same time as he looked forward to Zola and beyond.[8]

The opposition Fourier/Marx can also be seen as dovetailing to some extent with the debate in the 1930s between Surrealist and more orthodox Marxist approaches to political action. In the *Arcades* notes, Benjamin quotes from Emmanuel Berle's critical description in 1929 of the Surrealist position, which suggests that it draws rather upon Utopian than scientific socialist tradition:

As the Surrealists never ceased confusing moral nonconformism and proletarian revolution, instead of orienting themselves towards the modern world they try to put themselves back in time to a historical moment where such a confusion was still usual: to the climate prior to the Tours congress, even prior to the period of the development of Marxism in the 1920s, the 1930s and 1940s. (V, 852)

This is no accident, Benjamin comments, 'for...there are elements here that are refractory to Marxism – anthropological materialism, the hostility towards progress', and, as we shall see, his sympathies in such debates were by no means one-sided. That concept of 'anthropological materialism', which he unmistakeably associates with Fourier, had in fact already been employed in the essay on Surrealism as a name for an alternative materialist tradition in nineteenth and twentieth-century France and Germany, with which Marx's 'political materialism' must try to make alliance, even if its residue of idealist abstraction prevents it from ever entirely doing so (II, 309, 1040).

Yet, on the other hand, he could and did draw upon Marx's own reverence for Fourier in an equally telling context. Benjamin notes how, in his defence of Fourier against Karl Grün's attacks upon the 'immorality' of phalanstery life, Marx had seen the fundamental dialectical role of humour in Fourier's design. It was a kind of test, like that in Godard's *Vivre sa Vie*, where the philosopher Brice Parrain – a friend of Klossowski – insults the prostitute played by Anna Karina (and elicits the correct response of laughter) not to get hot under the collar and thereby betray, as Grün did, the philistine humourlessness that was quite unable to respond to the 'colossal conception of humanity' displayed in and through Fourier's *critical* satire upon existing social conditions (V, 771).

If Benjamin was affected by the Moscow trials, some important changes in the later career of Roland Barthes can be traced in similar fashion, as Calvet suggests, to his perception of the events of 1968. His essay, too, can be seen as balanced upon an opposition between a Fourierist conception of politics and a Marxist one – the Klossowski formula in fact resurfaces explicitly in an interview Barthes gave in January 1972, where he remarks: 'Utopia is the state of a society in which Marx would no longer criticise Fourier.'[9] For Barthes, Fourierism focuses upon the 'domestic' sphere and upon concepts such as 'pleasure' and 'desire', whilst the Marxist approach addresses the public arena and principles like 'determinism' and 'necessity'. He remembers ruefully how, in May 1968 at the Sorbonne, the students in search of a new social model thought at one point of studying Fourierist topics like that of a 'domestic Utopia', but eventually decided against such a course because it was decided that this was a bourgeois concept.[10]

Both Barthes and Benjamin, in their writing on Fourier, stress the *material* nature of Fourier's thought in contexts where, (1) the word is equated with concreteness and opposed to abstraction, and where (2) it connotes sensual gratification. Benjamin refers to Fourier's 'hedonist materialism' (V, 773), and Barthes writes that 'the motive of all Fourierist constructions or combinations is not justice, equality, liberty etc., but pleasure'.[11]

III Harmonizing the Passions

Fourier can be seen as a Riegl in the sphere of pleasures: he has no concept of perversity. Following Sade in his emphasis on the primacy of human passions, he leads these in a benign direction by asking what might happen to 'perversity' in a society willing to gratify even the most extreme and bizarre fantasies.[12] Writing between June 1935 and December 1937, and perhaps reflecting discussions with Bataille or Klossowski, Benjamin comments on how sadists and masochists might help each other find harmonious contentment in Fourier's Utopia: 'In his experiments the sadist might light upon a partner who is seeking precisely those sufferings and humiliations that his tormentor seeks to inflict upon him' (V, 786). Klossowski argues that the gratification of passions moves them in the direction of liberation, transforming them into play – as in the case of Fourier's deliciously culinary Lady Strogonoff whose cruelty towards her servant-girl is the expression of suppressed lesbianism: 'If someone had put the idea into her head that she was a lesbian and reconciled her and her victim, under these conditions they would have become passionate lovers.'[13]

Writing out of his own 'perversities', perhaps, Barthes has some splendid appreciative commentary and quotation on Fourier's insistence upon sensual gratification. One quotation seems almost Dantesque in its vision of felicity ('it is doubtless the case that many civilised people would be struck dead by the violence of their ecstasy' in the phalanstery) whilst another memorable sentence – 'what we have done wrong is not, as has been believed, to desire too much, but to desire too little' – elicits the remark that, for Fourier, 'pleasure is not subject to quantification, its essence is the *too much*'. Writing out of his Protestant theological background perhaps, he highlights the extraordinary *generosity* of Fourier's conception of bliss in the afterlife, which can't begin until the happiness of the living has been ensured: 'No religious eschatology has had such audacity.'[14]

As might be expected of someone with an intense interest in children (Susan Buck-Morss quotes Scholem's description of him 'attracted with almost magical force by the child's world and ways...his writings on the subject are among his most perfect pieces'[15]), Benjamin responded enthusiastically to Fourier's equally innovative ideas on the incorporation of the pleasure principle into education and the *Umfunktionierung* of children's 'perversities' in the phalanstery. He compares his pedagogy to that of Jean Paul, whose *Levana*, as the first essay on Hebel notes, recommends that infants be introduced to beer and schnapps (V, 779; II, 278). What it characteristically does is to manage children who, in Beecher's words, are 'naturally rebellious, obstinate, obscene, and – above all – irresistibly attracted to filth, excrement, and danger' by gratifying their tastes to the utmost degree, by organizing them into 'Little Hordes' and giving them such jobs as the collection of garbage and the cleaning-out of slaughterhouses and latrines.[16] As Gerhard Fischer points out to me, Benjamin makes memorable use of this item of the educational programme in his Fourierist reading of Brecht's poem 'Vom Kind das sich nicht waschen wollte' (II, 564–5), about the child who refuses to wash his face and so misses out on meeting the Kaiser when he comes to the family up seven flights of stairs and the mother can't find a towel in time. Too bad, the poem seems to say for Benjamin, in appropriately dialectical and satirical fashion – all that this means is that there's something wrong with a society that can't find a use for the love of dirt.

IV Matriarchy

Fourier is thus a Blakeian 'brusher against the grain', tireless in his crusade against the 'doxa' (in Barthes's phrase) of a 'civilization' dedicated to 'binding with briars my joys and desires'. Also like Blake, he asks the question in a two-way direction:

> What is it men in women do require?
> The lineaments of gratified desire.
> What is it women do in men require?
> The lineaments of gratified desire.[17]

The phalanstery would be nothing without the liberation of women's passions as well as men's. Moreover, this affirmation of female sexuality is made in full recognition of the issues of power that play into the whole question of women's rights: for Fourier, the motor of history is not the relationship of classes to the means of production, but the relationship of women to power. Consciously or unconsciously echoing Benjamin's habitual political phraseology, as used explicitly in the context of Fourier (V, 777), Evelyne Sullerot identifies a 'feminist explosion of 1831–2' in the wake of Fourier's work; Flora Tristan's use of Fourier's maxim, 'The extension of the privileges of women is the general principle of all social progress' as the motto of her *L'Émancipation de la femme* testifies to the contemporary acknowledgement of an explicit debt.[18]

Yet this is not the place to explore the relation of either Fourier, Benjamin or Barthes to feminist theory (it is, as one might expect, a contested issue, especially in the first two cases). What is perhaps interesting and relevant in the case of Benjamin is to explore the intertwining of the 1934 work on Fourier with his contemporaneous essay on the nineteenth-century Swiss classical scholar, Johann Jakob Bachofen, whose pioneering *Das Mutterrecht (Matriarchy)* enjoyed a considerable vogue at the time, disseminated through the Munich circle, Die Kosmische Runde (consisting principally of Klages, Schuler and Wolfskehl) at the turn of the century.[19] Bachofen's disciples believed in the idea of a universal matriarchy that had preceded the patriarchal system of classical and later modern Europe, whose existence could be demonstrated through the reading of myths that retained memory traces of the former regime and of the patriarchalist revolt against it.

Benjamin set great store by this essay, written in French for the *Nouvelle Revue Française* as a first contribution in his adopted country of residence to what he saw as the predominantly 'anthropological' bias of contemporary French thought (III, 508). Jean Paulhan's rejection of it was a severe blow to his hopes of establishing himself in France and making a public contribution to the struggle against fascism. For this essay is specifically aimed (with the aid of Fromm) at 'redeeming' Bachofen from contemporary fascist readings of his work and turning him round so that he may be of service to socialists and anti-fascists. It emphasizes Bachofen's 'evocation of a communist society at the dawn of history', a communism that he regarded as 'inseparable from gynocracy'. This 'archaic democracy' was based upon an entire, separate matriarchal concept of authority and system of law of a fundamentally 'feminine', sensual, materialist kind, based upon the cult of Dionysos, which (according to Bernoulli, in a quotation where Benjamin seems not to have spotted the irony of the word 'patrimony') was a fundamentally democratic religion, 'because that sensual nature which it addresses is the patrimony of all mankind'. This had later been overthrown and its memory submerged in the 'patriarchal revolution', the uprising of men against their subjection by women – according to Lehmann, Benjamin's former Mexicanist anthropological mentor, taking as their symbol the swastika, the ancient Aryan fire symbol, and turning its hooks from left to right (II, 228, 231–2)

Parallel to this essay, Benjamin was also much exercised at this time by the critical reading of Jung, another Swiss anthropological thinker who himself appeared to have submitted voluntarily to fascist appropriation. The *Arcades Project* was to have contained a major critique of the Jungian concept of the 'collective unconsciousness' – again involving a radical

Umfunktionierung – in which the connection between Fourier and Bachofen's idea of a primitive matriarchy would have figured centrally. For, as the early *Arcades* notes make clear, Benjamin saw Fourier's concern with the rehabilitation of the status and powers of women as a prime example of the 'collective unconscious' at work. At the dawn of the era of high capitalism, Fourier's Utopian dreamings represented a powerful progressive force because of their ability to tap memories of the dawn of history. It could be shown that their essential 'hedonistic materialist' content – their ability, for instance, to invoke traditional symbols of bliss and sensual excess like the cornucopia or the land of Cockaigne (Benjamin quotes a delightful 1832 theatrical parody of Saint-Simonism where snow is wine, rain is roast chicken, and ducks and parsnips regularly fall from the skies; V, 232) – was a symptom of deep chthonic roots. Utopian thought as a resurrection of 'anthropological materialism' was a form of re-invocation of early matriarchy, and in thus re-energizing opposition to the prevailing patriarchal social order, it offered the dialectical spark that might ignite a collective reawakening.

V For There is a Language of Flowers

Klossowski comments that there was in Benjamin in Paris in the 1930s 'a visionary with all the riches of the imagery of Isaiah at his disposal', and that his Fourier was steeped in mystical tradition: 'He [Benjamin] had a prodigious knowledge of all the esoteric currents and the arcanest secret doctrines of the period.'[20] The evidence of the *Arcades* notes supports this view – we find Benjamin in 1934 quoting Engländer and Lerminier comparing Fourier with Swedenborg in his prodigious powers of invention and description, and when he notes that, 'in England, the influence of Fourier is combined with that of Swedenborg', we are again manifestly drawn in the direction of Blake (V, 765, 770).

Menninghaus has shown that this side of Benjamin's work – expressed, for instance, in his researches into Romantic language theory, the work, for instance, of Creutzer and Hamann, who was translated by Klossowski and also found his way into very late surrealist-inspired ideas of the sacred[21] – is at bottom a preoccupation with mystical language, with hieroglyphs and the cabbalist tradition, with traditions concerning secret writings and the supposed signatures of things in the Book of Nature before and after the Fall. It is not hard to find corresponding preoccupations in Fourier. Beecher has a fine page or two on this feature of his work, showing how, in his system, the phases of history write out their meanings in natural hieroglyphs: reptiles, insects and sea monsters are part of the alphabet of 'civilization' and other corrupt eras of mankind, but 'Full Harmony' will produce new signifiers: anticrocodiles to provide river transport, antiwhales to tow stranded vehicles, and antilions to deliver the post.[22]

Thus Benjamin's Fourier notes bulge with quotations concerning allegory and hieroglyph. Gods and goddesses and the planets that are named after them 'plant' the significant vegetation of the earth – it was Venus who created the blackberry with its brambles as a symbol of morality, and the strawberry full of worms as a symbol of corruption (V, 776). The planet Mercury will teach us to read in Harmony: 'He will give us the alphabet, the declensions, in fact all the grammar of the unitary harmonic language spoken on the sun and the harmonised planets' (V, 768). And a comment on Fourier's own use of language – 'Fourier loves to dress up the most reasonable propositions in reflections of a fantastical kind. His discourse is like a higher language of flowers' (V, 793) – irresistibly reminds this reader, at least, of another glorious ornament of the language tradition in question – Christopher Smart:

> For the flowers are great blessings.
> For the flowers have their angels even the words of God's creation.
> For the flower glorifies God and the root parries the adversary.
> For there is a language of flowers,
> For flowers are peculiarly the poetry of Christ.
> For the right names of flowers are yet in heaven.[23]

Menninghaus, too, directs us to resemblances between aspects of Benjamin's preoccupation with language and Barthes's.[24] It is no surprise to find that Barthes's Fourier essay concentrates upon showing that his delineation of Utopia represents a kind of *writing*, in which the power and freedom of the signifier is vastly extended, and the role of the signified is very much shrunken (elsewhere, in the near-contemporary *Empire of Signs* in particular, there seems to be a relationship between the Barthesian distinction of signifier and signified with the opposition matriarchal/patriarchal). He, too, has a section entitled 'Hieroglyph', which proceeds from the premise that the decipherment of the world through nature's hieroglyphs that Fourier undertakes is a necessary preliminary to its alteration. It works in tandem with what Barthes calls 'systematization' (as opposed to 'system'), a classificatory activity which organizes the 'marvellous reality' that Fourier imagines in such intense detail in an openly-structured series of linguistic categories. He is the inventor of a language for this world, and it is significant in the context of Benjamin's work that Barthes should describe his method of classification as 'baroque': 'Inserted in the history of the sign, Fourier's construction puts forward the claims of a baroque semantics, which is to say one that is open to the proliferation of the signifier: infinite and yet structured.'[25]

But for Barthes, the most radical gesture of all in Fourier is contained in the neologisms. Benjamin notes them too, comparing this aspect of his work to Jean Paul: 'Fourier loves preambles, cisambles, transambles, postambles, introductions, extroductions' (V, 789). But he does not foreground them to quite the same degree as Barthes, for whom they are the essential vehicle of a destruction of the old order and a creation of the new, as the passage with which his essay concludes makes plain:

> The *impossibilia* of Fourier are his neologisms. It is easier to predict the overthrow of 'the weather as we know it' than to imagine, as Fourier does, a masculine equivalent of the feminine noun *fée* [fairy] and to write it quite simply as '*fés*': the sudden spring into being of a strange graphic configuration from which the feminine has been dropped, this is the real *impossibilium,* an impossible binding of gender and language, so that in *matrons* and *matrones* it is a new monstrous transgressive object that is brought to humanity.[26]

VI Writing Against: Against Progress and 'The Conquest of Nature'

Barthes's analysis of Fourier makes plain its fundamental repudiation of Enlightenment theories of human progress and perfectibility: 'Passion (character, taste, mania) is the irreducible unit of Fourierist combinations, the absolute grapheme of the Utopian text. Passion is *natural* (there's no way of improving it except by producing something that goes against nature, as has been done in Civilization).'[27] And Benjamin produces a quotation from Fourier that sneers at such doctrines as laughable from the perspective of phalanstery connoisseurs of pleasure who simply exist on another plane all together, even in such basics as selling wheat and baking bread:

> A phalanx doesn't sell a thousand quintals of wheat as one lot, it sells that thousand quintals in gradations of five, six or seven nuances of flavour that have been tried out at the bakery, distinguished according to the type of earth in which it's been harvested and the methods of cultivation...Such a mechanism will be the reverse of our upside-down world, our perfectible civilization. (V, 770)

His essay on Jochmann makes the point from another angle, as it discusses in a Hegelian context Fourier's belief that 'all partial improvements in the social constitution of the human race during the era of civilisation necessarily lead to a worsening of the whole status quo' (II, 583).

As Michel Löwy's fine essay on the subject effectively demonstrates, Benjamin was primarily a pessimist on the question of progress throughout most of his career.[28] The 'regressive' tendencies of Fourier – the fact that he took the opposite side to that of the Saint-Simonians in their passionate embrace of industrial development, that he preferred many features of small-scale early capitalism to large-scale modern enterprise and sought to preserve them in the phalansteries – were by no means entirely lacking in appeal to him, whatever the resulting contradictions both in Fourier and his own work. He saw that the phalanstery *was*, after all, dependent on very advanced methods of production (V, 456). Above all, perhaps, he was attracted to a theory of history that could contain *both* an idea of growth towards a future paradise on earth and a future decline. This running-down process would be ushered in by 'Harmony' itself, until after 80,000 years, the planet earth would simply be extinguished. In 1938, Benjamin sets down a passage from a letter from Hermann Duncker to Margrete Steffin, citing Engels's praise of Fourier in *Anti-Dühring* for introducing into his conception of history the idea of 'a future end of the human race, like Kant's idea of the future end of the solar system' (V, 432).

In discussing Fourier's conception of history, Beecher quotes Frank Manuel's characterization of it: 'Mankind was summoned to the worldly pleasures of the Phalanstery but was offered no promise of eternity. The earth's delights were real but necessarily transitory.'[29] These words closely approximate Benjamin's perspective on the matter, in so far as these can be gauged from the *Arcades* notes. 'Transitoriness and happiness closely intertwined in Fourier' is the terse comment at one point (V, 794). Something of what might have been made of it in a more finished state can perhaps be glimpsed in the memorable sentence in the essay on Gottfried Keller (another figure belonging to Benjamin's conception of 'anthropological materialism'), describing this writer as a 'passionate hedonist unwilling to allow his rendezvous with this life to be disturbed by any possible other life' (II, 286).

Susan Buck-Morss has commented most fully and brilliantly on the major theme of a critique of the idea of the 'Mastery of Nature' in the *Arcades* notes; all that need be done here is to demonstrate how centrally Fourier – again, in part, through his 'matriarchal' stress, that linking him back to chthonic roots and a primal 'Mother Nature' – contributes to it. His 'radically optimistic assessment of work', writes Beecher, 'was rooted in his denial of an irreconcileable antagonism between man and nature. He did not share Marx's Promethean vision of man as constantly engaged in wresting a living out of a hostile environment.'[30] Simmel had clearly influenced Benjamin in the same direction – he quotes his view that 'the idea of conquering or mastering nature is a childish one, for all conceptions of victory and subjection only make sense when some opposing will is broken. Natural events as such lie beyond the alternative of freedom and compulsion' (V, 812). Nietzsche is remembered, too, for his critical perception that it is Descartes who is the first to have 'compared intellectual discoveries to a series of battles fought against nature' (V, 467). Scheerbart is another major reference point, especially because he imagines a union of the forces of technology and of nature, on two conditions: 'That humanity must leave behind the low vulgar opinion that it is called upon to "exploit" the forces of nature; that, on the contrary it remain convinced that technology, in liberating human beings, will at the same conduct a fraternal liberation of the whole of creation' (II, 631). But it is in the very late French version of the *Arcades Project* exposé that the key role of Fourier is stressed: 'One of the most remarkable features of the Fourierist Utopia is that the idea of the exploitation of nature by man which later became so widespread is alien to it. Technology presents itself for Fourier rather as the spark which sets fire to the powderkegs of nature' (V, 64).

VII (Childs)Play

The Benjamin–Klossowski–Barthes line of descent is nowhere more clearly discernible than in the emphasis all three give to Fourier's importance as an apostle of play. In the two French writers, the emphasis falls more particularly on the psychoanalytic and therapeutic merits of ludic activity, perhaps because both are thinking of Fourier in connection with Sade: 'The seriousness of perversion has to be replaced by play' is Klossowski's stress,[31] whilst Barthes characteristically turns this idea in a linguistic direction, meditating upon the importance of conflict in the phalanstery: 'The aim of Harmony is not to protect oneself from conflict...nor to reduce it (by sublimating it or softening it or normalising the passions) nor yet to transcend it...but to exploit it for the greater pleasure of everyone and without hurt to anyone. How? by *making a game of it*, by turning conflict into a text.'[32]

Noting that Fourier, at the very outset, began formulating his vision of human happiness as a kind of game, as a means of whiling away the time during a period of four months in 1803 waiting for a job to start in Paris (V, 765), Benjamin ,by contrast, is again at pains to establish Fourier as the fount of an alternative socialist tradition to that of Marx, its separateness established along the oppositional axis of play and work: 'To have situated play as the canon of a form of labour that is no longer exploitative is one of the greatest merits of Fourier' (V, 456).[33] In Harmony, as both Benjamin and Barthes note (Barthes compares the regime to that of a sanatorium), no one wants to sleep for more than four and a half hours: waking-up time is at 3.30 a.m. because adults in the phalanstery become like children and work becomes like play – they want to get at those toy soldiers again. The same magnificent passage from the Baudelaire section of the *Arcade* notes continues with an evocation – again significantly centring upon the unlocking of the naming powers of a conventionalized word – of an unalienated version of work that *improves* nature rather than exploits it:

> Fourier's Utopia presents a model for it, one that can in fact be found realized
> in children's play. It is the image of an earth in which all places have become
> *Wirtschaften*. The double meaning of the word [economy/public inn] blossoms
> here: all places are cultivated by human beings, made useful and beautiful by
> them; all, however, stand like a roadside inn, open to everyone.[34]

The dialectical energies of the arcade-phalanstery as the quintessential
form of glass architecture resurface here in this highly characteristic
metaphor. Havens of light as well as warmth, these 'wombs with two-way
views' of the 1820s are way-stages or signposts that (as Benjamin remarks
elsewhere) echo Goethe's call in 1832, at the threshold of death, for 'More
light!' In Harmony, love-making never takes place at night ('detestable
habit of civilization', mutters Barthes with sympathetic irony[35]). There is
an eccentric, Fourier-style passage in Benjamin's essay on Fuchs that links
the visual pleasures of sex with a crucial historical transition in the chthonic
mists of the past. He speculates that the frontal position for intercourse, in
which the lovers can exchange auratic gazes, was a kind of perversion for
as long as the sexual act had the mere purpose of animal procreation, and
homo sapiens's ancestors still went on all fours, but that, as Bachofen's
primal 'hetaerismic' hordes began to enjoy orgies in a Kantian way, as ends
in themselves, in which all the pleasures of the senses combined, including
sight, might produce the *de trop* of sexual ecstacy, the evident attractions
of the frontal position had, as a subsidiary effect, the accomplishment by
the species of the crucial transition from walking on all fours to standing
and walking upright (II, 497)!

VIII Transitions

It should not be forgotten that arcades serve as passageways, that their noun
in French and German is in fact *Passage*. Though he admired Aragon's
Paysan de Paris, Benjamin distances himself from its 'mythical' approach
to the arcade: his own project is to serve as a transition or awakening out
of the sleep of capitalist modernity and commodity fetishism. He wants
to realise the name of the *Passage* as passage.

Fourier, of course, stands only at a point of 'origin'. An early Benjamin
fragmentary outline of the *Arcades Project* stresses that his imaginary
constructions are still places to live in (and both Blanqui and Heine did,
in fact, live in arcades): 'Transitory purposes of iron buildings. Moreover:
iron, as the first artificial building material, is the first that submits to a
process of development. This went faster and faster as the century went
on. In Fourier arcades are still to be lived in' (V, 1221). But Fourier himself

was interested in transitions. At one time, in his search for a benefactor, he considered Robert Owen; he even met Owen towards the very end of his life. Although this came to nothing, he was of the view that New Lanark 'merits the rank of 5 1/4, and that it provides a half-exit from Civilization, an ascending half-transition'.[36] Barthes has a splendid section entitled 'The Nectarine' on the vital importance in Fourier of 'special terms which permit transiting or enmeshing one classification to another' – ambiguous categories that 'impurely' (in the terms of Mary Douglas's *Purity and Danger)* mingle peaches and pears. It quotes a memorable passage from Fourier (applicable to Benjamin) on that exemplary 'trivial transgression', death, which 'will lose all the odium attached to it when philosophy will deign to study those transitions that they proscribe under the name of trivialities'.[37]

Perhaps what Benjamin valued above all in Fourier was that he was, like Jean Paul and Pestalozzi, a great educator: 'Educational theory as the root of Utopia', he notes (V, 1222). After the 1833 phalanstery had failed (the architect to blame, in Fourier's view), he went into something of a decline in his later years. But, as Benjamin notes, his spirits rallied again towards the end at the idea of designing a new phalanstery for children only: he thought that the people of Paris, Blois and Tours would be willing to let go of their children for the experiment (for they needed to be taken away from the malign influence of their fathers, if not entirely from their mothers; V, 786–7).

And the greatness of Fourier as an educator resided, for Benjamin, in the power of the example, a power that resided in his mastery of concretion. Barthes provides a good strategic illustration of that power – Fourier's metaphor for the importance of transition: 'Transitions in the harmony of the passions are like dowels and joists in the frame of a building.'[38] It is a habit of of his own work to work from a concrete example: it announces itself right at the beginning of his career in *Writing Degree Zero,* which opens with the instance of the swearwords in Hébert as 'signs of revolutionary writing', but is still in evidence in the Fourier essay, which starts with a delicious parable about eating rancid couscous in Morocco (a 'mania' that Barthes does not share, but which could be reconciled in the phalanstery with his own preference for fresh couscous through a cookery contest).

But it is Benjamin, who spent his exile in search of 'the utmost concreteness for the example' of the arcade, who is the supreme master of this dialectical and pedagogic mode. In his praise of Fourier, he distinguishes between useless moralistic examples in education and 'gestural examples' of Fourier's kind. He may have Brecht's great poem 'Das Waschen' in mind, written for Carola Neher during her imprisonment under Stalin in the Soviet Union, from which she never returned, urging her to continue in prison with the practice of exemplary gestures learnt during her training as an actress – dipping her face in ice-cold water, rubbing it on a rough towel with her eyes open (if so, the hypothesis of a Fourierist reaction against the Moscow trials would be marginally strengthened). At any rate, some of his own most powerful emblems, drawn most commonly from the behaviour of children, emphasize gestures of touching and grasping some person or object, which may be of glass. *Traumkitsch*, a piece on Surrealism written as early as 1925, notes how the Surrealists attempt to come at objects by approaching them from their most worn and used-out sides: 'This isn't always the right way to do it – children don't carefully clasp a glass in their hands, they clutch at it' (II, 620). But the most telling example is that which tries to characterize the Utopian strain, both in Fourier's politics and in his own: 'Comparison with the child who learns how to grasp things by means of an attempt to hold the moon in his hands' (V, 777).

NOTES

1. Benjamin takes an interest in this timetable of Fourier's predictions in his *Arcades* notes. Cf. *Gesammelte Schriften,* ed. R. Tiedemann and H. Schweppenhäuser (Frankfurt/Main, 1974–), V, 787. All quotations from Benjamin refer to this edition by identifying volume and page number. All translations are my own.
2. Jonathan Beecher, *Charles Fourier: The Visionary and His World* (Berkeley, 1986), pp. 355, 492. Cf. also Johann Friedrich Geist, *Passagen: Ein Bautyp des 19. Jahrhunderts* (Munich, 1969), p. 65.
3. Pierre Klossowski, 'Lettre Sur Walter Benjamin', *Mercure de France*, 315 (1952), p. 457.
4. In *Walter Benjamin et Paris,* ed. H. Wismann (Paris, 1986), p. 179.
5. Georges Bataille, *Oeuvres complètes I: Premiers Écrits* (Paris, 1970), p. 391.
6. Alain Arnaud, *Pierre Klossowski* (Paris, 1990), p. 188.
7. Cf. Denis Hollier's edition of *Le Collège de Sociologie* (Paris, 1979), which contains Pierre Klossowski's 'Entre Marx et Fourier' (pp. 586–7), and Chryssoula Kambas, *Walter Benjamin im Exil: Zum Verhältnis von Literaturpolitik und Ästhetik* (Tübingen, 1983) p. 221. Cf also Bernd Witte, *Walter Benjamin* (Reinbek, 1985), p. 128.
8. Cf. Julian Roberts, *Walter Benjamin* (London, 1982), p. 185. Roberts is wrong, I think, in his view that Benjamin's linking of Fourier with the 'colourful idyll of Biedermeier' is a disparaging one. Riegl is the mentor again, and he seems, in fact, to be praising Fourier for foreseeing Biedermeier a generation or so before it came into being.
9. Roland Barthes, *Le grain de la voix: Entretiens 1962–1980* (Paris, 1981), p. 164. Translation my own.
10. Roland Barthes, *Sade, Fourier, Loyola* (Paris, 1971), p. 90. Translations from this volume are my own.
11. Barthes, *Sade, Fourier, Loyola*, p. 86.
12. P. Klossowski, *Les derniers travaux de Gulliver, suivi de Sade et Fourier* (Montpellier, 974), p. 46. Cf. Barthes, *Sade, Fourier, Loyola*, pp. 83–4, which has a list that includes spider-eaters and heel-scratchers.
13. Klossowski, *Les derniers travaux de Gulliver*, p. 54. See also M.C. Spencer, *Charles Fourier* (Boston, 1981), p. 88.

14. Barthes, *Sade, Fourier, Loyola*, pp. 88–90.
15. Susan Buck-Morss, *The Dialectics of Seeing: Walter Benjamin and the Arcades Project* (Cambridge, MA, 1989), p. 262.
16. Beecher, *Charles Fourier: The Visionary and His World*, p. 267.
17. *The Poems of William Blake* , ed. W.H. Stevenson (London, 1971), p. 212).
18. Beecher, *Charles Fourier: The Visionary and His World*, pp. 118, 206, 439; cf. also Spencer, *Charles Fourier*, p. 157.
19. Martin Green, *The von Richthofen Sisters* (New York, 1974), p. 71.
20. Klossowski, 'Lettre Sur Walter Benjamin', p. 457.
21. Alain Arnaud, *Pierre Klossowski* (Paris, 1990), p. 202.
22. Beecher, *Charles Fourier: The Visionary and His World*, pp. 339–40.
23. Christopher Smart, *Jubilate Agno*, ed. W.H. Bond (New York, 1969), p. 105–6; these lines, except the last, are used in Britten's *Jubilate Agno*.
24. Winfried Menninghaus, *Walter Benjamins Theorie der Sprachmagie* (Frankfurt, 1980), pp. 127–31.
25. Barthes, *Sade, Fourier, Loyola*, p. 103.
26. Barthes, *Sade, Fourier, Loyola*, p. 124.
27. Barthes, *Sade, Fourier, Loyola*, p. 105.
28. Cf. *Walter Benjamin et Paris*, ed. H. Wismann, pp. 629–39.
29. Beecher, *Charles Fourier: The Visionary and His World*, p. 320.
30. Beecher, *Charles Fourier: The Visionary and His World*, p. 295.
31. Klossowski, *Les derniers travaux de Gulliver*, p. 41.
32. Barthes, *Sade, Fourier, Loyola*, p. 104.
33. Cf. Buck-Morss, *The Dialectics of Seeing: Walter Benjamin and the Arcades Project*, p. 276.
34. Buck-Morss, *The Dialectics of Seeing: Walter Benjamin and the Arcades Project*, p. 276. Cf. also *Walter Benjamin et Paris*, ed. H. Wismann, p. 879.
35. Barthes, *Sade, Fourier, Loyola*, p. 118.
36 . Beecher, *Charles Fourier: The Visionary and His World*, p. 366.
37. Barthes, *Sade, Fourier, Loyola*, pp. 111–3.
38. Barthes, *Sade, Fourier, Loyola*, p. 112.

8

The Messiah Complex: The Angel of History Looks Back at Walter Benjamin from its Perch on the Ruins of 'Socialism as it Existed in Reality'

John Milfull

'Benjamin:', writes Peter Demetz, 'all agree that he was a man of quiet, fastidious and extremely polite manners, and yet there was in his character and in his thought a half-hidden thirst for violence (more poetic than political), ill according with his life in the library and his later will to believe in revolutionary discipline'. And, quoting Ernst Fischer: 'Benjamin contributed much to an interpretation of capitalism but little to changing the world...his philosophy, sustained by utter loneliness, rather than by the concerns of the masses, particularly attracts those intellectuals who restlessly search for a better world and yet shy away from the grubbier commitments of a political kind.'[1] This distinction between the lonely intellectual and the 'man of affairs' has a long history in German culture, dating at least from Goethe's *Tasso*; with characteristic irony, history has abolished the distinction in the Tohubohu of the last few years, and Fischer's political aims seem no more worldly than Benjamin's Messianic dreams. Malamud's perception that in the twentieth century we have all become Jews is in need of an update; since 1989, those of us, at least, who cling to such Utopias have all become Benjamins. The long sight of his angel of history, which used to penetrate to the rubble of earlier catastrophes, must surely be blocked by the vast mass of decaying masonry and social fabric, reaching beyond the horizon, of 'socialism as it existed in reality'. I like to think that the angel, who only a few years ago seemed petrified and wingless, has come to perch briefly on top of a pile of rubble, breathless and confused from the sudden blast of the last triennium, which no longer blows from the beginning of time, hidden behind the towering wreckage, but swirls and eddies between the ruins. We, too, sit in our privatized libraries and wonder whether the economic storm is really 'what we call progress'.

I was one of many Westerners who shared a strange and deep-seated feeling of solidarity with the embattled protagonists of the vanished world of state socialism, state capitalism or proto-socialism, as we variously termed it, depending on the time of day and our metabolism. It was not a particularly romantic solidarity, not at least in the sense that any of us expected a new society to emerge fully-formed from the brows of real socialist Jupiters or dissidents; we saw too clearly the greyness, the losing streak and its compensations, bureaucracy run amok, Alzheimerian paternalism and empty political gesture. But this world, which defined itself mainly *ex negativo*, as that which it was *not* (in more than one sense) seemed nevertheless the matrix of the future, if we had one. Biermann, Müller, et al.: at heart they longed for the embrace they spurned; the hint to depart, whether gentle or brutal, cut right to the Utopian quick. To resist it was the ultimate point of honour. And we, in the West, rehearsed the excuses for socialist *tristesse*, kept troth with the friendships that seemed so much more giving than the passing alliances of intersecting self-interest we knew at home. Somehow, we filled and over-filled our moral norm by siding with those within the whale, wearing the badge of our solidarity with pride and accepting the minor sanctions it incurred almost as a sign of grace.

I would have no qualms about claiming, with true Postmodern chic, that history is wrong and we were right, if I had not become convinced in the great wash-up that followed that there is more to it than that. Benjamin's *Theologico-Political Fragment*, written perhaps as early as 1920, but still so much in his mind at the end that Adorno co-dated it mistakenly with the *Theses on the Philosophy of History*, presents a paradox so crazy and yet so deep that I fell into it many years ago:

> If one arrow points to the goal towards which the profane dynamic acts, and another marks the direction of Messianic intensity, then certainly the quest of free humanity for happiness runs counter to the Messianic direction; but just as a force can, through acting, increase another that is acting in the opposite direction, so the order of the profane assists, through being profane, the coming of the Messianic Kingdom. The profane, therefore, although not itself a category of this Kingdom, is a decisive category of its quietest approach.[2]

In good Australian: if you believe that, you'll believe anything! Yet the fascination of a dialectic which teaches you that the negations of history contain their own negation is endless; as Demetz again points out, Benjamin's 'movement back and forth between romantic metaphysics and Marxism' is perhaps unexceptional, 'closely bound' as they are 'to each other by Hegel's philosophy.'[3] Yet the fascination with paradox masquerading as dialectic which exercised such potent sway over German and German–Jewish intellectuals alike, and lies perhaps at the very heart of the ill-fated German-Jewish 'dialogue', goes deeper than that. A culture that for nearly two thousand years had compensated the catastrophes of history through the belief in its Messianic *telos*, which saw this *telos* as unknowable, unforecastable and containing in itself not only the reversal of history but the reversal of the Law itself, the iron companion of exile, dismissed its heirs into the secularised world of modernity with a paradox not easily forgotten. This *tikkun*,[4] this transvaluation of all values, finding its deepest expression in the Kabbalist writings of Isaac Luria and his followers, could not be worked towards or anticipated; the end must not be hastened, it might come at any moment, when least expected, at the nadir of history or in the paralysis of inaction. Benjamin's secularized Messianism is no idiosyncrasy; one might almost claim that it was the essential baggage with which this new generation of Jews set out on the greatest adventure of all, the attempt to survive and flourish in the realm of Count West-West, the final descent into the world of the other, mirrored and rationalized in the apostasy of the false Messiah, Sabbatai Zwi, four centuries before. Writers as diverse as Kafka, Feuchtwanger, Schnitzler and Toller, separated already by worlds from literal religious belief, return again and again to the image of the end, an end not justified nor prepared by their own ungratified search for acceptance, but holding the age-old promise of a sudden epiphany, the emergence of the solution when it seems at its most remote. It is hard to read the *Theses on the Philosophy of History* without succumbing to the spell of a hope so deep, so paradoxical and profound, that it still articulates itself at the dead point of personal and historical defeat.

Yet the German colleagues who welcomed or spurned these newcomers were not averse to such paradoxes themselves; the curious waiting game of Christianity, the Messiah who had come and not yet come, whose transformation of life seemed exiled into as distant a future as its Jewish variant, gave way with the rise of secular thought to an even more troubling dilemma. The pseudo-Messianism of revolution, and its belief in the capacity of human reason to end the waiting and transform the world, was soon assailed by the recognition of reason's own apostasy, the new breed of monsters to which its dreams gave birth. Perhaps nowhere more than in Germany, where the new could not easily ally itself with the brash certainties of modernization, and gazed with a mixture of fascination and repulsion across the borders of time and place. It is no coincidence that Goethe responded to the French Revolution with a fairy-tale, nor that the Early Romantics constructed their potent visions of the marriage of natural and human seasons in the world of art; locked in the stifling embrace of the old, the new became for them a Messiah who would suddenly and miraculously transform the world, without the complex process and problems of a social transformation both near at hand and impossibly remote. An idea of 'progress' as uncomplicated and straightforward, at least on the surface, as in England and France could never take root in Germany. The deep ambivalences of the German Enlightenment, whose tethered falcon could never range far afield, were echoed a century later in the age of industrial take-off: the 'idealised kingdom [of reason] of the bourgeoisie'[5] had shown its spots unmistakably enough, and a whole generation of German writers turned against the belated and naked fulfilment of its promise in a search which put them at odds with the bullish progress of Wilhelmine society. Its Jewish subset, acutely mapped by Hans-Dieter Hellige,[6] experienced this rejection in telescoped form; the fathers, the *Geldmenschen* they rebelled against, were themselves both agents and products of the modern. For better or worse, there was little to distinguish the passion with which they denied the present and sought its redemptive reversal from that of their German colleagues; in an irony which has been often remarked, the high point of their assimilation was also the point of secession. These 'double outsiders' bought admission to a 'realm of pure spirit' as surely divorced from the real as the post-Hegelians Marx had ridiculed. As Weimar Germany spiralled to its doom, they sought its *tikkun* in their libraries, troubled, no doubt, by the sound of stamping feet, but apt enough to equate them with the birth-pangs of the Messiah, whichever humane or inhumane shape he might come to adopt. It is a matter of record that some few pursued the paradox to its end, and declared themselves for the millennium of the man from Braunau, only to be flung into outer darkness with no small despatch.

The allegory of reversal may have its deepest historical roots in Jewish Messianism, but it has long since become the common property, not only of German Jews and Germans, but of all those who can no longer envisage a change for the better, grounded, and taking its source, in the present. This dream of reversal has elements both of destruction (and self-destruction) and betrayal: it can only release the new by destroying the old, including the self which, as Brecht wrote in an early gloss on his own pseudo-Leninist reversal, *The Measures Taken*, is 'the last bit of rubbish you have to get rid of',[7] formed as it is by the same rejected present. And this self-hatred, throwing oneself on the pyre with the rest of the world, becomes the moral excuse for invoking the apocalypse. In an unfinished play, *The Great Flood*, Brecht's Nahaia, an anti-Noah, taunts old Jahwe: 'But it's important not that they cease to sin, but that they're eradicated...instead of destroying them you always hope...Now the time has come when he will destroy them. He's come with his water. But I shall go down to the cities, for I want to perish and be destroyed myself, so that *nothing is left*.'[8] This nihilist pose, as Benjamin would have recognized, is only the other side of the Messianic coin; it challenges history, God or whatever to cancel its own botched job and start again, like the extra-terrestrials of *2001* – send a new star-child to get it right this time.

Of course, it is quite a serious business to call down the wrath of God, Messiah or Mao on the Sodom and Gomorrhas in which we writing ones have lived by choice, and not without good urban fun, since our species emerged. The verve, the panache of a text like Benjamin's 'ironic self-exploration',[9] *The Destructive Character*,[10] demands contradiction, only to dismiss it in the name of the 'future', the ways through the passless barriers destruction will find. According to all the best logic of reversal, the destructive character is, of course, the only true constructor, he creates the empty spaces on the negative of the Messianic film. Yet it's hard nowadays to watch this literary *salto mortale* without some kind of shiver, and not for the performer, but for those mute others to whom Benjamin so often appealed. The human sphere seems as fragile, as easily wrecked beyond recall as the outside world on which we have practised our domination, our virulent mix of construction/destruction merged into one and steadily 'sawing the branch on which we sit' (another cheerfully nihilistic image of Brecht's).[11] I had cause, recently, to turn to the story of Jahweh's next trial apocalypse, the burning of those first cities of the plain with fire and brimstone.[12] It is a text as subtle, as multivalent as any of Benjamin's: the quiet shame with which Lot begs permission to move to the city of Zoar, only 'a little one',[13] gladly surrendering the cause of Bedouin virtue to his brother, speaks across millennia – the gentle irony of some urban scribe. But even more vivid is the plea of Abraham, not to destroy if there are only 50, 45, 40, 30, 20 or 10 just men in Sodom[14] – an arithmetic progression which fights the demand for reversal, the destructive character, and leaves us with the conviction that 0 (*Nought*) is enough; in that absolute glare, which of us is just?

But even if we can purge ourselves of such eschatological inhumanity, a further catch remains. The logic of reversal estranges, alienates in a way more powerful and insidious than industrial work; it makes us regard the daily injustice that surrounds us not as something requiring our own action, however limited, but as the sign of a need for reversal so thorough as to remove both act and actors. To invert the Marxist critique of charity: any support which must wait until the whole system is changed will wait far longer than any of us has time for. Of course, the appeal of reversal may stem not so much from a secret lust for violence – the mesmerized gaze of bespectacled Isaac Babel at Budjonny's Cossacks – as from inbuilt fear of the effort needed to cross the borders of self, hated and loved, and try to help. The hopelessness of the present may become not a ground for our own intervention, however apparently hopeless, but a paradoxical comfort, the ultimate alibi for inaction, which only the Messiah – who never comes – could challenge.

Of course, the Messiah *came*, as foretold, when least expected, with the mother mark on his brow, with considerable blowing of trumpets and crumbling walls, but like most of his predecessors, brought a reversal, not to a future world, but to one that seemed past, *only more so*. I imagine we all will return again and again to the age-old question, *what went wrong?* – constructing our explanations and rationalizations with all the frustrated fervour of latter-day Sabbatians. The matrix of the future, the puzzling black hole that was neither capitalism nor communism, is filled now with dreams of a different kind, the unresolved national gripes which wormed their way under the cold, hard tundra of Stalinism.

My friends and I, I now see, were *late* early Christians: the revolution, already remote, our First Coming, the signal of ultimate reversal; the Second Coming, the realization, delayed again and again, blocked by all manner of forces, external and internal. The crumbling edifice Stalin built was paradoxical proof of its own need for transformation, while none of us dared to forecast the day, to hasten the end. We saw the future only in negative, its banning of so many things we guiltily knew, like Lot, did not really belong in the Kingdom. We do not need to reproach ourselves for denying the status quo, which remains in need of denial, great or small; but for that fixation which let us believe in the future rather than turn our critique of the present to actual use. Should I meet Walter Benjamin's angel, panting somewhere in the ex-GDR, I shall look him/her/it as squarely as possible in the clouded eye, and say that we both should *walk* from now on. The wings that we spread and the storm which filled them were both illusions; we can stay and help, at the price of accepting that such time travel was only a myth, to rescue the movement we hoped to find in history, contradictory or paradoxical as it might be, from entanglement in a present which seemed to deny such ends. Kafka's crows are right; there is no heaven, and crows are real enough. The conclusion that there are no ends of history but those we reach ourselves is a daunting one, but it is time to face it and free ourselves from the lure of the Lurian, the Messiah complex.

NOTES

1. Walter Benjamin, *Reflections: Essays, Aphorisms and Autobiographical Writings*, ed. Peter Demetz (New York, 1986), p. *xli–xlii*.
2. *Reflections*, p. 312.
3. *Reflections*, p. *xli*.
4. Cf. Gershom Scholem, *Die jüdische Mystik in ihren Hauptströmungen* (Frankfurt/Main, 1967), especially Chapter 7.

5. Frederick Engels, 'Socialism: Utopian and Scientific', in Marx/Engels, *Selected Works* (Moscow, 1962), p. 117.

6. Hans-Dieter Hellige, 'Generationskonflikt, Selbsthaß und die Entstehung antikapitalistischer Positionen im Judentum', *Geschichte und Gesellschaft* 5, 4 (1979), pp. 476–518. See also Demetz, *Reflections*, p. *ix*.

7. *Bertolt-Brecht-Archiv*, Mappe 1422/12.

8. Quoted in John Milfull, *From Baal to Keuner: The 'Second Optimism' of Bertolt Brecht* (Basle, Frankfurt/Main, 1974), p. 25 (my translation and italics).

9. Demetz, *Reflections*, p. *xv*.

10. *Reflections*, pp. 301–3.

11. Bertolt Brecht, 'Anmerkungen zur Oper', *Gesammelte Werke* (Frankfurt/Main, 1967), vol. 17, p. 1016.

12. Genesis 18:16–19:29.

13. Genesis 19:20.

14. Genesis 18:23–33.

III
Literature/Epistolography

Walter Benjamin as Literary Critic

Manfred Jurgensen

In his authoritative anthology, *Deutsche Literaturkritik im zwanzigsten Jahrhundert*, Hans Mayer includes two critical essays by Walter Benjamin: his polemical response to Fritz von Unruh's travelogue, *Flügel der Nike*, 'Friedensware' (1926), and his paradigmatic interpretation 'Karl Kraus' (1931).[1] Mayer has little difficulty demonstrating the antithetical character of two literary cultures in Germany during the twentieth century: a continuing, albeit ever-decaying 'bourgeois' orientation challenged by an emerging 'proletarian' ideology. In German literary criticism, the assertion of a Marxist school of thought began with Franz Mehring, specifically with Mehring's polemics against Arno Holz in their discussion of revolution in poetry. Yet Mayer has also shown how these opposing positions frequently overlapped, and that it was not always possible to define the place of writers and critics in exclusive specificity.[2] Germany's sociopolitical development during this century has brought about a wide range of complex and contradictory cultural positions, especially among literary critics. As a result, Hans Mayer does not hesitate to speak of a change in the very typology of criticism ('eine Wandlung des Kritikertyps'[3]). Among these new types of literary critics, Walter Benjamin was to prove historically the most outstanding, in the assertions, impulses and directions of his work the most representative, and in the scope, perspective and precision of his writing the most authoritative.

Twentieth–century literary criticism is inextricably linked to the technology of communication, especially the print media. Benjamin's own thesis of 'art in an age of reproduction'[4] applies equally to the critical reception of literary works of art. Academic critics in the tradition of the eighteenth and nineteenth centuries quickly drew a distinction between literary history and literary criticism. Increasingly journalistic critics began writing for a newspaper readership identifiable in its sociopolitical and cultural commitments. Mayer's inclusion of Benjamin's polemic against

Unruh is, by the editor's own admission, the documentation of an exception: employed by the *Frankfurter Zeitung*, the critic attacks an author sponsored by the newspaper's own publishing company. Hans Mayer sees in that evidence of financiers' and publishers' belief in the relative insignificance of newspaper criticism.[5] Walter Benjamin took some part in the radical transformation of academic to journalistic criticism, but his insistence on detailed work analysis and his commitment to the objectivity of philological research meant that he did not represent the general trend of modern German criticism. Indeed, his aim was to counter the emergence of a critical subjectivity which was to culminate in the celebrity status of the critic over the second half of this century. So we are dealing here with the exceptional nature of Walter Benjamin's literary criticism, a writing that was, and saw itself as being, in conflict with the mainstream of twentieth-century German criticism.

In such a context Benjamin's essay, 'Literaturgeschichte und Literaturwissenschaft', first published in *Die literarische Welt* on 17 April 1931, holds a position of special significance. He states his major assertion early, namely: 'Literary history is not merely an academic discipline; in its genesis it is itself part of general history' (III, 284). In his following analysis, he proceeds to confirm the latter, in order to challenge the former. For to him, literary history has been guilty of 'a false universalism in the methodology of cultural history' (III, 284). Germanists failed to place their own historical methodology in a concrete, materialistic sociohistorical context. Hovering between prescriptive aesthetics and an intrinsic enactment or realization of the literary work itself, German literary history took refuge in cultural or artistic generalities such as 'the beautiful', 'values of imaginative experience' and 'the ideal' (III, 287). Benjamin reminds these so-called literary historians that they have failed to think historically; in particular, 'the technical aspects of literary production' (III, 288) deserve greater attention, such as writings by non-artists and non-professionals, a sociology of the reading public, distribution and sales of literary works, relationships of writers and new literary forms. He accuses the literary historians of consciously anti-philological practices and what he calls an exorcism of history. To Benjamin, the literary work exists in a context of multilayered historical specificity and can only be understood in these terms.[7] Literary history has to include in its deliberations the genesis of the work, its reception by contemporary society, its translations and, finally, its fame and after-effects. Literature is not only an art form which has to be understood as an expression, often contradictory, dialectic and volatile, of the time in which it was created; it is also, by its critical reception in later times, a revealing self-reflection of the critic's own age. To Benjamin, this means that literature becomes 'an agent of history' (III, 290). A true history of literature would therefore deal with a double reflection of at least two stages in sociopolitical history.

In his own *Kritiken und Rezensionen* from 1912 to 1940, Walter Benjamin presents models of more or less journalistic reviews which demonstrate the kind of historical sensitivity he is advocating. In his review of Georg Keferstein's *Bürgertum und Bürgerlichkeit bei Goethe*, for instance, he highlights the shortcomings of the study in quite programmatic terms:

> The study fails to consider that this bourgeoisie consisted of academics and cattle dealers, lawyers and stewards, clergymen and factory owners, public servants and manual workers, farmers and shopkeepers, and that since the turn of the century it had experienced trends and crises of the most diverse kind – and that Goethe participated in these conflicts. (III, 420)

In another review, of Hermann Schneider's study, *Vom Wallenstein zum Demetrius*, Benjamin emphasizes that the author's analyses 'have emanated from two decades of academic teaching' (III, 420), thus reinforcing his earlier statement in 'Literaturgeschichte und Literaturwissenschaft': 'What matters is not renewal of academic teaching as a result of research, but vice versa, a revival of research inspired by teaching' (III, 288). Benjamin's newspaper criticisms and reviews must therefore be read as paradigmatic examples of the author's theoretical writings on the relationship between literary history and a 'science' of literature. In characterizing and opposing the development of German criticism in the early twentieth century, Benjamin gave his own publications in this area the character of alternative models. The thematic range of his reviews runs counter to the trend of specialization, their sociopolitical orientation forms part of a programmatically materialistic analysis of literary culture. Together they amount to a practical demonstration of a new Marxist criticism, a left-wing opposition to the art and political establishment in Germany from before World War I to the outbreak of the World War II. Its main concern is to convey to authors and critics a sense of historical responsiveness and responsibility which extends beyond the incestuous, aesthetic and 'timeless' concerns of literary history. Benjamin's 'Retrospective on Stefan George' ends with the symptomatic observation: 'Such a statement may once have merely remained part of literary history. In the meantime, it has become a historic statement carrying its own historical weight.'[8]

In his various essays on individual authors,which Benjamin had planned to collect in one volume,[9] he continues to make a number of categorical statements which together add up to certain basic principles and assumptions, values and beliefs of his own literary criticism. His introduction to Carl Gustav Jochmann's *Die Rückschritte der Poesie* addresses itself to what he calls the 'place of intellectual production in historical tradition' (ÜL, 7). Benjamin's point is that it is not only the immediate reception which determines the nature of historical mediation of art, but also its indirect acceptance by correlated media and genres: 'Often they are integrated indirectly, via media of elective affinities - adopted from predecessors, contemporaries or successors' (ÜL, 7). Benjamin thereby broadens the scope of literary history; he evaluates traditions, influences, 'elective affinities', interrelationships, indirect, 'dialectic' identifications, allusions and cross-references among artists and art forms of different ages. As such, he advocates something like a comparative art history which acknowledges art's own historical force operating within and across specific periods of social and cultural epochs. The literature of different times can therefore prove a more or less powerful factor in determining the historical formations of the present; art itself can be a contributing force of history, with its unique ability to create influence by reviving consciousness from correlative concerns across periods and cultures. This view can be tested in Benjamin's essay on Gottfried Keller,[10] in which he addresses himself to the subject of re-invocation in art of earlier periods of cultural history. 'Frequently painters and poets of the early Renaissance aimed to portray classical antiquity when in fact they were expressing the characteristics of their own age' (ÜL, 27), he reminds his readers. With Keller, Benjamin believes the opposite is true. In formal reduction he sees the Swiss writer reinvoke classical antiquity: 'Keller's writings are full of this kind of authentic and distorted antiquity. His world has contracted to an 'Homeric Switzerland'; it is a landscape of parables and analogies' (ÜL, 27). It is a form of cultural 'simultaneity', a revival of affinities which makes the placing of 'intellectual productions' (ÜL, 7) in history a complex and synchronic as well as diachronic undertaking. Benjamin writes: 'The spirit of nineteenth century classical antiquity manifests itself in Keller's language' (ÜL, 27). Yet in that language he also recognizes 'a strong hint of the baroque', and in addition, sees Keller's use of dialect as 'the currency of many centuries' (ÜL, 28). Finally, he interprets Keller's descriptive prose as a narrative poetic quality which Post-Romanticism helped to shape: 'The major contribution of German Post-Romanticism is the penetration of the narrative by the poetic' (ÜL, 29). It can be seen, then, how Walter Benjamin identifies a number of literary relations as historical agents, leading to a much more embracing, more dynamic assessment of an author's position in contemporary culture.

In his essay on the narrator, Nikolai Lesskow[30] Benjamin speaks of the artist's 'living influence' (ÜL, 33) – or the lack of it. He interprets our age as a period of narrative decline because experience itself has been negated by technology and a lack of moral authority. There is nothing we have left in common; nothing, therefore, to communicate, to share, to narrate. In a happy paradigm, Benjamin can return to his earlier thesis of historical cross-references and updated references or cultural orientations: he speaks of the social archetypes of 'settled farmer' (countryman) and 'trading sailor' (seaman), or 'the resident master and wandering journeymen' (ÜL, 35). Benjamin brilliantly unites an analysis of narrative decline based on a concept of epic truth with its genre-related origin in the history of literature. The 'epic character of truth and wisdom' has 'died out', and the birthplace of the novel 'is the lonely individual' (ÜL, 37). Epic form and literary (sociocultural) history are correlated. It could be argued that Benjamin's paradigmatic interrelationship between art and history as creatively and culturally generative forces is itself a kind of 'reproduction', anticipating his concern over a mere duplication of art by technology. In his Lesskow essay, he links an age of mass communication to the negation of narrative art. The demand for 'verifiable information' (ÜL, 39) calls for an explanation of literary narration. And he stresses the short-lived effect of informative communication in contrast to the long-term design of the story. Not surprisingly, Benjamin declares the narrative 'a tradesman's craft of communication' (ÜL, 42) and reminds his readers that Lesskow 'had a close affinity for the tradesman's craft but little understanding of industrial technology' (ÜL, 43). Benjamin defends the craftsmanship of literary art against the mass-produced information products of the new age. Only as non-industrialized, individual works can literary art remain 'alive', retain a 'living influence' (ÜL, 45). All creative narration emanates from, and relates to, death. Narratives are, in that sense, reports of social and natural history. It is in the treatment of history, in the historical consciousness of a specific narrative form, that living values or qualities of death are propagated. Literature itself constitutes a quality of history.

What about Benjamin's own language, especially in his readings and historical interpretations of literature? On Paul Valéry, he writes: 'The ideas of his poems rise like islands from the ocean of speech' (ÜL, 69). He speaks of Proust's 'River Nile language flooding and fertilizing the plains of truth' (ÜL, 72). And he declares that the author 'built a home from the honeycomb of memory for his swarm of reflections' (ÜL, 74). Little has been made of Benjamin's penchant for imaginative analogies in the form of genitive metaphors (a construction Günter Grass calls 'all-purpose glue'[12]). As a critical tool, he may have attempted to invoke historical dimensions intrinsic to the language of art; if so, his metaphorical analogies would have to be characterized as conservative, essentially Romantic. In his essay on Surrealism, Benjamin himself warns of the dangers of metaphorical criticism: 'Nowhere do analogy and metaphor clash as drastically and irreconcilably as in politics' (ÜL, 101). If, as Benjamin asserts, thinking in images has not served the revolutionary intelligence well, it must be conceded that Benjamin's own critical style occasionally reveals the imaginative limitations of historical conservatism. This peculiar mixture of revolutionary thought, complex historical specificity and conservative imagery characterizes the language of Benjamin's literary criticism. Thus, he can say of Karl Kraus: 'His silence is a dam measuring the level of his ever-rising consciousness' (ÜL, 108). Yet, in the same essay, we find short and precise definitions such as: 'The phrase is a product of technology' (ÜL, 106). Benjamin can thus be both 'the messenger of old engravings' (ÜL, 139) and a revolutionary *Angelus Novus,* Paul Klee's 'New Angel', employing generalities such as 'Now we all know', and indulging in *bon mots* such as: 'Art means reality brushed the wrong way. To polish it up is wall-papering' (ÜL, 144). A critic who delights in formulations of social and aesthetic wit, for example, 'Hope is the *ritardando* of fate' (ÜL, 149), aspires to the status of creative writer, rather than literary historian in the academic sense, or journalistic reviewer celebrating his own subjectivity.

Another characteristic feature of Benjamin's literary criticism is his delight in paradigmatic comparisons of individual writers. Thus, he claims: 'Zola's [naturalism] invokes man and his relationships as only a contemporary could, Green's [naturalism] updates them in a manner no contemporary would have been able to' (ÜL, 150).Or he defines: 'Proust evokes the magic hour of childhood; Green imposes a kind of order onto our earliest terrors' (ÜL, 153). Analogies and contrasts are not confined to creative or narrative writers: 'As Lukács thinks in terms of historical periods, Kafka thinks in terms of the history of the world' (ÜL, 155). Fictional characters are included in this methodology of comparisons. Quoting the figures of Schweyk and K., Benjamin explains: 'One is surprised by everything, the other by nothing' (ÜL, 183). At an important stage, correlatives, analogies and coincidings reveal fundamental cultural relations; Benjamin's criticism extends beyond the purely literary: 'Film and phonograph were invented in the age of man's highest degree of self-alienation, a period of exclusively incalculable, indirect mediation' (ÜL, 183). Benjamin's critical terminology derives from ever–widening comparatives which determines symptomatic formulations, such as the following: 'Kafka's work is an ellipse, the distant focuses of which are determined by a mystical experience which is, above all, the experience of tradition, and by the experience of modern metropolitan man' (ÜL, 199). It is not merely the image of his intellectual parallelisms which defines the nature of Benjamin's critical language. A close analysis of his writings reveals a constant, almost manneristic search for stylistic balance. Benjamin delights in sentences of structural counterpoise: 'There is no teaching which could be learnt, no knowledge which could be preserved' (ÜL, 200). Benjamin's criticism seeks extensions and correlatives; it reaches out from a specific work or author, phenomenon or problem to a more embracing vision, a totality of sociocultural interrelationships.

In his address *The Author as Producer*[13] Walter Benjamin applies this pattern in almost formula-like precision. Discussing the possible conflict between ideological commitment and artistic quality he writes:

> *On the one hand*, it is reasonable to expect of a literary work an ideologically sound basis, *on the other hand*, its literary quality is to be expected from this very disposition. Of course, such a formula must remain dubious until one *appreciates the casual interrelationship* between bias and ideological commitment and literary, artistic excellence. (II, 684)

Benjamin's own italics emphasize a progression of understanding through interrelationships, linking concepts and judgement in such a way that a new logic of reason emerges. That is precisely the critical structure of Benjamin's literary analysis: it extends questions and evaluations beyond an either/or to an analogous composition, an interrelationship of seemingly disparate subjects or values. The ultimate target of such broad investigation is renewal, an artistic regeneration and revaluation in the historical context of sociocultural and political developments. The new form is to grow out of the dialectics of totality. Art is to redefine its own function by a creative innovation of its nature. It is literature's self-reflection in the overall context of cultural production which leads to its renewed originality.

Historically, Benjamin sees the evolution of an artistic avant-garde in its identification with the 'progressive forces' of communism, indeed with the ideological values of the Soviet state (II, 695). In his usual manner, he draws together this *Sowjetstaat* and the *platonic* in an attempt to define the specific place of writers in an ideal society. Soviet communism lost its credibility, even in this context, long before the collapse of the Soviet Union (at the latest, over the revelations of Stalinist terrorism). What remains valid in Benjamin's attempt to define originality and creative renewal in literature (and the arts) is his definition of an 'organizing function' in a work of imaginative innovation. To him, it is 'the model character of production' (II, 696) which makes an author's contribution valuable. Originality in art thus originates from interrelated, ever-changing forces operating in social history. Benjamin sees in that an art-specific quality of *Aktivismus* (II, 689). Ultimately, he minimizes the distinction between author and reader, between citizen and artist. It is the imaginative enactment of sociopolitical values which makes a work of literature public property and part of the general production process of culture. Benjamin knows that 'we are involved in a major historical transformation of literary form' (II, 687). Genres, aesthetics, art itself, are in terminological and functional flux. What Benjamin fails to see – and there are verifiable historical reasons for his inability to do so – is that the terms of production of art have not only led to its reproductability, but in the end, also to a trade in its commodity which makes the work of literature a mere demonstration of the power of its technological means of production. How to resist this tyranny of mass reproduction by the development of a new originality independent of technology yet representative, expressive of its culture is a challenge contemporary literature has failed to meet.

Rolf Tiedemann and Herman Schweppenhäuser offer a philological report on Walter Benjamin's overall output and concept of literary criticism.[14] Benjamin's overview of the subject is contained in the following sketches: 'A Programme of Literary Criticism' (ÜL, 161), 'The Characteristics of the New Generation' (ÜL, 167), 'A Tip for Patrons' (ÜL, 168), '(Antitheses)' (ÜL, 169), 'The Task of the Critic, (ÜL, 171), 'False Criticism' (ÜL, 175), and the brief list of 'motives': 'Schemes', 'Changing the Functions', 'Resistance Against Changing the Functions'; 'The Creative Force', 'The Technological Question', 'On the Crisis of Art' and 'On Döblin's *Berlin Alexanderplatz*' (ÜL, 181–4). These fragments amount to a shorthand summary of Benjamin's central views on the nature and function of literary criticism, and may serve as a programmatic guide to his own work in this area. Benjamin aimed to revitalize the role and quality of criticism. In his aphoristic listing of critical tasks, he employed polemics in an attempt to redefine the discipline in a sociocultural context. He warns of a critic's corruption as part of a broader commerce of art. Honesty, to him, means a recognizable ideological strategy which dictates its own truth and logic. Benjamin clearly sees literature and literary criticism as part of the social politics of an age, a nation and a culture. More specifically, this means that criticism has to function as political enlightenment. In its identification of the consumers of literary culture, Benjamin sees the task of criticism as revealing a 'sectarianism' (ÜL, 162) among the twentieth-century (German) reading public. From the vantage point of the final decade of the millennium, it must be said that Benjamin's assessment of a sectarian readership has proved wrong. It may be that 'communism did not take over' (ÜL, 162), but in its place, a capitalist consumerism has negated the difference between Benjamin's definition of 'general readers' and 'reading circles' (ÜL, 161). The 'age of technological reproduction' has reproduced not only works of art but, along with it, its audience, its readers, its consumers. Benjamin's claim that 'criticism has to legitimize itself by developing a proper understanding of the workings of literary production and distribution' (ÜL, 162) has therefore assumed even greater justification. Yet his attack on publishers of 'bad books' (ÜL, 162), whether on commercial or on idealistic grounds, has not only proved futile; in the last quarter of the twentieth century, publishers and the internationalized (German) literary market have produced authors as much as books. Benjamin relates his concept of criticism back to universities and what he calls the 'handing down of knowledge' (ÜL, 163). He laments the loss of 'an authoritative consensus of themes and terminology' (ÜL, 163). Like the English literary critic F.R. Leavis, Benjamin sees criticism as part of a 'great tradition'.[15] Not surprisingly, he regrets that, in his own age, there is little 'ideological commitment' or 'critically informed debate' among contemporary authors. 'Literary life' suffers as a result.

Literary criticism, then, is a continuing public dialogue among writers, publishers, critics and readers, redefining the tradition and reflecting on the nature of contemporary society. The recurring question must be: 'Whose interests are being served by what prevailing concerns?' (ÜL, 165). The task of criticism is to search for and expose the 'hidden tendencies' (ÜL, 165) of a work of art. All criticism is in that sense contemporary, as is literary creation. 'Classical aesthetics manifested the profoundest perceptions of contemporary criticism', Benjamin reminds us (ÜL, 166). It is essential, he notes, to have a critical 'programme' (ÜL, 166); an 'impartial honesty' in critical judgement he considers to be 'of no interest and ultimately abstract' (ÜL, 161). Georg Lukács's 'Partiality' (*Parteilichkeit*)[16] thus corresponds closely to Benjamin's 'Programme'. Ideally, literary criticism fulfils a vital function in the continuing life of the work of literature: 'Criticism is therefore an intrinsic function in the history of a work of art' (ÜL, 170). It should, accordingly, operate with as many quotations as possible: the work thus speaks for itself through programmatic criticism as much as the ideological position of the critic is revealed by quotations from the literary work. This is what Benjamin means when he states: 'Criticism is a dimension intrinsic to the work itself: art is merely a transition stage of great works. In their genesis they have been something different, and in their critical unfolding they will become something different' (ÜL, 172). There is a genesis dimension and a critical evolution of a work of art. Hence, there cannot be a categorical separation between literary history and criticism. Benjamin calls for 'deductive aesthetics' (ÜL, 179) because he believes that, at the centre of a creative work, no art resides. In frustratingly general terms, he defines that place as 'inside the work itself where there is a fusion in the substance of truth and fact' (ÜL, 179). It is this target of his criticism which makes Benjamin's analyses so challenging and so provocative. In denying the idea of a literary work exclusively or primarily aesthetic status, he defines its character and the function of criticism as demonstrations of ideology and social politics.

NOTES

1. H. Mayer, *Deutsche Literaturkritik im zwanzigsten Jahrhundert* (Stuttgart, 1965), pp. 405–12 and pp. 697–737. All quotations in this paper are my translation.
2. Mayer, *Deutsche Literaturkritik im zwanzigsten Jahrhundert*, p. 22.
3. Mayer, *Deutsche Literaturkritik im zwanzigsten Jahrhundert*, p. 23.
4. *Das Kunstwerk im Zeitalter seiner technischen Reproduzierbarkeit*, in W. Benjamin, *Gesammelte Schriften*, ed. R. Tiedemann and H. Schweppenhäuser, 7 vols (Frankfurt/Main, 1974–), I, 431–69.
5. Mayer, *Deutsche Literaturkritik im zwanzigsten Jahrhundert*, p. 34.
6. W. Benjamin, *Gesammelte Schriften*, III, 284. References in parentheses identify volume and page number. Quotations from Benjamin refer to this edition unless indicated otherwise.
7. Cf. Benjamin, *Gesammelte Schriften*, III, 289.
8. W. Benjamin, *Angelus Novus* (Frankfurt/Main, 1966), p. 481.
9. Cf. the 'Editorial Note' in W. Benjamin, *Über Literatur* (Frankfurt/Main, 1970), p. 203. Hereafter, references to this volume are given in parentheses, abbreviated ÜL, followed by page number.
10. Walter Benjamin, *Über Literatur*, pp. 21–32.
11. Walter Benjamin, *Über Literatur*, pp. 33–61.
12. Cf. *Alleskleber,* 'Schreiben', in G. Grass, *Gesammelte Gedichte*, (Darmstadt/Neuwied, 1971), pp. 171–2.
13. 'Der Autor als Produzent', in *Gesammelte Schriften*, II, 683–701.
14. *Gesammelte Schriften*, VI, 731–46.
15. F.R. Leavis, *The Great Tradition* (London, 1948).
16. Cf. G. Lukács, 'Tendenz oder Parteilichkeit', in *Die Linkskurve,* IV, 6 (1932), pp. 13–21.

10

The Essential Vulgarity of Benjamin's Essay on Goethe's *Elective Affinities*

Anthony Stephens

The title of this paper is, of course, in part a joke – a homage to that unnamed idol of my student days who was said to have published an essay entitled *The Essential Vulgarity of Henry James*. This was, in turn, quite likely a homage to an earlier study entitled *The Essential Vulgarity of Spenser's Faerie Queen*, and so on back to a clay tablet inscribed with a work whose title might translate as *The Essential Vulgarity of the Epic of Gilgamesh*. In other words, my title belongs to a trope, one which expresses the irritation of literary scholars with the charisma of the objects they professionally venerate.[1]

The title has its serious side as well, for it conveys my reservations about the awe in which Benjamin's thought is held today, a phenomenon resulting in devout exegesis where a healthy scepticism seems to me more appropriate. For if Benjamin, as a thinker, was frequently original, he was just as frequently incoherent, and I am not persuaded that so much confusion was the price he absolutely *had* to pay in order to produce his brilliant *aperçus*. As far as the existence of Postmodernism is concerned, I am an agnostic. It is, I suspect, nothing more than a label attached promiscuously by members of our guild to whatever takes their fancy. The only common trait I can discern among those who are willingly described or describe themselves as Postmodernists is a preference for messy thinkers over neat ones. Benjamin's discourse is irremediably, at times gloriously, messy, but then so is that of the Bible, if for slightly different reasons.[2] Jahweh was, perhaps, the first Postmodernist – unfair competition, to be sure, for other aspirants to the title.

The purpose of this paper is to give some insights into the early phase of Benjamin's thought by offering a critique of a substantial essay he completed in the second half of 1922, many years before those works which have made his name a byword today in the English-speaking world. Benjamin's essay has received a lot of attention in German literary scholarship, and the present paper would not be written as it is if I had not been equally fascinated and confused when, as a student thirty years ago, I sought the aid of Benjamin's gnomic statements in trying to come to an understanding of one of the greatest European novels, Goethe's *Elective Affinities*.

But why 'vulgarity'? I confess that, once the joke had paled and homage had been done, I despaired of the title. The prospect of having to tease out a definition of the vulgar for fifteen minutes and then wrap it around a bunch of examples was dispiriting. I was about to change the title to something wholly safe and meaningless, like 'Benjamin and the Dawn of Postmodernism', when a genuine piece of vulgarity came to my rescue. The Vice-President of the United States, Mr Dan Quayle, was quoted as passing moral strictures on the conduct of a fictional character in a popular TV series who had decided to have a child out of wedlock. Is it not vulgar, I thought, to pass moral judgements based on a confusion between fiction and reality? The answer must be yes, since otherwise the author of a novel in which a rape occurs might, in serious intellectual discourse, be accused of being a rapist. But does Benjamin treat the characters of Goethe's novel differently from the way Mr Dan Quayle treats Murphy Brown? I am afraid he does not.

Viewed critically, large tracts of his essay consist of the proceedings of a kangaroo court he holds to judge the behaviour of the wraiths of this fiction as if they were real people. In doing so, he commits the same vulgar errors as those early opponents of Goethe's novel who saw in his profound study of the interplay of circumstance and human passion, and of the anguish this may create, nothing more than a glorification of adultery, 'the apotheosis of illicit desire'.[3]

As a moral judge of fictional characters, Benjamin is unswervingly dogmatic. To impose his dogmatism on the reader, he uses the strategy of deploying concepts such as 'myth', 'destiny' and 'guilt' in specific but quite esoteric senses, as if these were axiomatic to any reader, whereas in fact, an understanding of their approximate meanings presupposes a knowledge of their elaboration elsewhere in Benjamin's early essays, notably in *Towards a Critique of Force*. There are various other strategies by which Benjamin sets out to intimidate the reader into sharing his moral strictures, but, to stay with the quality of his dogmatism for a moment, it is hard for me, on re-reading Benjamin's essay of 1922 today, to believe that it is a work of post-Nietzschean criticism, for its moral stance is curiously anachronistic.

According to Helmut Pfotenhauer, Benjamin had an acquaintance with Nietzsche's thought, and could even find grounds for cheer in the doctrine of the 'eternal return of the Same', which surely makes him one of the most unlikely optimists in twentieth-century European thought.[4] Yet even the stereotyped Nietzsche who was familiar to German intellectuals of the 1920s, and decisively influenced their thinking, had so thoroughly lambasted the moral dogmatism of Wilhelminian Germany that it had lost all credibility in more sophisticated philosophical and literary circles.

Today, since the publication of the Nietzsche edition of Colli and Montinari made a wealth of early, unpublished fragments accessible, we are much more aware of the extent to which Nietzsche's castigation of moralizing extends into a critique of language itself. But a late work, such as *Beyond Good and Evil*, was in vogue in the Germany of the 1920s, and in the prologue to it we read:

> To be serious for a moment, there are good reasons for hoping that all dogmaticising...no matter how solemn, how ultimately and finally valid it may have presented itself as being, may have been no more than high-flown childishness and the work of amateurish beginners; and the time is perhaps very close when it will be understood, again and again, what little was really necessary to serve as the foundation stone of such exalted and absolute philosophical monuments as the dogmatists have constructed to date...some play on words, perhaps, some seduction that stemmed from grammar or an arrogant generalization of a very narrow, very personal, very human – all too human – selection of data.[5]

Nietzsche, like Baudelaire, was one of the greatest connoisseurs and critics of nineteenth-century vulgarity. He was even able to perceive the vulgar fallacy underlying the very same revolutionary apocalyptics, to which he was himself prone, but only, naturally enough, when it was exemplified by others.[6] To read, by way of contrast, some of Benjamin's moralizing in his essay on the *Elective Affinities* is to find oneself transported into a world of pre-Nietzschean sanctimoniousness: 'And so we have no option but to pronounce the verdict: that it is not true love that prevails in Eduard and Ottilie. Love only becomes perfect when, elevated above its own nature, it is redeemed by God's intervention' (I, 187). If Benjamin's second sentence merely echoes the Christian dogma of Original Sin, we might still ask of the first: how do we know 'true love'? What gives it legitimacy in a work of fiction?

Benjamin's answer could only be tautological: what exists between Eduard and Ottilie cannot be 'true love', because, if it were, it would redeem them, as it does the young man and woman in Benjamin's interpretation of the *Novelle* which Goethe includes in the second half of the novel. This concerns the problematic love between the son and daughter of neighbouring households, who have to undergo a vicarious experience of death by drowning before being able to accept their love for one another.

It is clearly meant as a reflection or refraction of the main plot of the novel, but there is still no consensus among critics as to how this relationship is to be taken. Most see it as highly ambivalent.

Benjamin decisively – one might say courageously – opts for an interpretation of the *Novelle* that makes it a simple reversal of the unhappy loves that bind the novel's central characters. His identification of 'true love' in the *Novelle*, and its opposite in what Eduard and Ottilie feel for one another, is a stratagem to enforce this reading of the work. Part of this ploy is to deny the figure of Ottilie any chance of 'redemption' (*Erlösung*), and so her death must be portrayed as a spurious sacrifice: 'And thus it [Ottilie's death] may well be atonement in the sense of destiny, but not holy reconciliation, which humanity can never attain by a freely chosen death but only by one that has been divinely ordained' (I, 176). This cosmic law of Benjamin's own devising is, in turn, invoked only so that he can free the *Novelle* from all the ambiguities that abound in the rest of the novel: 'Even if all its [the *Novelle*'s] details only reveal their significance in the full light of the main narrative, those that have been mentioned so far show unmistakably: the motifs of the *Novelle* stand in contrast to the mythical ones of the novel itself by virtue of being motifs of redemption' (I, 171).

Until I analysed Benjamin's essay for the purposes of this paper, I had been entirely mystified by the lengths to which Benjamin goes to denigrate the figure of Ottilie, even to the point of falsifying the plot. As Ulrich Schödlbauer points out, Benjamin depicts her as wrapt in silence, when the novel itself has her being extremely articulate about her past and future attitudes to Eduard and Charlotte, notably in the fourteenth chapter of the second part.[7] Most readings of the *Elective Affinities* see Ottilie as being to some extent idealized, though not so much as to cost her the sympathies of a reader of the late twentieth century. At the end of the novel, she undergoes a transfiguration in death which is surrounded by so many complex ironies that most critics still fight shy of assigning it one clear import – not so Benjamin. In order to establish the terms of the encapsulated *Novelle* as being unequivocally positive, all the positive attributes of Ottilie in the second part of the work must be disqualified as 'illusion'. Hence, Benjamin's dogma of 'true love' as that emotion which Ottilie *fails* to embody has all the elements of a strategy of denial in psychiatric terms.

The *Novelle* itself concludes with a rhetorical question that may be answered positively or negatively, according to one's conclusions as to what the whole work makes more probable. The beginning of the eleventh chapter of the second part lays a number of trails which may be true or false: Charlotte is excessively upset by the narration of the *Novelle*; something very similar has happened long ago between the *Hauptmann* and a 'neighbour', who may or may not have been Charlotte herself; the narrative voice of the whole novel comments equivocally: 'In the end, it is mostly the case that both everything and yet again nothing remains as it was.'[8] Thus, the novel seems to endow the extremely succinct narrative it encapsulates with a wealth of tantalizing ambiguities, but Benjamin wants nothing of them.

In the paradigms which determine what aspects of the text Benjamin is prepared to acknowledge, 'ambiguity' is placed firmly in the same column as 'myth', and, in Benjamin's view, anything 'mythical' is marked negatively. To make plausible a simple opposition, where Goethe's text presents a wealth of ambiguity, all the motifs of the *Novelle* must converge in the concept of 'redemption'. Hence, the young couple in the *Novelle* must perforce be, in contrast to Eduard and Ottilie, *die wahrhaft Liebenden* (those who love truly); hence, Benjamin goes to extraordinary lengths to deny any similarity between the impetuosity of the young woman in the *Novelle* and Charlotte's daughter, Luciane: 'The wildness which deforms the girl's behaviour is also not the vapid, pernicious wildness of Luciane, but the urgent, wholesome quality of a more noble creature' (I, 185–6).

If too many ambivalences creep in, then Benjamin restores order and simplicity by referring the whole matter to God. In the following passage, one may see him getting into deep water on the subject of Ottilie's beauty, which the text of the novel does emphasize, and then finding firm ground again by a direct appeal to divine authority:

> Through the illusory quality that determines Ottilie's beauty, the salvation which the friends win from their struggles threatens to become insubstantial. For if beauty is only apparent, so is also the reconciliation it mythically promises in life and death. Its sacrifice would be as unavailing as its flowering, its reconciling an illusion of reconciliation. In fact, true reconciliation can only be with God. (I, 184)

To pair 'true love' with 'true reconciliation' seems quite expedient to start with, until one looks at the last sentence of the *Novelle* in these terms. Benjamin insists on understanding the *Novelle* in exclusively positive terms. At the conclusion of the *Novelle*, the young couple seek reconciliation, not with God, but with their respective parents: hence, another case of 'illusory' reconciliation? In his excursus on Kant's definition of marriage, Benjamin has left the reader in little doubt that neither he nor God have any interest in conventional morality. Since the ending of the *Novelle* does nothing to disturb convention, Benjamin's doctrine of 'true reconciliation', for all its portentous tone, appears simply inconsistent.

But Benjamin's familiarity with God still retains some strategic value. As Ulrich Schödlbauer puts it: 'The theological trope of salvation reinforces the forensic trope of suspicion.'[9] But why does the authority Benjamin appeals to have to be divine? The appeals to God are, in my view, a way of eluding the constraints of historicity. Peter Gebhardt, who has written informatively on the genesis of Benjamin's theory of literary criticism, sees Benjamin's early approach as a variant of that of the Romantic, Friedrich Schlegel, but with the following important difference: 'Whilst Schlegel's point of departure is the historicity both of the critic and of the object of criticism, for Benjamin the truth of the work, which it is the purpose of criticism to reveal and develop, remains outside history.'[10] This foreshadows the later Benjamin's vacillations between a dogmatically materialist view of history and a penchant for irrationalist epiphanies. It also accords with his endowing his essay on the *Elective Affinities* with an oppressive religious dimension that is missing from the novel itself, where all religious motifs are caught up in the complex play of ironies that defy reduction to a simple code. If Benjamin, in opting for concepts of 'true love' and 'true reconciliation', is much more metaphysical than Goethe expects any reader to be, then we must ask, given that Gershom Scholem attests no profound religious conviction on Benjamin's part at the time he wrote the essay, what further strategic advantage a leap outside history gains for the author of what is, at heart, a polemic, rather than a devout exercise in critical discourse.

Once more, an observation by Nietzsche, directed against nineteenth-century dogmatists, provides a perspective on Benjamin's strangely anachronistic approach: 'The "Will to Truth" needs psychological investigation: it is no moral force but a form of the Will to Power. This could be proven by the fact that it avails itself of *every immoral* means: the metaphysicians ahead of the rest.'[11] Does it make sense to interpret Benjamin's metaphysics as part of a power play? I think it does, since one of his overt intentions is to discredit Friedrich Gundolf's interpretation of the novel in particular, and of Goethe in general. Gundolf's view of Goethe was influential and far more in accord with the academic and literary orthodoxy of the times than Benjamin's. Cutting Gundolf down to size is thus the first of Benjamin's power plays.

The second goes beyond the demands of refuting Gundolf and is directed towards suborning the reader. This is not the technique of seduction-by-complicity that is characteristic of Nietzsche's rhetorical blandishments, but Benjamin tries rather to compel belief from out of the reader's confusion. I have observed above that Benjamin treats the very specific meaning he has developed for key terms, such as 'myth', 'destiny' and 'guilt' in his other early writings, as if they should be immediately obvious, yet neither explains nor justifies them in his essay on Goethe's novel. Moreover, these meanings have a tendency to shift without warning. Any budding scepticism on the part of the reader is kept down by bewildering changes of terminology, and the ultimate intention is clearly to choke it off altogether by the author's easy familiarity with the mind of God – far less tentative than anything Paul Davies has to offer us today, but distinctly more bombastic in its certitude.

Benjamin's dominant message in the sub-text is, effectively: trust and obey, or mistrust and rack off! This perhaps helps to explain the unique position of Benjamin's essay in scholarly writing on Goethe's novel to date, which Ulrich Schödlbauer summarizes as follows:

> As little as one can imagine present research on this novel without Walter Benjamin's study on Goethe's *Elective Affinities*, its author has, for all that, just as effectively precluded the simple adoption of its conclusions by successive researchers. Benjamin's methodological reflections on the distinction between *criticism* and *commentary* remain, even today, the reason that the influence of certain details of his study stands in contrast to the complete lack of acceptance of its overall import. These two terms are positioned at the beginning of the essay as if they had the task of preventing the uninitiated reader from penetrating any further.[12]

But these are only the first of many terminological Symplegades that the intrepid reader will have to pass without getting squashed in order to reach the heart of Benjamin's argument. It is as if Benjamin, being aware of the imperfect match between his central concept and the novel itself, wants the reader as confused and intimidated as possible at the moment when a credulous acceptance of 'true love' and 'true reconciliation' will be demanded.

The third, and much more subtle, power play is directed against Goethe himself. The opening move in the game is Benjamin's distinction between the 'truth content' of a work and its 'material content'. Very early in his essay, he uses this to imply that a critic's perception of a work may, in some circumstances, be superior to that of its creator:

> Thus the critic inquires as to the truth whose living flame keeps burning above the heavy logs of what has existed and the light ash of what has been experienced. Though the being [*Dasein*] of a work may not conceal itself from its creator, as also from the readers of that time, yet the realities [*Realien*] in a work mostly will. But since it is only by contrast with these that the eternal aspect of the work becomes visible, any contemporary criticism, no matter how high its status, comprehends the work's effect in its own time, rather than its eternal being. (I, 126)

Benjamin is here advancing a variant of Friedrich Schlegel's idea that a work of literature is enhanced by being read and written about. Few would disagree today that a great work of literature, seen from the perspective of a few centuries of critical reception, is a different entity from the same work shut away forever in a drawer. At its most neutral level, Schlegel's claim is no more than an extension of the Kantian theory of perception to the work of art. The problems arise in the evaluative mode. Schlegel at one point describes criticism as 'poetry of poetry', meaning 'poetry raised to a higher power'.[13] The young Schlegel, naturally enough, did not imagine that pedestrian scholarship could raise its objects to a higher power, for in the 117th *Lyceum* fragment, he insists that 'only poetry can criticize poetry'. For him, the work is translated to a higher plane only if the genius of the critic matches the genius of the creator.

Benjamin takes this argument in a different, if no less radical, direction. As Peter Gebhardt concludes from an analysis of Benjamin's doctoral dissertation: 'Criticism acquires the task of extinguishing the historical life of works of literature in favour of the concerns of philosophy and its objects: knowledge and truth.'[14] The critical reception of a work is thus, for Benjamin, like a refining fire. The dross of historically-determined misreadings, including those of the work's creator, is burnt away, and an unmediated truth shines forth.

If we pursue the *ignis fatuus* of Goethe's own misreading of the *Elective Affinities*, then we find the following in Benjamin's text:

> That over which the poet has conscious control, in the sense of his artistic craftsmanship...may indeed be in contact with the realities [*Realien*] in the material content, but at the same time constitutes the line of demarcation *vis-à-vis* the truth content, which can never be entirely present to the consciousness of the poet or the critics of his day. (I, 145)

To be consistent with the rest of Benjamin's theory, the truth can scarcely be present to their consciousness at all. From here, it is but a step to confusing Goethe with his own fictional creations. Note, in the following, the appeal to an extra-textual authority, in this instance, Goethe's younger contemporary, the novelist Jean Paul Richter, and the adroit insertion of the fatal adjective 'mythical', which Benjamin consistently uses as a negative marker in his evaluation of aspects of Goethe's novel: 'In this manner, Goethe confronts all criticism in his old age: as an Oympian...This term – it is attributed to Jean Paul – denotes the dark, self-absorbed, mythical nature which, in speechless rigidity, is inherent in Goethe's artistic character' (I, 146–7). If one takes the trouble to follow up Jean Paul's description of his first evening in Goethe's house in Weimar in June 1796, then it is to recognise once more how perversely selective Benjamin's reading is.

Jean Paul's beautifully-crafted letter begins with Goethe's formidable reputation, the 'Olympian' effect of the house itself, and then goes on to the coldness of Goethe's formal manner. But then, thawing, Goethe reads one of his own poems aloud, and all is transformed. Jean Paul offers the reader the striking image he has prepared all along: volcanic fire – 'of the heart' – bursting forth from beneath an ice-field:

> Ostheim [Charlotte von Kalb] and everyone else depicted him as quite cold towards all persons and things on earth – Ostheim said that he admires nothing any more, not even himself – that each of his utterances was pure ice, especially those addressed to strangers, whom he was rarely willing to receive – there was something stiff in his matter, the kind of pride we find in Imperial cities – only matters that touch on art can still slightly thaw the nerves of his heart...I went to him without any warmth of my own, purely from curiosity. His house [~~palace~~] is most striking; it is the only one in Weimar decorated in Italian fashion – with such staircases! – a whole Pantheon of paintings and statues, a chill of anxiety oppresses the heart – finally the God approaches, cold, monosyllabic, with no liveliness in his speech. For example, if Knebel says the French are marching into Rome – 'Hmm!' says the God. His body is robust and vital, his eyes shine (but in no pleasing hue). But finally, not only the champagne but also the discussions of art, the attentive guests etc. stirred the coals to life in an instant and – we were in the presence of Goethe. His speech is not as ornate and fluent as is Herder's, but incisively clear and calm. Finally he read to us – that is: he acted for us* – as yet unpublished poem – a splendid piece, and, as he did so, his heart drove tongues of flame through the crust of ice...When I left, he took my hand once more and invited me to come again. He thinks his literary career is over. But, by God, we shall learn to love one another...He is also the most appalling gormandizer. He is dressed in the most elegant of fashions.
>
> * His manner of reading is nothing but a rumble of thunder intermingled with the pattering of raindrops: there is nothing like it.[15]

Benjamin dispenses with the fire, to say nothing of the gluttony, and opts for 'speechless rigidity', a quite one-sided extrapolation from Jean Paul's image – indeed a falsification of his account. One knows from other memoirs that Goethe tended to make abundant use of the formulae of polite discourse to keep others at arm's length, but Jean Paul insists beyond the least doubt on the epiphany of reversal: wine and poetry ignite the fire of genius, and the unapproachable Olympian becomes human. But the strategy has worked – for the purposes of Benjamin's essay. Goethe has become as 'mythical' as those aspects of the novel Benjamin needs to mark as negative to make his own reading plausible. This is probably because Goethe, in a conversation with Sulpiz Boisserée dated 5 October 1815, expressed a totally different set of attitudes towards his own fictional character, Ottilie, from those on which Benjamin's interpretation depends.[16] It is therefore useful to discredit Goethe's perceptions of his own work by situating him in the 'mythical' stratum of Benjamin's cosmos, upon which both the critic and God may look down with like superiority. That Benjamin should have devoted two whole pages of his essay (I, 160–1) to attacking Gundolf for confusing Goethe's biography with his works is surprising to no one familiar with basic techniques of propaganda: always accuse the enemy of crimes one commits oneself.

The value of Benjamin's essay is that it succeeds in making more individual aspects of Goethe's novel intriguing or worrying to the reader than many longer treatments of the text with impeccable academic credentials. It could also scarcely be the work of the Benjamin who is today so cherished, indeed canonized as a subverter of ideologies *par excellence*, if it did not contain a few elements that tend to undermine its own dogmatism. Perhaps the shifting quality and obscurity of Benjamin's own concepts has its pedagogical value in eventually confronting gullible readers with proofs of their own gullibility. Moreover, he introduces two concepts which are themselves so opaque as to suggest that the truth *cannot* be articulated with the complacency with which Benjamin himself prates about 'true love' and 'true reconciliation'. These are, firstly, the 'expressionless', *das Ausdruckslose* (I, 181), and secondly, the concept of a caesura or hiatus in normal discourse which permits an intuition of something that must be left unsaid.[17]

Last but not least is the fact that he quotes the sonnet by Zacharias Werner entitled 'Die Wahlverwandtschaften' of the year 1811, which a young writer, whose filial bond to Goethe was about to be broken, composed with an uncanny mixture of aggression and insight.[18] Benjamin is dismissive of Werner's poem, since it goes quite against the grain of his own reading, but at least he quotes it in full. In my view, Werner's sonnet conveys a much better sense of the ambivalences of the novel than Benjamin's basic argument that the encapsulated *Novelle* is a simple corrective of what the novel's four main characters get wrong. That Benjamin should quote it, when it serves his main purpose not at all, may properly be designated a subversive element in his own text.

But when all such allowances are made, the vulgarity of Benjamin's approach resides in the claim that literary criticism – at some arbitrary point of a work's historical reception – can unveil the 'truth content' of a work, and in the pathos which accompanies this claim. It is the self-aggrandizement of the middle-class intellectual taken to an absurd extreme. Nietzsche succumbed to the same vulgarity in *Thus Spake Zarathustra* and subsequent writings, but these were markers that signal the approach of his complete and final mental collapse. Benjamin, by contrast, is thirty, and has his best work still before him. Until Nietzsche himself fell prey to the vulgar errors of revelation and prophecy, 'the pathos that stems from the conviction that we possess the truth' is denounced frequently enough in his earlier writings for Benjamin to have taken notice.[19]

One of Nietzsche's more salutary maxims on the relationship of art and truth reads: 'We have art so that we do not perish of the truth.'[20] If we contrast this with Benjamin's claim that literary criticism can effect a revelation that transcends the historicity both of the work and its reception, then there is a liberating quality in Nietzsche's words.

Earlier in this paper, I suggested that Benjamin affects a pre-Nietzschean innocence, as far as the elusiveness of truth is concerned. Winfried Menninghaus, in his study of Benjamin entitled *Schwellenkunde: Walter Benjamins Passage des Mythos*, makes two more pertinent criticisms of Benjamin's essay. Benjamin's concept of 'myth', he points out, displays both common prejudices of the time and an ignorance of the significant work that had been done on myth in anthropology and ethnology by the early 1920s. Still worse, he says, some of Benjamin's thinking seems to have been taken over uncritically from the doctrinaire approach to Greek literature instilled into him in his schooldays: 'More strongly even than the theological discrimination against 'false gods', one senses the Classical high-school with its stock concepts for understanding Greek tragedy: destiny, guilt and atonement.'[21] When Benjamin completed his essay on Goethe's *Elective Affinities*, he was thirty, too old to be decorating the prejudices of his schooldays with the trappings of divine revelation.

He was to go on to develop into one of the most confused thinkers in the German language since Richard Wagner – and to be canonized for it. Let us not begrudge him his canonization, for he was, in his confusion, from time to time, what so few of us are: namely, original. It would be rewarding to counterpoint the vulgarity of his study of Goethe with the sophistication of his later writings on Baudelaire, since these are not driven by the same imperative to assert the superiority of 'the critic', a clone of Benjamin himself with Jahwehistic overtones, over such easy, if prestigious, victims as Friedrich Gundolf in the 1920s and, quite bizarrely, the great Goethe's understanding of his own work. Baudelaire himself was iconoclast enough not to provoke Benjamin into bouts of gratuitous iconoclasm. It is strange that the Goethe of the *Elective Affinities* was not, for nowhere in his writings is Goethe further away from that heavy sententiousness to which he was quite prone and which provides abundant material for 'thoughts for the day' in desk-diaries and similar publications. But he was, in the 1920s, even more of a national monument than he is today. In his attempt to outdo Goethe, Benjamin becomes even more sententious than Goethe at his most self-consciously 'wise', and all the obscurantism of which he was capable and which fills the pages of his essay cannot, in the long run, mask its underlying vulgarity.

Anthony Stephens

NOTES

1. Walter Benjamin, *Gesammelte Schriften*, ed. R. Tiedemann and H. Schweppenhäuser, 7 vols (Frankfurt/Main, 1974–), I, pp. 125–201. References in parentheses identify volume and page number. All translations in this paper are my own.
2. Cf. H. Bloom, *The Book of J* (London, 1992), pp. 23–36.
3. *Goethes Werke: Hamburger Ausgabe* (Hamburg, 1960), vol. 6, p. 645, quotes a letter, dated 12 January 1810, by Friedrich Jacobi, which contains the verdict: 'What totally disgusts me is the apparent transformation, in the ending, of carnality into spirituality; one might well call it: the apotheosis of illicit desire [*die Himmelfahrt der bösen Lust*].'
4. Cf. H. Pfotenhauer, 'Benjamin und Nietzsche', in *Walter Benjamin im Kontext*, ed. B. Lindner (Frankfurt/Main, 1978), pp. 120–1. Pfotenhauer quotes the following passage from Benjamin: 'The idea of the eternal return conjures forth from out of the misery of the times the speculative idea (or the phantasmagoria) of happiness. Nietzsche's heroism is an antithetical counterpart to the heroism of Baudelaire, who conjures forth from the wretchedness of philistinism the phantasmagoria of the Modern' (I, 683).
5. F. Nietzsche, *Werke in drei Bänden*, ed. Karl Schlechta (Munich, 1966), vol. 2, p. 565.
6. Cf. A. Stephens, 'Nietzsche's Apocalyptic', in *Myth and Mythology*, ed. F. West (Canberra, 1989), pp. 101–17.
7. U. Schödlbauer, 'Der Text als Material: Zu Benjamins Interpretation von Goethes "Wahlverwandtschaften"', in *Walter Benjamin – Zeitgenosse der Moderne*, ed. D. Harth (Kronberg/Taunus, 1976), pp. 103–4.
8. *Goethes Werke: Hamburger Ausgabe*, vol. 6, p. 442.
9. U. Schödlbauer, 'Der Text als Material', p. 113.
10. P. Gebhardt, 'Über einige Voraussetzungen der Literaturkritik Benjamins', in *Walter Benjamin – Zeitgenosse der Moderne*, p. 74.
11. F. Nietzsche, *Werke in drei Bänden*, vol. 3, p. 764.
12. U. Schödlbauer, 'Der Text als Material', p. 94.
13. P. Gebhardt, 'Über einige Voraussetzungen der Literaturkritik Benjamins', p. 72.
14. P. Gebhardt, 'Über einige Voraussetzungen der Literaturkritik Benjamins', p. 77.
15. *Jean Pauls Sämtliche Werke: Historisch-kritische Ausgabe, Dritte Abteilung. Zweiter Band – Briefe 1794–1797*, ed. E. Berend (Berlin, 1958), pp. 211–2, letter dated 18 June 1796.
16. *Goethes Werke: Hamburger Ausgabe*, vol. 6, p. 624.
17. Cf. Benjamin (I, 182): 'Such power has scarcely ever become more evident than in Greek tragedy, on the one hand, and in Hölderlin's hymns, on the other. In tragedy, as the hero's suddenly falling silent; in the hymn as an audible hiatus in the rhythm.'
18. Benjamin calls it 'such crazy praise and blame, lacking all decorum' (I, 142).
19. F. Nietzsche, *Werke in drei Bänden*, vol. 1, p. 727.
20. F. Nietzsche, *Werke in drei Bänden*, vol. 3, p. 832.
21. W. Menninghaus, *Schwellenkunde: Walter Benjamins Passage des Mythos* (Frankfurt/Main, 1986), p. 112.

–11–

A Man of Letters: Walter Benjamin as Correspondent, Editor of Letters and Theorist of Epistolography

Gert Mattenklott

A prominent feature of Walter Benjamin's work is that from every passage you can prove the whole. This is not to minimize all the important changes which actually characterize his writings in the course of three decades. It is also not intended to minimize the variety in Benjamin's work, the different views which appear when one approaches either the position of Benjamin as a critic, essayist and philologist, as the author of *Städtebilder* and *Berliner Kindheit*, or of Benjamin the correspondent. Yet, there are certain *idées fixes* which can be found throughout his work, although in changing disguises and masks. Many of these can be discovered in Benjamin's letters, in those he wrote to Florens Christian Rang, Hugo von Hofmannsthal and Gershom Sholem, as well as in the letters to Bertolt Brecht and Theodor W. Adorno.

Only a small selection of Benjamin's letters has been published. So far, his correspondence has been used only as reference material by scholars working in the extensive field of Benjamin philology. These authors, however, have not realized that letters had a rather singular meaning for Benjamin: the letter is a literary form that is situated between, perhaps beyond, art and life. Benjamin used this form frequently throughout his life. His interest in correspondence resulted in the publication of *Deutsche Menschen*. He also commented on epistolography in various scattered theoretical reflections in which the letter is characterized as a chimerical form that contains the best of both worlds: it participates in everyday life, but also in the sphere of thought and reflection. This balance between vital and moral ethics is always determined by the circumstances of everyday life, by the author's moral scrutiny in using this symbolic form of living spontaneity. If one follows this definition to its end, than one can picture Benjamin's oeuvre as a letter which always begins anew, and his real correspondence as the work *en miniature.*

Benjamin himself invites speculations of this kind. If one reflects on his letters in the context of his ideas on linguistics, for example, it appears doubtful whether the people he wrote to were really the addressees of his messages. In Benjamin's philosophy, the letter aims at pure language, in opposition to the implementations of an instrumentalized use of language. In the light of this idea, letters are never out of date; thus, Benjamin did not cease writing letters in favour of more modern means of communication. With each letter, he testified to the desire for an ideal dialogue, a dialogue which was not determined by the omnipresent system of mass communication.

Amongst Benjamin's posthumous papers, there are a number of theoretical comments on the uses of letters. They derive from a letter he wrote to Ernst Schoen in 1919 (19 September). The reflections are connected with a reference to Goethe's correspondence with Count Reinhardt. Benjamin praises it for its 'remarkable, most noble and unswerving certainty of the tone of voice with which they speak of and to each other'. He continues:

> Nowadays correspondences are underestimated because they are usually connected wrongly with the notion of the work of the author and of authorship. In fact, they belong to the sphere of testimony, and their relation to a person is as insignificant as the relation of any pragmatic-historical testimony (inscription) to the person of its creator. Such testimonies belong to the history of the *afterlife* of a human being, and therefore in correspondences one can study the way how a life with its own history extends into afterlife. (This is not possible with a person's works: they are like a watershed in which life and afterlife never mingle.) For posterity, a *correspondence* appears somehow condensed (while the *single* letter loses of its life in relation to the writer): the letters, when read in sequence and very short intervals, change their character, they change objectively with their own life. They live in another rhythm than the rhythm of the past when the addressees were alive; and in other aspects they change likewise. (VI, 95)[1]

Benjamin's manner of speech is apodictic. He does not mention the supposedly self-evident purpose of letter-writing: letters as means of communication for the exchange of information. He excludes this aspect from his reflections, because he objects to it for the same reasons he objects to linguistics as a science of communication: it is limited to the pragmatic relations between empirical persons, it wrongly implies that there is a proportionality between real human beings and their linguistic representation. However, in the moment of speech, the word no longer belongs exclusively to a singular and private relationship between sender and addressee, but to a third realm created by dialogue. Benjamin emphasizes the aspect of exchange in the afterlife of letters. It is not the dialogue he stresses, but the objective form of the letter, which makes its secondary aspects – the letter as a source of information or as a document – less important.

Whatever two correspondents have to say to each other, they cannot express it except by giving it away to a third instance, which secretively is the first. They are unable to influence the result of the correspondence; the letter gains an autonomous existence the moment it is posted. This describes the situation of the correspondents: either they do not realize themselves in the letter, or they acquire by letter what they lack in their personality in real life. Therefore Benjamin states that there is no symmetry between the letter and an author's life or work. He characterizes the special feature of correspondences as *Fortleben,* a kind of autonomous afterlife. Rudolf Kassner would probably have described this notion as chimerical: it bears a likeness to a cocoon where someone has changed in order to escape at any moment as someone new and different. Instead of reflecting life, the letter exchanges the life of the author for a fictitious second nature, which, inspite of its abstract and fictitious nature, is so dominant that it overpowers the life of the correspondent. Thus, the letter provides an opportunity, or rather more compels a writer, to construct the shape of his or her own afterlife which has to be invented anew with every letter, and perhaps always in a different shape.

The ever-changing character of the letter leads to another of Benjamin's affinities: to an elective affinity. All his life, Benjamin was fascinated by Goethe. It is no mere accident that he chose one of Goethe's correspondences as an occasion for a theoretical reflection on the nature of correspondence. It is not so much the romantic aspect of the letter as a diversity rich in contradictions that fascinated Benjamin, but the stability of a second ego acquired by letter-writing. The writer can confide in this second ego without reserve, because he can rely on the metamorphic power of the medium of the letter/correspondence.

The praise of 'noble, unerring certainty of the tone of voice' in Goethe's and Reinhardt's letters is not only a praise of a model correspondence, but also a glorification of the form in general. Noble and distinguished: Benjamin likes to use these words of praise, not only in the comments on the letters he has collected for his anthology of letters, where the reference to a *Klassikerbibliothek* suggests such epithets (he describes the anthology as a kind of 'Golden Treasure of German Letters').[2] The desire for *Haltung,* which can be only inadequately translated as style and composure, as the dignified form of the natural being and the natural form of the man of letters, was cherished by Benjamin as much as by any member of the

George circle. In this respect, he is closer to George than is suggested by the distance which he often expresses elsewhere.

If the letter does not testify to the correspondent's pragmatic context of life, what else do correspondences testify? Letters are testimonies of an intellectual life on which the correspondent can only take out a loan. The testimony of a letter touches all profane and situative circumstances only peripherally. However, for a volume of letters, it is still necessary that the actual context of writing be annotated, not in order to disclose private matters, but to neutralize them with factual information so that the letter – as testimony – can gain a clearer profile.

A characteristic aim of Benjamin's theory of the letter is to establish the importance of small and insignificant items, of fragments. So, if we do not read a letter only as a source of philological information or as a biographical document, but regard it differently, we shall notice a way of thinking which is not primarily interested in being a witness *of* its time, but in being a witness *against* its time. Reading a correspondence in this way, finally, testifies to a physiognomy of thinking that aims, above all, at being testimony.

There seem to be many objections that could be raised against this approach to correspondence: letters contain merely private communication or merely communication about things, just to mention the two most extreme prejudices, in the names of subjectivity or objectivity. Both objections fail to come to grips with Benjamin's idea of the letter as testimony. His ideal of the letter contains both spheres: letters have to belong to life, but they are not founded in life, because life never has its foundation or its reason in itself. The letter also has to refer to the reality of intellect without betraying life. In this respect, the letter is a true medium, a go-between, which testifies to the possibility of a balance between nature and intellect.

Adorno, who edited the first collection of Benjamin's letters together with Scholem in 1966, has characterized Benjamin as a correspondent precisely in this manner: 'The letter was in accordance with Benjamin's ideas because it encourages a mediated objectified immediacy. Writing letters simulates life in the lifeless solidity of words. In the letter you can deny remoteness and simultaneously remain remote and distant.'[3] By its own means, the letter cannot point to a third instance as a possible realm where both spheres are reconciled. This is the reason for the performative nature of the letter, which neither follows the rhythm of natural life, nor permanently remains in the sphere of abstraction, in a sphere remote from life. The character of the letter is appellative, it constructs its own reality, at least for the duration of the correspondence. Therefore, Eros is a discreet participant in every long-lasting correspondence. On the basis of this idea, Benjamin connects the concept of testimony with a non-sexual form of productivity: creation as a para-erotic, written act which carries no resemblance to the physical sexual act of procreation, but rather takes its place. In dialogue, and even more in the letter, Eros is present and has a legitimate and undenied position in the intellectual sphere. These ideas are the ideas of the German *Jugendbewegung*, the youth movement of pre-World War I. Benjamin does not only adapt them, but surpasses them. Because his idea of testimony carries a multitude of diverse meanings, its relevance is not limited to a history of culture.

It is not simply a question of replacing a pragmatic biographical interpretation of correspondences with a reading guided by an interest in cultural or intellectual history. Consistent with this view, the letters of Karl Wolfskehl, which were nearly never answered, would no longer be read as records of learned admiration of George, but as testimonies of a monological and bacchanalian language of passion. Kommerell's letters, this elegant subterfuge from a scholar's orderly life, could bear witness to the subversive power of humour confronted with the stilted language of the sublime, as it was practised in the George circle. With an altered approach, Benjamin's correspondence would no longer be read as a document commenting upon the genesis of his work, but as an ambitious attempt to find a *tertium datur*, sought in order to escape by letter the dilemma the contemporary intelligentsia had to face, of having to choose between the political-intellectual alternatives of the time in favour of a third, nameless option.

However, Benjamin is neither Blei nor Friedell. The substitution of individual, private life as an idea of universal value for a more generalizing approach was hardly his main concern. His idea of testimony is not rooted in empirical reality, which, on the other hand, he is not willing to abandon. More than any of Stefan George's disciples, Benjamin searched not for an idea, but for a form, as a stronghold against the corrosiveness of time, against the *Furie des Verschwindens*, as Hegel described the horror of losing the past.[4]

Deutsche Menschen (subtitled *A Sequence of Letters*) was first published in Switzerland.[5] The anthology is not only very instructive in relation to Benjamin's concept of testimony and his theory of letters generally, which gains a new dimension here, but also because of its context. Twenty-seven letters from this collection were published in the *Frankfurter Zeitung* in 1932. They were numbered consecutively, but carried no reference to Benjamin, who was the editor. According to a manuscript from the posthumous papers, Benjamin intended to discuss and comment on them in a radio essay.[6] In this manuscript, he mentions Gundolf's image of the tectonic character of the artistic world: at the *base* there are dialogues and conversations, leading to a *massif* of letters, which lead up to the *summits* of individual works. Benjamin mentions this idea in order to question it, especially with reference to the reception of German classicism. 1932 was Goethe's jubilee year. Retrospectively, the idolization of Goethe and of the *Kulturnation* seems pathetic or even absurd, because it was celebrated by a nation which was simultaneously preparing an apotheosis of barbarism. Against the 'glaciating hero-worship' (*vergletschernden Heroenkult*) of classical poets, Benjamin mobilizes a different idea of classicism. Letters, especially Goethe's letters, are used to support his thesis. Benjamin's approach implies to read Goethe's letters as such, not as monuments. Goethe's work was frozen into a 'glacial' monument by hero-worship, a kind of reception of Goethe which Benjamin regarded as extremely unproductive. His approach neither implies reading the letters out of an interest in gossip, nor constructing an opposition between individual concerns and the sublime; he also does not intend to popularize classicism through letters. Quite the contrary, for the sake of physiognomic recognizability, his solemn sobriety tends towards the distance of historiography:

> Historical distance, however, dictates the laws of our reflections. The first principle is that the differentiation between the private person and the author, subjective and objective, person and cause, will become void with increasing historical distance, which means that if you do justice to one of these important letters and illuminate it in all its factual references, its details and allusions, you will get right to the core of humanity. (IV, 944)

Das Menschliche (the human) is not the profane of mere living, however, which will remain when you remove life's intellectual sphere. It is situated in the sphere where, in the language of the eighteenth century, the real human being (*der allgemeine Mensch*) is placed. Eighteenth-century language served as a model in *Deutsche Menschen*, where Benjamin mimetically adapted it. The passage quoted above was very important to Benjamin. He repeated it literally in his 'Memorandum on the Sixty Letters', a kind of self-review for promotional purposes, adding the following sentences:

> The short commentaries which precede the letters have nothing in common with the stereotypical comments one can usually find in anthologies. There will be nothing which could detract from the concrete physiognomical appreciation of the individual writer. None the less, these letters represent an extensive account of German intellectual history of the period in question. (IV, 950)

The historical distance from classicism Benjamin assumes in *Deutsche Menschen* is not related to the social ethics of German idealism. Benjamin would also have signed the contract for the foundation of the nation which the poets of German classicism, above all Goethe and Schilller, had agreed on. In Germany, aesthetic education was held in high esteem, more than in any other nation. Their programme is a much an aesthetic as a moral programme. For no social stratum in Germany did it have as much appeal as for the Jewish minority; no other group adopted it as wholeheartedly as the German Jews. In his belief that aesthetic and moral values spring from the same source, that they are two manifestations of the same substance, Benjamin was true to Jewish tradition. However, Goethe or the other German classicists would not have disagreed. Among the Jewish German-language authors, this idea gained an importance for the choice of a specific form within the ensemble of art forms, and within the genre, it was the reason for the preference for certain forms.

In German literature, there are many more Jewish artists than in fine arts or music. Within literature, Jewish artists and intellectuals prefered forms related to pedagogy. In the history of aestheticism, on the other hand, there are hardly any Jewish writers at all. Aesthetic immoralism, or even mere aesthetic indifferentism, have no roots in Jewish tradition. Therefore, Jewish authors opted for genres or art forms that allowed them to propagate the transformation of their lives for the better. This approach was very close indeed to German idealist aesthetics, and it promoted an alliance between idealist aesthetics and Jewish intellectuals. The basic idea was to ground philosophy in the arts, which was regarded as a means of moral improvement. The result was not only an admiration of the literature of the German classics, but also an opting for Hegelian aesthetics which marked a period of Jewish thinking that lasted from Heine to Lukàcs, i.e. a decision that implied commitment to moral progress. That this idea of progress had to be promoted strenuously was realized by the young participants of the movement for Jewish emancipation which took place during the first decades of the twentieth century. It was the course of Jewish history that forced them to come to this conclusion.

These young Jews attacked art in the name of morality: Max Nordau did so at the beginning of this century, and later, Walter Benjamin doubted the aura of artworks, favouring art that could be copied by means of mechanical reproduction. Guided by the same intention in *Deutsche Menschen*, Benjamin opts for the letter as a form of comparatively meagre aesthetic value, compared to the gilted-edged volumes of classicist literature, which represents autonomous and pure art. In contrast, the letter is not such a 'pure' form of art, because it belongs to the sphere of intellect as well as to the sphere of life. From the very beginning, Benjamin created his own moral portrait in letters, because he felt their testimonial aspect would be more reliable than either art or life, which are equally frivolous when moral self-determination is in question.

NOTES

1. W. Benjamin, *Gesammelte Schriften*, ed. R. Tiedemann and H. Schweppenhäuser, 7 vols (Frankfurt/Main, 1974–). All quotations from Benjamin refer to this edition, unless otherwise noted. Abbreviated references identify volume and page number.
2. 'Eine Art goldener Klassikerbibliothek in nuce': see the posthumous 'Memorandum on the Sixty Letters' (IV, 949).
3. T. W. Adorno, in the preface to Walter Benjamin, *Briefe* (Frankfurt/Main, 1966), vol. 1, p. 15.
4. The 'fury of disappearance' is a term used and probably invented by Hegel in *Phänomenologie des Geistes*, in the chapter 'Absolute Freedom and Horror' (!), in which he deals with the after-effects of the French Revolution. See G.W.F. Hegel, *Werke* (Frankfurt, 1970), vol. 3, pp. 435–6.
5. Under the pseudonym Detlef Holz (Luzern, 1936).
6. Cf. 'Tracking down Old Letters' (IV, 942–4).

Translated by Christina Ujma (Berlin).

–12–

Walter Benjamin and Children's Literature

Klaus Doderer

I Benjamin's Diverse Interests in Children's Literature

Walter Benjamin showed more than an occasional interest in children's literature. Having grown up in an upper-middle-class family, surrounded by literature, he was, on his own admission, even as a child, fascinated by the 'second reality' which was hidden in the written word. The reasons for his interest in literature for young readers were varied, however, and they changed with time.

As an adult, Benjamin expanded his childhood library into a superb collection of children's books. He often wrote texts explicitly directed at a young audience, particularly around the year 1930. He also continued to examine the importance of young people's culture, both past and present. In doing this, his attention was drawn again and again to children's books. Observations based on his own childhood experiences can be found in many of his essays and reviews.

Interestingly, Benjamin's approach towards literature for children was very much in opposition to the conventional approach taken by educators, writers and publishers. For example, if Benjamin collected old children's books, it meant for him collecting objects of aesthetic beauty which gave him detailed information and insight into a way of life now lost. If he wrote a script for the radio programme *Jugendstunde* (children's or youth hour), he specifically directed his pieces towards young people, but he was also trying, within the medium of broadcasting – a new medium at the time – to use the narrative form to provide explanations which would be equally understandable, entertaining and interesting to young and old audiences alike. If he concerned himself with theory – for example, that of the proletarian children's theatre – he considered the question of how communication could be learned through play with the aim of developing the ideal democratic society.

Such efforts far exceeded the usual demands of superficial research into children's books. Benjamin observed the field of past and present-day children's culture, he commented on it in writing, tried to make a contribution to it within the new media channels, and, at the same time, he remained a critic of the literary scene of publishing for young readers.

II Collecting Children's Books as Objects of Beauty

In 1918, the year his son Stefan was born, Benjamin wrote to his friend, Ernst Schoen, that he 'had chosen a special area of interest, just like any true book collector. It is old children's books, fairy-tales and legends', and he added: 'The nucleus of the collection stems from a raid which I made on my mother's library, my old childhood library.'[1] The story of Benjamin the collector of children's books is easily told. His collection was expanded now and then by purchases, it played a part in his plan to open a second-hand bookshop specializing in rare and valuable books in 1924 (*Antiquariatshandel*), it led to contacts with other collectors (in particular, Karl Hobrecker) whose collections he studied, admired and reviewed. He lost access to his own collection in 1930 after his divorce from his wife, Dora.

Benjamin's collection then moved to the South of France with his son, Stefan, and Dora, in 1939, and from there to London. On his mother's death in 1964, Stefan Benjamin inherited the collection. In 1985, it was bought by the Institut für Jugendbuchforschung at the University of Frankfurt, where it has now found a permanent home. The collection comprises in total 204 titles of old German, French and Dutch children's books, mostly from the nineteenth century. Some are older, from the eighteenth century, and some stem from the early twentieth century. In terms of subject matter, the collection is not really specialized; it contains Aesop's fables in several editions, ABC books, Campe's *The New Robinson* (*Robinson der Jüngere*), Orbis-Pictus editions, Thekla von Gumpert's *Die Herzblättchen,* books for girls, non- fiction books, collections of fairy-tales, well-known and lesser-known titles. Above all, Benjamin was interested in owning particularly beautiful and, if affordable, hand-coloured illustrated editions.[2] Benjamin the historian above all preferred the children's books of the Biedermeier era.

However paradoxical it may seem, the question arises as to whether Walter Benjamin's primary interest as a collector of children's books was indeed an interest in children's literature. There are comments which show that, to him, the times of a past age were never more clearly shown than in the illustrations of old children's books. To him, these books were a wonderful window through which the history of everyday life could be observed and studied. At the same time, however, Walter Benjamin was always busy as a collector and a bibliophile, seeking out unusual, beautiful and previously undiscovered books.

III Writing for Young People

Apart from planning to become involved in publishing children's books, Benjamin also wrote plays for children and appeared on radio as a story-teller. We know from a letter which he wrote to Gershom Sholem that, in the mid-1920s, he wanted to compile and edit a book of fairy-tales and an anthology of legends. The idea was never realized. He did, however, write the script of a radio play in the form of a traditional puppet show, *A Row over Punch* (IV, 674–95), and we also know of another piece for younger audiences, a radio play he wrote together with Ernst Schoen, based on Wilhelm Hauff's fairy-tale *The Cold Heart* (VII, 316–46), which was supposed to have been broadcast in 1932.[3] Since 1985, Benjamin's manuscripts written for the youth programme *(Jugendstunde)* of the Frankfurt and Berlin radio stations, between the years 1929 and 1932, have become known and accessible to researchers.[4]

Walter Benjamin dealt firstly with that branch of children's literature which reached into the magical and the mythical: fairy-tales, legends, children's rhymes and songs. He wanted to preserve them without interfering as a writer. Secondly, he dealt with *Kasperl*, the German equivalent of Punch, a popular comic figure in children's puppet theatre, and thirdly, he was heard on many radio programmes as an enlightened narrator of stories written for children. Benjamin did not consider stories concerning magic or mythology, such as fairy-tales and legends, to be purely children's literature, but rather he saw them, as the early Romantics would have done, as a form of 'universal poetry'.

Walter Benjamin's *Kasperl*, or Punch, is the old *Hans Wurst* character, but relevant to people of all ages, and not only to children. Benjamin's Punch does battle with modern technology, rather than with devils and crocodiles. There is thus a clear departure from what is usually considered specifically children's literature. If one searches Benjamin's works for special children's texts, we find only the scripts written for the radio. They were broadcast as part of the so- called *Jugendstunde* programmes; but are they specifically children's literature?

Benjamin used the medium of radio as a means of direct address. From the condition of the typescripts and the comparison of tapes and scripts, we know that Benjamin himself spoke to his listeners. He began his lectures with 'Dear Invisible Listeners' (*Verehrte Unsichtbare*). He frequently deviated from his prepared script and improvised. This kind of liberation from the constraints of a script was an attempt on Benjamin's part to actually converse with his listeners. In this, he saw a fascinating opportunity, a means of deriving, from the text written on paper, some reality of life in communication.

It is not by chance that in these texts Benjamin followed the style of the classical German story-teller in the tradition of Johann Peter Hebel, author of the didactic-popular calendar tales (*Kalendergeschichten*). Hebel's 'gentle readers' (*geneigte Leser*) became 'gentle listeners' (*geneigte Hörer*) in Benjamin's radio scripts. He happily used the familiar form of speech to them (*Du* instead of *Sie*), but not only because he was addressing listeners of the 'youth hour' programmes. Rather, he treated his listeners as adults, posing questions, telling jokes, offering notes and passing on theories and knowledge them. He believed that 'knowledge that is truly alive' must be spread by the new mass medium, broadcasting. The radio also gave Benjamin the opportunity to critically question this 'living knowledge'. So, for example, the listeners to his radio programme, entitled *Berlin Dialect*, are told a series of jokes typical of the metropolitan city; through many examples of urban Berlin wit, the listeners came to realize how mentality, environment and historical events have left their mark on the language of the people of Berlin (VII, 68–74). At the same time, they were made aware of other dialects – such as Gotthelfs Swiss German, Reuters Mecklenburg Low German, and Hebels Southwest German-Swiss-French *Allemanisch* – and in a subtle and entertaining way, Benjamin the story-teller released his young listeners from the conventional way of thinking learned at school. The listeners discover, as a matter of course, how marvellously expressive the Berlin dialect can be. Intellectual connotations are suddenly recognizable in apparently minor details.

Hebel's style of mixing world history and personal history also appears in Benjamin's 'youth hours' for the 'dear invisible listeners'. As a narrator, he strolls through the past. He enlightens, but he also questions and destroys opinions based on prejudices – for example, concerning Gypsies. He makes his listeners think – for example, about the quality of life in Bijerlin, in the radio talk 'The Tenement House' (*Die Mietskaserne*; VII, 117–24). Benjamin's basic aim is to try to provide a popular explanation appropriate to the medium. However, the message is not only directed at young people, but also at the older generation, to anyone, in fact, who is willing to go beyond the narrow-minded, conventional way of thinking. Thus, Benjamin speaks into the microphone of the Berlin radio station:

> Open up yours ears, you could just hear something that you won't so easily hear in your German class or your geography class or in your social science class, and which could at some time be important to you. Because you should all understand what the war against the tenement slums, which Berlin has been fighting since 1925, is all about. (VII, 118)

Around 1930, Walter Benjamin set about presenting a critical knowledge of life to young people in a clear and amusing way. The twofold intention on the part of this archaic narrator still remains: that of the teacher who teaches by telling stories, and that of the destroyer of second-hand knowledge.

IV Fragments of a Critical Theory of Children's Literature

Benjamin's theoretical-critical comments on the subject of children's literature are scattered throughout his work. They first appear in 1918, in a letter to Ernst Schoen, and continue during the 1920s and 1930s, when they are to be found in newspaper articles, reviews, radio scripts and also in *Berlin Childhood*. Several basic ideas of Benjamin's views regarding children's literature can be distinguished. As in his remarks concerning 'advanced literary studies' (*fortgeschrittene Literaturwissenschaft*) in one of his 'Listening Models' (*Hörmodelle*), entitled 'What the Germans read as their classic authors wrote', he raises rather than lowers his attention to children's literature (IV, 641–70). What interested him were the readers, their reasons for reading and their reading material. Benjamin could also have asked 'What did the children read while their educators were writing?' His reply to this, based on his personal childhood experiences, was always that children were inspired readers who were more attracted by the 'stillness' of the book which 'enticed further and still further away'. The content of the book is not of major importance to them, since they 'still make up their own stories when they are in bed'.[5] Respect for the written word had not yet triumphed over the child's natural curiosity and inventiveness.

To the ears of philosophers, that may sound like heresy, but in a review of a collection of Frankfurt children's poetry, published in the *Frankfurter Zeitung* in 1925, Benjamin writes: 'Right here one can see how the child "models", how he "builds" and how, in his way of thinking as well as of feeling, he never accepts the given form as the only one' (IV, 792–3). In other words, Walter Benjamin allows his young readers a high degree of independence regarding literature. He considers the child to be an independent reader. From this position, his remarks concerning literature written specifically for children prove to be rather negative. Again and again he complains about the omnipresence of the educational lobby. He speaks out vehemently against attempts by some writers and educators to modernize, to remove some of the magic, some of the irrationality from fairy-tales, in a misguided attempt to bring them up to date. He speaks out, in a newspaper article of 1930, against what he calls 'giving up what is the most genuine and original' (*'Kolonialpädagogik'*; III, 273).[6] In 1924, he states that the pride in knowing about children's innermost lives has resulted in a form of literature that is published in an attempt to attract the public's attention. The 'sweet gesture' of the writer criticized by Benjamin was not suited to children, but to the author's incorrect *idea* of children.[7]

On the one hand, Benjamin attacks the rewriting and adaptation of texts to be read specifically by children, and, at the same time, he stresses the independence of the young reader. Looking back to the history of children's literature, he realizes, of course, that it is very much governed by the 'encyclopaedia of coincidence and chance'. His view darkens when he examines examples of that type of specific children's literature in which the original and true form is sacrificed in the search for the moral of the story, and in which adults have turned children's literature into a branch of 'colonial pedagogy'. In his radio talk on 'Children's Literature', Benjamin says:

> We read not in order to increase [*mehren*] our experiences, but ourselves. In particular, and always, children read in this way: by way of imbibing rather than by way of empathy. Their reading stands in the most intimate relationship much less to their education and knowledge of the world, but to their own growth and power. Therefore, children's reading is equally as important as all the genius that is contained in the books they take up. And that is the particular character of the children's book. (VII, 257)[8]

In these sentences of Walter Benjamin, which contain the rudiments of a realistic, critical and emancipatory theory of children's literature, children are seen as independent readers who face the genius that hides in books in a superior way. The notion of childhood, so extraordinarily significant to Benjamin, is paraphrased here and seen as a sort of philosophical place in which knowledge is absorbed and assimilated. Benjamin's plea for children as independent readers is also a criticism of the notion of children's literature as 'colonial literature' that aims to subjugate young readers through didactic moralizing. His appeal is for childhood to be saved, to become a refuge where children, through reading books, can gather knowledge of life and of themselves.

NOTES

1. Letter dated 31 July 1918, in W. Benjamin, *Briefe*, ed. Gershom Scholem and Theodor W. Adorno (Frankfurt/Main, 1966), vol. 1, p. 198. References to Benjamin's works are to *Gesammelte Schriften*, ed. R. Tiedemann and H. Schweppenhäuser, 7 vols (Frankfurt/Main, 1974–). Abbreviated references in parentheses identify volume and page number.
2. See the catalogue, *Die Kinderbuchsammlung Walter Benjamins*, an exhibiton of the Institut für Jugendbuchforschung at the University of Frankfurt, edited by Stadt- und Universitätsbibliothek Frankfurt, March 1987. On Benjamin as a collector of children's books, see Theodor Brüggemann's essay, 'Walter Benjamin und andere Kinderbuchsammler – Karl Hobrecker, Arthur Rümann und Walter Schatzki', in *Walter Benjamin und die Kinderliteratur*, ed. K. Doderer (Weinheim, Munich, 1988), pp. 68–92.

3. Cf. the *Rundfunkgeschichten for Kinder* ('Radio Stories for Children'): VII, 68–249. On *A Row over Punch*, see Uwe Lothar Müller, 'Radau im Rundfunk', in *Walter Benjamin und die Kinderliteratur*, pp. 113–19.
4. Walter Benjamin, *Aufklärung für Kinder: Rundfunkvorträge* (Frankfurt/Main, 1985). See also (VII, 68–249).
5. *One-Way Street* (V, 113).
6. The essay on *Kolonialpädagogik* is a review of a book by Alois Jalkotzky, *Märchen der Gegenwart: Das deutsche Volksmärchen in unserer Zeit* (Vienna, 1930).
7. Cf. the article 'Alte vergessene Kinderbücher', dated 1924 (III, 14–22).
8. Final lines of the radio talk entitled 'Kinderliteratur', broadcast by Southwest German Radio on 15 August 1928 (VII, 250–7).

Translated by Anne O'Connor (Darmstadt).

IV
Performing Arts/Children's Theatre

–13–

An Interrupted Performance: On Walter Benjamin's Idea of Children's Theatre

Hans-Thies Lehmann

I

It was probably at the beginning of 1929 that Walter Benjamin wrote the *Programme of a Proletarian Children's Theatre* for Asja Lacis.[1] This essay, which is full of allusions and which formulated its essential motifs in a secretive way, represents a strange case of mimicry, of loving disguise, of the attempt to forge a link between communist practice and Benjamin's esoteric thoughts – an impossible task, as it turned out. It develops a complex idea of 'proletarian' education, inextricably bound up with implications relating to metaphysics, moral philosophy and the philosophy of language. There is an astonishing continuity between this idea and positions that Benjamin had developed in the ideologically very different context of his 'idealistic' involvement in the area of youth movements and reforms in educational theory before World War I. On the artistic level, the notion of theatre implicit here corresponds to the radical avant-garde of Brecht's didactic plays (strongly rejected by the communists), which Benjamin was to analyse not long afterwards in essays that are still among the best written on the didactic play model.

The present essay is related to a project examining the significance of the motif areas connected with childhood and the child in the thought of Walter Benjamin. It is concerned with his ideas on a children's theatre he called 'proletarian' which, if they are to be read in a non-reductive way, make it necessary to examine in greater detail some inconspicuous formulations which initially seem unproblematic in their context. This applies particularly to the notion of 'observation' as the real 'genius of education', of the difficult concept of 'gesture', which is used almost without explanation, of the description of the child as 'dictator', of the concept of the performance as 'carnival,' and of the demand that the influence of the educator on the child be only 'indirect' and never 'moral'. If we follow these clues, we shall find that, behind the communicative façade of this text, which is apparently endeavouring to be simple and clear, there is, in reality, a concept that is not communist, but rather – if one were to make a political classification – an anarchistic, or at least anarchic one. It is a concept which, despite all the evident style of argumentation, presents an image of the child and its education in a Nietzschean or, in Benjamin's understanding of the term, Surrealistic light, but certainly not a Marxist one. This leads to a decisive correction of the way the essay was largely read in the 1970s, when it was possible to think that Benjamin's 'programme' lay within the same 'framework' as the principles of communist children's theatre, as formulated especially by Edwin Hoernle.[2]

The political fate of the programme is not without an element of unintentional comedy. When Benjamin put the principles of Asja Lacis's work on children's education into point form, they were 'presented in a tremendously complicated manner'.[3] At Liebknecht House, the Communist Party 'read and laughed', whereupon Asja Lacis asked Benjamin for a second, more comprehensible version. This is the only surviving one, in a single typewritten copy. The *Programme* had no genuine chance of being put into practice. But it does have special significance as a complex document of Benjamin's aesthetic and pedagogical thinking, particularly as evidence of its astonishing continuity, despite all the contradictions resulting from Benjamin's turning to radical communism.

The first published text Walter Benjamin signed with his own name was an essay entitled 'Moral Education' in Gustav Wyneken's series, *Die Freie Schulgemeinde* ('The Free School Community').[4] In this text of 1913, he demonstrates, with strict neo-Kantian deduction, that a direct moral education is unthinkable. A truly moral will, strictly defined, the 24-year-old Benjamin argues, is determined by its total lack of external motives, and for this reason, it cannot be influenced by external factors. Education can therefore not be the subject of a branch of science, nor is it rational, nor is it possible to conceive of it systematically. Pedagogical influences by example will necessarily remain unsuccessful and fruitless. If, for instance, a child is encouraged to love his or her neighbour by referring to the many working people to whom children owe their daily bread, then this reference will only be effective for a child who *already knows* the concepts of 'sympathy' and 'love of one's neighbour'. And Benjamin concludes: 'The child can learn this only in the community, not in a lesson on morality.' This thought recurs almost verbatim in Benjamin's *Programme* essay: it is solely the 'tensions' in the children's 'collective' itself that constitute the 'medium' of education, and not the didactic, let alone the ideological, influence of the teacher. This collective alone has the capacity to provide 'the inevitable moral adjustments and corrections'. Thus, children's theatre can become a moral authority for adults, but not vice versa.[5]

Nor is it the task of the group 'leader' to teach the children proletarian discipline. Instead, all disciplining of the children is totally condemned in the spirit of educational reform; necessary social discipline is 'postponed' until later. The untroubled growth of the children, their individuality, the anarchy of their development are *unconditionally* more important than the demands of socialization. It is obvious that here, in addition to other sources, ideas from Gustav Wyneken's concept of *youth culture* continue to have an influence, even though Benjamin distances himself from his former teacher in the text. Childhood and education had long been important in his thinking. Numerous texts and fragments written between 1911 and 1914, including the important *Metaphysics of Youth*, show that Benjamin had made an intensive study of the youth and school reform movement and of questions of university students' education long before the pedagogical aspect became the dominant feature of his later texts. It is therefore not surprising that, when he met Asja Lacis in 1924, he evinced an immediate interest in her work for the children's theatre she had founded in Orel.[6]

II

His meeting with Asja Lacis brought Walter Benjamin both a great passion (the third in his life after Dora and Jula Cohn) and an awareness with far-reaching consequences, a double event, 'a vigorous liberation and an intensive insight into the topicality of radical communism',[7] as Benjamin wrote to Scholem in July 1924. In hindsight, it is not without irony that Benjamin, working on his book on tragedy in Capri, met Asja Lacis in the company of her daughter, Daga, with whom he immediately became good friends and whom he later immortalized in *One-Way Street* as the child who refuses to wash.[8] A later phase of his long courtship (over years) of the 'Bolshevik Latvian from Riga, who acts and directs at the theatre, a Christian' (as he wrote to Gershom Scholem from Capri), and one 'of the most outstanding women I have met'[9] is recorded in his Moscow diary. On 20 December 1926, Benjamin disclosed to Asja Lacis his wish for a child by her, a wish that remained unfulfilled. Under the same date, however, he also noted his 'fear of inimical elements in her' and his doubt as to whether, even if he were 'ideally...allied to her by a child', he 'would be a match for a life with her with its amazing hardness and, despite all her sweetness, her lovelessness'.[10] At the same time, he was seriously considering joining the Communist Party in Moscow; the entry for 27 January 1927 lists the 'immense advantage...of being able to project my own thoughts, as it were, into an existing force field'[11] as a particular attraction. This kind of phallic-political fertilization was to be denied him, both personally (with Asja) and politically, and also to his programme for a children's theatre.

These details from Benjamin's life are more than an incidental biographical curiosity. What justifies their being mentioned here is the factual fusion of the motifs of 'generation', continuous effect, and didactic fatherhood with the conception of a strict, Utopian, sober theatre of the collective beyond individual morality. Scarcely any other realm was of such great significance for Benjamin's thinking as the dialectic of tradition and 'generation', topical relevance and future. It is in this dialectic that his ideas of history are grounded, as is his politics (he would have been very aware of the derivation of the word 'proletarian' from the Latin *proles*, meaning offspring), his lifelong interest in the world of the child as well as his theory of the continuing life of artworks (not least in translation) and the 'fruitfulness' of intellectual relationships. Jacques Derrida, discussing Benjamin's double obsession during his Moscow stay in 1926 (on the one hand, the desire to be tied to Asja by a child, on the other hand, Benjamin's unborn work-child, the great 'presentation' of Moscow), emphasizes the need to 'examine the motif of the seed, of conception and continuing effects which is related to conceiving and giving birth as well as surviving or living on in the whole of Benjamin's work'.[12]

Despite the uncertainties in his relationship with Asja Lacis, Benjamin asked his wife, Dora, for a divorce at the beginning of 1929, 'in order to marry Asja'.[13] The final point of this story of the background to the *Programme of a Proletarian Children's Theatre*, a story not devoid of tragic elements, can be seen in the fact that, in the following year (1929/30) – not long after the text was written – Benjamin's relationship with Asja came to an end (she left Berlin and returned to Moscow at the end of 1929, while Benjamin's divorce was still proceeding). However, a second attempt to initiate a friendship between Benjamin and Brecht, which Asja Lacis had first mediated in 1924, but which failed then, was now successful.

III

The children's theatre programme demands nothing less than that children's theatre form the framework for the *entire* education of the proletarian child between the ages of four and fourteen,[14] admittedly in such a way, however, that it is not the performance that is central. A theatrical performance is not the goal; it happens, as Benjamin emphasizes, 'incidentally, you might say by mistake' (II, 765). The *Programme* defines the performance as a 'prank' and a 'carnival', while the theatre and the theatre work are seen as the place and framework of continuing 'study'. We can add a note to the effect that this only apparently pedagogical re-evaluation of the performance aspect identifies completely changed principles which, especially since the beginnings of *action art*, have been acknowledged even by the mainstream theatres which define their work in terms of the process of their productions, not the finished product, which stress their work as a project and activity, not as an aesthetic object. To this extent, one question that Benjamin leaves open in his essay can be answered positively, at least for the most recent time, namely: 'whether or not the kind of children's theatre of which we shall be talking, has the closest parallels with the mainstream theatre at the highest points in its history' (II, 764).

Almost as an inversion of the curious emphasis on schooling processes in Benjamin's work on modern art, and especially on film, we can observe an extreme negation of all ideological and pedagogical influences precisely for the proletarian children's theatre: 'The hasty...over-tired educational work the bourgeois producer performs on the bourgeois actor is abolished in this system...There is no moral influence here' (II, 765). Any attempt by educators to have a direct effect as 'moral personalities' is rejected in the strongest terms. Instead, 'materials, tasks, events' of the children's collective are the medium of the only possible influence, that is, 'indirect influence' of the 'leader'. But what do the leaders have to do, what is their task? Benjamin answers this question with the surprising statement that it is (nothing more than) 'observation', which is defined as 'the true genius of education', and he continues: 'All educative love which (in nine out of ten cases, due to knowing better and wanting better) discourages and spoils the pleasure of observing the child's life is worthless. It is sentimental and vain' (II, 766).

Asja Lacis herself speaks of her work in terms that appear identical to Benjamin's at first sight. When, in 1918, she came across the *Besprisorniki* in Orel, hordes of neglected children and young people who, uprooted by the civil war, were roaming about everywhere in Russia, when she saw the war orphans sitting around in a stupor in homes, sad and tired 'like old men', she realized that it was necessary to 'seize these children *completely* and to liberate their traumatized abilities'. She chose to work in the theatre because this required all of a person's capacities. But the main goal is not the *première*: no alien will of a producer should be forced upon the children, an already-finished piece was not to restrict their imagination. Instead, the work was divided into 'sections': painting and drawing, music, 'technical training', rhythm, gymnastics, diction. 'By means of *improvisation*, we combined hidden strengths that were being liberated by the process of work with newly developed capacities.'[15] On one occasion during just such an improvisation – and it just happened to be on the topic, 'Robbers are sitting around a fire in a forest and boasting about their deeds' – a band of *Besprisorniki* joined them and boasted about murders, robberies and arson, but in much crueller terms than the children had done before, so that at first they were very frightened. Asja Lacis did not intervene: 'According to all the rules of education I ought to have interrupted their wild and brazen talk – but I was wanting to gain an influence on them. I really did win the gamble – the Besprisorniki came back and later became the core team of our children's theatre.'[16]

Asja Lacis defines the centre of her pedagogical practice in the following terms:

> The point of departure for educators and those to be educated for us was *observation*. The children observed things, their relationships between each other and their changeability; the educators observe the children to see what they have achieved and how far they can apply their abilities productively…Early in the morning and again in the evening we went outside with the children and drew their attention to the way in which colours change with distance and different times of day, how differently tones and noises sound in the morning and evening, and that the silence can sing.[17]

No doubt the readers of Benjamin's *Programme* at Liebknecht House did not pay any particular attention to the word 'observation', they would have understood it the way Asja Lacis used it. It must be immediately obvious, however, that Benjamin, unlike Asja Lacis, applies the term *only to the educators*, and never to the children, even though, at first sight, it would appear much more plausible from a pedagogical point of view for it to apply to the children.

The proximity of observation to Benjamin's notions of topicality and attention ought to lead us to suppose that we are dealing with more than just a rule of thumb taken from the book of educational reform. And indeed, the concept of observation is closely related to an essential motif in Benjamin's thought, namely, the *concept of experience* (*Erfahrung*, in contradistinction to *Erlebnis*) as a kind of practical knowledge which includes, in Benjamin's understanding, *the failure to process impressions consciously*. In a note dated 1928, he writes concisely: 'The identity of experience and observation has to be demonstrated. Cf. the concept of "Romantic observation" in my thesis – Observation based on meditation.' If we pursue this reference to the treatise on art criticism in German Romanticism, we come upon Benjamin's explanation of an Early Romantic theory of observation and experiment, magical and ironic observation, in which the crucial idea is to regard the object of knowledge not as merely 'passive' with regard to the process of investigation, but as something active, 'which creates knowledge out of and through itself'. Therefore, observation does not aim at 'anything individual, anything definite' as its object, it only 'aims at the burgeoning self-awareness in the object'. Observation does not lead, as one would initially have to suppose, to specific knowledge but occurs as *suspension of all knowledge*. Only and precisely in 'not knowing, in watching' does a mimesis take place in which one 'knows better – and is identical with the object'.[18] What children do, especially when they are playing in the theatre, what the adult 'learns' from them, is the truth, not of a social insight, but of a mimetic form of behaviour which strictly *interrupts* the positing of knowledge.

Humility and respect for the object (youth, the child), the justification for which the text itself only hints at, virtually obliges education to abandon all formative norms. In 1921, Benjamin noted down another difference of Late Romantic theory of observation in comparison to that of the Early Romantics, in that the emphasis changed from reflection to love. In this fragment, loving observation is a power which 'the father's look claims in education':

> The growing child must be aware not only of the watchfulness of the paternal eye but also of the power of its sparkle or its sorrow. And just as this non-violent guidance, which must of course start no later than at birth, has more power over the child in all important things than anything else (more than physical violence and, above all, more than the power of the much-lauded example), it is also more meaningful than considered educational planning. For while his look follows, his eye learns to see what is appropriate to the child. And only the man whom the look has taught a great deal has the power of contemplation.[19]

The adult learns while educating. And what he or she learns, what is appropriate to the child, is nothing less than the suspension and delay of knowledge and the positing of norms altogether. It is not a question of considered educational planning, which would tend rather to lay an opaque covering over the object of the looks. Instead, this thesis, in which the concept of 'non-violent guidance' makes indirect reference to Benjamin's essay on violence, is directed at contemplation that is comparable to 'suspended attention' in Freud's sense: the technique of being passively open, receptivity to impulses which arrive unpredictably, cannot be planned or become usable. It is this 'suspension' alone that opens our eyes to images from the future which will materialize in childlike 'gestures'. The concept of observation implants an idea of practical knowledge into the model of theatre and education – far beyond the renunciation of ideological indoctrination – an idea that stands in sharp contrast to the positions adopted by the German Communist Party (KPD), because it requires the suspension of all norms, even political ones, and the suspension of the thetic approach as such.

IV

It is more than just a rejection of communist pedagogy, which would only replace a bourgeois indoctrination with a Marxist one, when Benjamin speaks about the 'energies of youth – and especially of childhood – that can never be stimulated politically' (II, 768). Benjamin wants an education that does without ideology altogether until puberty. Against the 'theatre of today's bourgeoisie', which he sees as 'above all an instrument of sensationalism' both in front of and behind the scenes, Horace's *delectare* in its purest form, so to speak, there is the proletarian children's theatre as one of *prodesse*. Education must proceed out of class consciousness, but not by way of ideological influence – 'because the ideology, extremely important in itself, reaches the child only as empty phrases' (II, 763).

It is striking that the text does not deal at all with the most important authority on questions of socialist education of the time, Edwin Hoernle, except indirectly and negatively: Hoernle speaks of acting in the theatre as the culmination of all the child's artistic activities and of the fact that the 'accumulated tensions' in the child are 'relieved'. Benjamin's notion of tensions and resolution refers to the children's collective. There is nothing about Hoernle's wish for the 'recruiting' effect that would motivate children to become adult theatre-goers, nothing about a 'communal battle song', and above all, nothing about 'integrating the proletarian children into the class front of the adult workers', as Hoernle envisaged. Nor does Benjamin's conception have much to do with agit-prop-theatre which was flourishing in 1928/29, the young people's 'drummer groups', with 'living newspapers', nor with the 'Blue Blouses' following the Russian example.[20] What is worth noting is that there is no reference at all to these types of theatrical forms, which were much in favour with the KPD at that time. Benjamin insists on his anarchic approach to education. In a manner that seems very bourgeois at first sight, he demands that 'proletarian education...guarantees children their childhood' (II, 768). What he does not elaborate on here is his conviction that the 'child's picture of the world', like 'popular art', is to be regarded as a 'collective entity', and in order to understand it, it is necessary, above all, to give up 'the individual psychological image of the child'.[21]

Benjamin's opposition to theoretical moralism – he speaks of 'removing the "moral personality" in the leader' (II, 766) as a condition of observation, which is thus asserted to be a quality *outside the moral realm* – is one of the most prominent aspects of his thinking in these years. *The Author as Producer* gives a striking formulation of the result of the 'examinations' and 'evaluations' that the epic theatre makes about 'today's people': 'The result is this: the course of events can be changed not at its high points, not by virtue and decision but only in its strictly habitual manner, by reason and practice' (II, 699). The concept of practice (*Übung*), which, in contrast to continuous learning, is intermittent and 'unsteady', requires some explanation. In his *Brecht Commentary*, Benjamin defines 'practised, that is, noticed first, understood later' (II, 507). Taking this only a little further, one could describe practice as *suspending understanding through bodily praxis*. In place of 'moral' acculturation of the child's consciousness, and in place of consciously-reflected behaviour, we find what Benjamin calls signals and gestures, both in the theatre and in the child. It is their unconscious certainty that contributes to their 'despotic' aspect. Dismissing the 'bourgeois' moral dimension in favour of the idea of *interrupting* intentional consciousness – it is only from here that we can come to an understanding of the mysterious 'signals' which the child gives from its own world and from the future at the same time.

V

It is useful to quote Benjamin's explanation of 'signal' in full:

> For observation…every action and gesture of the child becomes a signal. Not so much, as the psychologists would have it, a signal of the unconscious, latencies, suppression, censoring but a signal from a world in which the child lives and gives commands. The new knowledge of the child developed in the Russian children's clubs has led to this proposition: the child lives in its world as a dictator. For this reason, a 'theory of signals' is not an empty phrase. Almost every gesture by the child is a command in an environment into which men of genius have but seldom opened a perspective for us. More than anyone else, Jean Paul did this. (II, 766)

And Benjamin concludes: 'Truly revolutionary is the effect of the *secret signal* of the future that speaks out of the gesture of the child' (II, 769).

Instead of an explanation for what the hidden world of the child and the signals emerging from it are, Benjamin quotes the name of Jean Paul. Perhaps we may think of Jean Paul's formula, 'children are little orients', or of the end of *Levana* where the children's souls come down to earth on the Last Day, and the end of the world is sealed by the children's paradise – a gruesomely beautiful image that may have been an emblem of the world revolution for Benjamin. But what is the meaning of this gesture which is also a command? Benjamin defines: 'Every gesture of the child is creative innervation in exact relation to receptive innervation', and makes a comparison with a painter 'who looks more closely with his hand when his eye flags' (II, 766). What is required is precisely not artistic consciousness, but a necessarily unconscious interaction of bodily innervations, optic muscles, hand and tactile sense – just as, with the acrobat, Rastelli, hand and ball 'communicate with each other behind his back', because 'the will in the internal space of the body abdicates once and for all in favour of the organs'.[22] With practice, the acrobat becomes the master of allowing things to happen; he knows how to make himself into the pure medium of the events.

Benjamin's insistence on unconsciousness is strictly distinguished from the concept of the unconscious by the collective element, by its involvement with the material world and by 'topicality', which is tied to 'corporeality'. A link has to be made between the innervation of the child's gesture and the later theory of the gambler in order to understand that the child's gesture and its 'development', as Benjamin puts it, imply a formation and unfolding of the capacity to react to the environment pre- and unconsciously, just like the gambler who makes a successful throw because he senses, in a bodily reactive manner, what is in the air without having to let it first enter his consciousness, which operates much too slowly. A person may either be able to take advantage of an opportunity with a sense for topicality, *or* may be able to understand it. The two are mutually exclusive. This thesis of Benjamin's casts light on the statement: 'The topicality of the child's forming and behaviour is indeed unequalled' (II, 766). As shown above, one collective (objective) solution and a resolution of the 'tensions', as in an electrical force-field, was morality, which Benjamin understands not in terms of consciousness and theory, but as behaviour. In the same way, the gesture turns out to be the name for a specific, unconscious behaviour – and to that extent, also outside the moral realm – whose direct 'topicality' now becomes closely related to the curious figure of the ruler, or even dictator.[23] However much this thought may link the child with the dictatorship of the proletariat in playful irony, the emphasis with which the dictatorial element is moved into the centre must strike one as odd. Without glossing over its political ambiguity, we should like to attempt to come to terms with the dictatorial aspect of the 'gesture', which mirrors Benjamin's own thought-gesture, which in turn brings together the idea of sovereignty (its significance for Benjamin between the theories of Carl Schmitt and Georges Bataille would need to be discussed separately), judging word, pure force, topicality and promise for the future.

If it is true that despotic command and signal, characteristic features of the child-dictator, form part of the same sphere in Benjamin's thoughts as the 'state of being wide-awake after sleeping one's fill' (*ausgeschlafenes Wachsein*), the flash of the only appropriate image in a moment of danger, the sure trajectory of the tiger's jump, the pre-conscious innervation of the gambler, then a common motif dominates all these figures of the lucky grasp of the moment: namely, the absence of inhibition. Benjamin is less interested in the fact that the child's desire to shape the world, as in the formula 'If I were king', is linked to a certain 'absolute power', and despite (or because of) this, always remained Utopian. In the context of children's theatre, education means above all the 'development' of the child's gesture into forms of expression in which 'improvisation' (with the decisive element of the original sense of the word, the unforeseen, *all' improviso*) remains central: the task is 'to bring the child's signals from the dangerous magic realm of mere fantasy to the executive on the material-matter' (II, 766).

The significance of this thesis is, however, revealed only by what Benjamin writes in connection with children's drawings: 'The child does not express itself through things, but things through itself. In the child, creativity and subjectivity have not yet celebrated their bold meeting.'[24] Profound, like so much in Benjamin's thinking about the child, the notion of 'boldness' (*verwegen*) in the meeting also suggests losing one's way, which has separated the adult who has attained subjectivity from the magical force-field of physical energies. The creativity of the child is situated in a realm before this meeting/separation, where Benjamin's ideas on the philosophy of language materialize: namely, that things attain *their* language *in* the person. Things, that which is real, are supposed to become manifest without any interference from 'subjective' culture. The pre-subjective signalling of the child's gesture transfers the expression from the realm of subjectivity into the 'objective' collective realm of the body. In between *vouloir-dire*/meaning to say and the body, lies the realm of the gesture, an intermediate realm in which, unhampered by 'culture', that which is mute becomes eloquent. (This is presumably the same realm in which things put on their 'surrealistic face'.) This is the moment of Benjamin's 'lack of inhibition'. Through it, the child's gesture becomes a figure of 'presence of mind', as Benjamin saw it: 'Having presence of mind means letting oneself go in the moment of danger.'[25] Inhibition, blending, translation by means of subjectivity – which is necessarily characterized by moral and rational attitudes – play no role. This is where the secret of the child's 'signals' lies.[26] Reflection and moral considerations, delay, planning ahead and thinking, spoil everything in a situation where the main point is child-like, playful, bodily innervation. *Decisive experiences are formed before or beyond intention, in interrupting it.* It is tempting to speak of irrationalism here, but in contrast to the vitalistic and 'philosophy of life' ideologemes of programmatic irrationalism, Benjamin is concerned with localizing non-conscious impulses and structures in the realm of practical expressive behaviour, not with their ideological hypostatization. They have a concrete place, such as the theatre, the text, and the child's gesture. Benjamin attempts to give this de-subjectivization a political name when he describes the child itself, and not merely the community of children, as the 'child's collective' (II, 766).

VI

The uninhibited is, however, also ruthless, without any consideration, and for this reason, the second political name for the bodily and linguistic *caesura* of the gesture is the dictator. It is extremely significant that the pedagogical concepts of Benjamin's *Programme* correspond in many ways to that of his critique of violence. Just as there 'pure violence' is distinguished from the decay of the world of parliamentary compromise, so here he talks about parliamentary mindlessness, about how necessary it is to reject the 'pattern of parliamentary discussion' (II, 763). Just as there the question of 'direct' or 'indirect' solutions to conflicts is discussed, so here the issue is the 'direct' instead of the 'indirect' effect of the teacher. The child moves in a realm described in the violence essay as 'mythic', because in its world of the unprogrammatic despotic gesture, it symbolises an 'anarchism', the power of which could never be justified generally or in principle but, as behaviour outside of demonic law, always remains singular as a 'gift of divine power, as *absolute power* in an individual case'.[27]

Against this background, what Benjamin writes about the carnival of the performance becomes clear. Here Rang's theory, which had interpreted the carnival (like tragedy) as *agon* and a break with the order of destiny – 'escaping from the stars' destiny' – is in the background. The apparently 'revolutionary' signal at the '*wild* release of the child's fantasy' is witness in the child's gesture of 'what is to come', literally in the sense of something that is always only the future, not thinkable as ever being present. The dangerous nature of this future interests Benjamin:

> The bourgeoisie regards nothing as more dangerous for its children than the theatre. This is not only a residual effect of the old bogey of the middle classes, the child-stealing travelling players. It is more that their frightened awareness balks at seeing the strongest power of the future appealed to in the children by the theatre. And this awareness makes the bourgeois education system outlaw the theatre. How then would it react if the fire – where reality and play merge, become so completely one that acted suffering can turn into genuine suffering, acted thrashings become real – could be felt from close up. (II, 764)

Since children's theatre in no way envisages a concrete Utopia, the main point here is not primarily the danger of the revolution, as one might at first think. The danger is that state in which the oppositions of logic fuse into a 'fire', of which it cannot be said with certainty whether it ought properly to be called 'real' or metaphorical. The gestural aspect of children's theatre is threatening for the 'frightened awareness', although, or precisely because, it is 'pure' and graceful on account of the dangerous (revolutionary) removal of the opposition between fiction and reality, active and passive, doing and omission. For it is this logic of awareness that gives justification to the forms of suppression. The gesture is not revolutionary because it envisages a 'concrete Utopia', it can 'only' ever give an *instruction* of what would be different: in a letter to Adorno in 1940, Benjamin writes of the 'gracefulness of children' as a 'corrective of society'. This gracefulness, he says, is 'one of the instructions that have been given to us for "non-disciplined happiness"'.[28]

But why is the all-levelling fusion of fiction and reality in the fire of the game discussed with reference to thrashing and suffering? Why is it that the examples Benjamin chooses for the possible repeated filming of the actions of the actors in *The Work of Art* essay are a 'leap out of the window' or the startled reaction of the actor after a knock on the door which looks as genuine, as 'desired', as the result of a pistol shot behind his back, why cries for help and actors being thrown to their death? Because in the children's theatre performance, just as in the film, we are basically dealing with 'surrealist' action, a *fantasy of destruction* that cannot be separated from the notion of *interruption* and *caesura*. We note the close proximity in which this places proletarian children's theatre, the 'carnival' of the performance, to the 'proletarian' general strike, which Benjamin understood as a moment of pure – not intentionally purposeful – suspension of the entire social mechanism of the law and its norms, and in this sense, as a 'pure means' (i.e. a means outside of the means-end relationship): that is, precisely as an 'interruption'. In turn, and in an exact parallel, the gesture, for Benjamin, also means 'pure' setting of norms, a calling up, a pro-vocation that posits nothing fixed. This kind of variation of positing norms, of the pre-formative, for which Werner Hamacher in his interpretation of Benjamin's *Critique of Violence* suggests the term 'afformative', occurs in the gesture as a language (that of things through the child), which can only ever 'announce itself, speak ahead of itself, speak as one that is only ever coming, future, as one that has never arrived, that is never already language itself'.[29]

We also note that, as early as 1912 (!), in an essay on education reform, Benjamin had written that everything the school accomplished was no more than 'contribution and achievement of the past', and: '[School] can bring nothing to the future apart from strict attention and respect. Youth however, which the school serves, sends it the future.' He sees the rising 'generation' of youth as being 'full of the images it brings with it from the land of the future', and: 'The culture of the future is, after all, the goal of school – and so it must remain silent when faced with the future embodied in youth. It must allow youth to be effective by *itself*, it must content itself with giving and encouraging freedom.'[30] The texts of the end of the 1920s remain faithful to those of Benjamin's beginning to a remarkable degree. Ima*ges from the future* which youth brings, and the 'coming things' in the signal of the children do not refer to any Utopian notion, let alone a vision of something better, but to the nature of *the (only ever) future, which is not susceptible to normative forces of any sort*. For this reason, one can agree with Giorgio Agamben, and see the gesture as being an eternally potential movement between potentiality and act, a 'potentiality that is not transferred into an act and exhausted in it, but remains and dances as a potential in the act'.[31] At the same time, it would be the occurrence of the other, thinkable only as interruption, omission, pause, caesura, but manifest in the dimension of language as pure communicability and indirectness, beyond the mythical demonic nature of means–end rationality, exchange and law/justice.

The children's performance, which, as 'the great creative pause in the work of education', is what the carnival would have been in ancient cults (II, 768), is certainly not harmless. In many ways, Benjamin's ideas on the children's theatre are founded on a Nietzschean kind of innocent cruelty of becoming – this is also an overlooked central theme in Brecht's didactic plays, incidentally. In his Surrealism essay, Benjamin thinks highly of Dostoevsky because he 'found inspiration in the lowest activity and precisely there. He understood even malice as something so pre-formed in the way of the world but also in ourselves, something suggested to, not to say commanded us, in the way that the idealistic bourgeois understands virtue'. Benjamin interpreted 'meanness, revenge, cruelty', in short, the 'cult of evil as a somehow or other Romantic disinfection and isolation technique of politics against any moralising dilettantism'.[32] Just as he differentiates political action again and again from any moralizing, so, for him, education must serve to harden children against moralizing bourgeois sentiments. It was precisely in the anti-moral and amoral phenomena such as cruelty, the desire to destroy, treachery and mendacity that he sought the mental picture of the revolution.[33]

In the *Conversation above the Corso*, as Lorenz Jäger points out in connection with the carnival theme in Benjamin's work,[34] Benjamin emphasizes that the 'uncivilized, inhuman', indeed the 'cannibalistic' side of children (IV, 770) must not be overlooked. Benjamin enlarges on this in *Old Toys*.[35] Here he talks about 'the cruel, the grotesque, grim side in the life of children' – reminiscent of the brothers Grimm and the grotesque film. According to Benjamin, artists like Ringelnatz or Klee – as distinct from those dreamers who follow Rousseau – have 'understood the despotic and dehumanized aspects of children'. As Benjamin shows with quotations from Salomon Friedlaender, 'the little ones laugh about everything, even the negative sides of life'. Things they love are:

> wonderfully successful little bomb assassinations with princes that go to pieces and are easily healed. Department stores with automatic arson attacks, break-

ins and theft. Victims that can be murdered in many different ways and the dolls who do the murdering equipped with all the requisite instruments...At least my little ones can no longer do without the guillotine and the gallows. (IV, 515)

Benjamin's addendum about the children who transform even the most royal doll – 'mislaid, broken and repaired' – into a 'hard-working proletarian comrade in the child's playing commune' shows once again the political connection between the child's despotic gesture with 'pure' violence, that is, one not corrupted into a means to an end. It is hardly possible to miss the connotation of the child's play which relates it to anarchistic assassinations, and the superimposition over the dictatorial signals of the child with pure violence, the idea of politics of pure means, as Benjamin develops it in his *Critique of Violence*.

VII

The key words 'collective' and 'improvisation' distinguish proletarian from bourgeois education (individual morality and achievement). What counts in the performance itself is not exact reproduction, rather the 'genius of the variant' unfolds in front of the audience. The whole course of 'educational schooling' is turned around, the performance appears 'as the radical release of play that the adult can only ever watch' (II, 767). The child's gesture needs the 'unexpected uniqueness' of improvisation as its 'real space', improvisation is the 'state from which the signals, the signalizing gestures rise up'. 'What matters to all the achievements of children is not the eternal lasting quality of the product but the moment of the gesture. Theatre as the transient art is children's theatre' (II, 767). It would not be doing justice to this idea to see it merely as a pedagogical thesis (the supremacy of improvisation in children's theatre over the so-called polished performance). Rather, the notion of the gesture points to Benjamin's work on Kafka, and especially on Brecht. Benjamin's thinking moves between the theory of the carnival, avant-garde theatre and children's playing, and with surprising ease, as Lorenz Jäger observes, 'theories can alter their scale and are changeable in their dimensions. Human experiences from antiquity can gain new life in the play of children. This is one characteristic of Benjamin's entire theory, a theory that has absorbed children's experiences to an extent that is probably unique and that often projects children's experiences on its horizon'.[36] Similarly, children's theatre here becomes an allegory for another kind of theatre, that of Brecht. We need to make a detour through Benjamin's reading of Brecht if we are to understand the article on children's theatre, and especially its central notion of the gesture.

If we follow what Benjamin's concept of 'gesture' means, the dynamics of children's theatre and Brecht's theatre, at least as Benjamin understood it, become clear: dynamics that are *deconstructive* in every sense of the word. 'Epic theatre is gestural' (*gestisch*) is a key phrase in the essay W*hat is epic theatre?* (II, 521). This is the point at which Benjamin begins his deduction; he then defines gesture as a third element in between language and action. If language in one of its dimensions is a means (to the end of expression), and action is also a means (to ends), then the gesture proves to be a 'pure means', a means before or beyond the end, 'language' in the dimension that is basic to Benjamin. Agamben describes Benjamin's idea precisely, when, in the context of the dance as gesture, he says: 'The gesture is the presentation of something indirect, the means becoming visible as means.'[37] In the same context, he refers explicitly to Benjamin's political notion of the 'pure means' (or, more precisely, to Hamacher's essay on it) and draws a parallel to 'communicability' as such, which, according to Benjamin, manifests itself in the dimension of 'pure language' before and beyond any communication. Agamben rightly concludes:

> Once these two images have been retrieved into the realm of the gesture, they lose their puzzling aspects and become transparent. The whole theory of interruption and the 'Messianic stopping of activity', which represents the real intention of Benjamin's ethical-political thinking, must be related to the theory of the pure means and thus interpreted in the light of the gesture.[38]

It is precisely because it retains its distance from the logic of communication that the 'framing' interruption of epic theatre renders the dominant power visible, and its own power as representation at the same time, as well. In a surreal, absurd, cruel or comic fashion, it suspends rational understanding in gesture, laughter (the 'most revolutionary emotion'[39]), silence, paradox.

The crucial point is therefore that Benjamin sees gesture in Brecht not as *scenic representation on the stage* – not even that of the dialectic (of social contradictions) – but describes the gesture itself as the 'mother of the dialectic' in the first instance (II, 530). In the threshold realm that is the gesture, the dialectic (conceptual knowledge, contradiction, sublation) does not yet exist; it is from the gesture, a realm of the undifferentiated, that *theory* can have its first beginnings: the rationality of ends and means, logic, exchange, justice, and especially all political norms. Benjamin reads Brecht's gestures more like those of Kafka (rightly, though this cannot be shown in detail here). It is not as though Kafka's gestures have 'a fixed symbolic meaning for the author from the start'.[40] Rather, Kafka removes 'the traditional supports…from human gestures', and in this way lets them develop into puzzles.

Epic theatre is constituted in gesture, and this does not mean only that, in it, gestures are the principal means of representation. It is constituted in gesture because it is never a representation of knowledge (theory), but it is the praxis of suspending the concept. Just as, in children's theatre, the true character of reproduction is opened up in improvisation, variation and the 'wild release' of play, so in the gesture, this happens in an absolute way. A moment of perception occurs which transcends the real, which is not enlightened by intellectual concept or conscious reason: of the surreal which refers to the necessity for radical change only indirectly.

This immediately becomes obvious in the idiosyncratic manner in which Benjamin interprets Brecht's concept of 'alienation'. For him, gesture in this context is the term for a manner of representation which creates a 'tableau' out of the 'living flow' of the action by means of interruption, pauses and exclusions. The gesture is characterized by 'being strictly enclosed in a frame' (witness the return of allegorical destruction, of the absence of expression, of the caesura). It translates 'actions' (*Handlungen*) into 'states' (*Zustände*). But the text declares the notion that epic theatre represents social relationships (*milieu*) in a superficial sense to be a misunderstanding. The concept of 'states' does not represent what is normally understood by this term in social discourse at all; what Benjamin means is what is 'discovered' for the first time 'by means of interrupting the sequence of events' (by bringing them to a halt). And now follows Benjamin's extremely strange example, not taken from any Brecht piece, but deliberately allegorically constructed (in 1934, Benjamin would take it up again in *The Author as Producer*, with some interesting modifications):

> The most primitive example: a family scene. A stranger suddenly enters. The woman was just pressing a pillow into a ball in order to hurl it at her daughter; the father was just opening the window to call the police. At this moment, the stranger appears in the doorway. 'Tableau', as they used to say around 1900. That is, the stranger comes upon a state that includes: rumpled bed-clothes, open window, devastated furnishings. But there is a perspective from which even the more accustomed scenes of bourgeois life are not so different from this. The greater the extent of the devastation of our social order (the more we ourselves and our capacity to justify this to ourselves are under attack), the more pronounced the distance of the other will have to be. (II, 522–3)

The child, the parents, family and state power, threats of punishment, conflict of the generations and the sexes – the tableau depicts reality as an all-encompassing civil war. At the same time, one can see the 'primacy of the material over the personal' – bedding, pillow, window, door, furnishings. It is in these things above all that the 'state' the stranger comes upon in his shock is most clearly manifest. (Conversely, it is the stranger who 'appears' as the personification of the moment of another perspective, framed in his turn by the door, on the threshold of this framed painting.) This scene would repay more detailed interpretation, but this much is clear: isolating the continuity of the events by a 'gestural' frame means symbolically interrupting it in such a way *that it is shown and not interpreted*: 'This stage no longer presents its audience with "the boards that represent the world" (that is a space under a spell), but a conveniently placed exhibition space' (II, 520). What in particular is interrupted by the frame is understanding. In the gesture, conventional sense is expunged, is subjected to a fade-out, because in the silent, merely bodily figures, the unthinkable becomes manifest as a linguistic accident, as the disappearance of concepts as such, as something inexplicable that arouses 'astonishment'. In other words, here in the sober, socialist, didactic theatre, just as in children's theatre, we encounter the *dialectical optic* of the Surrealism essay 'which recognizes the everyday as impenetrable and the impenetrable as the everyday'.[41]

It was with great insight that Benjamin noted the aspect of Brecht's theatre that was to be decisive for the future. Just as the child's gesture has to be seen as one which suspends all rational understanding but permits us to recognize that which is out-standing (*Ausstehendes*) or yet to come, Brecht's theatre is oriented towards a manner of production in which the gestural setting comes into conflict with a situation, and torpedoes itself by sublating (interrupting, suspending) mimesis and interpretation as knowledge. It is never a performance without ironically being a *performance of its performance*: that is, without preventing the 'superiority' of the audience (which does not exist in the children's theatre either).[42] This implies a concept of theatre as an event, of a performance and thorough-going self-reflection, which Benjamin first perceived in the alienation technique, and especially in the didactic play that was meant to stimulate social action. In the first version of *What is epic theatre?* (1931), he says about 'the true dialectic of epic theatre:'

> The following relationships are dialectic in the first instance: that of the gesture to the situation and vice versa; the relationship of the actor acting the role to the figure he is portraying and vice versa; the relationship of the action performed to the action that can be observed in every kind of performance. This list is sufficient to show how all these dialectic moments are subordinated to the highest dialectic, which has here been discovered anew for the first time in a long time, and which is determined by the relationship of knowledge and education. For all knowledge achieved by epic theatre has a direct educational effect, but at the same time the educational effect of epic theatre is directly translated into knowledge, which may of course be different for individual actors and members of the audience. (II, 1382)

The centre of all this is the self-reference of the performance to itself as performance, and thus the 'ironic' subversion of any 'thesis', any mimesis which must also appear as an effect of the performance. Epic theatre is dialectical because it absorbs into its formal constitution the fact that 'the entire Marxist education programme is determined by the dialectic that prevails between teaching and learning behaviour' (II, 529), that is, by the dialectic of education and knowledge. For this reason, it never forgets for one moment that it is theatre – a basic aspect of all avant-garde theatre. In *What is Epic Theatre?*, Benjamin refers expressly to 'Tieck's old dramaturgy of reflection', only to reject it again explicitly at once, admittedly in somewhat indefinite terms. For whatever reasons, this 'negation' of the connection seemed to him to be necessary, though mentioning it was no less so.

When he talks about 'filling in the orchestra pit', that is, removing the aura of the *prcoscenium arch* stage, the result is that the theatre loses its character as object and becomes an experience. The decisive thing is no longer the work but the model, and the measure of the model is single and unambiguous – namely, the degree, as Benjamin puts it in *The Author as Producer*, to which the theatre 'brings consumers to the production, in short, its capacity to turn readers or an audience into participants. We already have a model of this sort, which I can only mention but not discuss here. This is Brecht's epic theatre' (II, 696).

It would be more precise to speak here of the didactic play (*Lehrstück*), which Benjamin did not distinguish from the epic theatre as clearly as we need to do today. But Benjamin recognized the high standard of the form and the explosive force of those plays which Brecht research ignored for a particularly long time. He recognized the *didactic play as an artistic principle* (Adorno). Neither at that time nor in the present time is it obvious to the majority of researchers that the central aspect of epic theatre is 'the relationship of the action performed to that given in performance as such' (II, 529), that this 'dialectic' led to a radicalization in the didactic play model in which mimesis and the representation of knowledge take a minor role in favour of participation (with all its unpredictability) and the 'acquisition' of knowledge (rather than its representation). The didactic play has its place in exactly that line of theatre which leads from forms of action art in classical avant-garde to performance art and happenings, to integrated theatre and essentially to a conception of theatre which has precisely this real or 'virtual participation' of the audience as its specific centre, and thus proves to be an aspect of a profoundly altered idea of communication.

'There is no possible place for a superior audience in children's theatre. Those who are not yet utterly stupid will perhaps be ashamed of themselves' (II, 765). Without going too deeply into the specific use

Benjamin makes of the word 'shame', we can say that it refers to the shock experienced when faced with the other power which is in the child's gesture and its undomesticated inventive power, and simultaneously, the shame that marks the loss of paradise and the entry into the world of law, compromise and subordination. Just as the unpredictable signals of children's theatre are reminiscent of paradise, they also, like the 'great theatre' of Modernism, point to the future; this, of course, only in the form of an interruption to time, an interruption of the continuum, of language, of rational understanding.

NOTES

1. W. Benjamin, *Gesammelte Schriften*, ed. R. Tiedemann and H. Schweppenhäuser, 7 vols (Frankfurt/Main, 1974–), II, 763–9. All quotations from Benjamin refer to this edition, unless otherwise noted. Abbreviated references in parentheses identify volume and page number.
2. See my article 'Remarques sur l'idée de l'enfance dans la pensée de Walter Benjamin', in *Walter Benjamin et Paris*, ed. H. Wismann (Paris, 1986), 71–90; or the shortened version in German: 'Die Kinderseite der Geschichte – Walter Benjamins *Passagenwerk*', *Merkur*, 2, 1983, pp. 188–96.
3. Cf. M. Schedler, *Kindertheater: Geschichte, Modelle, Projekte* (Frankfurt/Main, 1977), p. 216. The value of this informative account is considerably reduced by too superficial sorting by ideological criteria, which was admittedly very common at the time.
4. A. Lacis, *Revolutionär im Beruf* (Munich, 1971), p. 30. Further references to the relationship between Benjamin and Asja Lacis can be found in 'Walter Benjamin 1892–1940', *Marbacher Magazin*, 55 (1990), 161–70.
5. Cf. 'Der Moralunterricht' (II, 48-54).
6. During the all too simplifying political reception of the text in the 1960s and 1970s, ideas of this sort, mostly only half understood, were put into the 'metaphysical' category. Schedler implies that Benjamin believed in a 'state of social innocence among children', although Benjamin never mentions anything like it. It was only when it came to be understood that Benjamin's position is neither Marxist nor simply that of an educational reformer that it was possible to reject the banal opinion that Benjamin still embodied vestiges 'of bourgeois-romanticizing consciousness'. Cf. M. Schedler, *Kindertheater: Geschichte, Modelle, Projekte*, pp. 248–9.
7. Benjamin visited her on the day after their first meeting, which had evidently made a deep impression on him. Asja Lacis writes: 'He arrived the next day...A lively conversation developed, I talked about my children's theatre in Orel, about my work in Riga and Moscow. He was immediately full of enthusiasm for proletarian children's theatre and for Moscow.' Cf. A. Lacis, *Revolutionär im Beruf*, p. 46.
8. W. Benjamin, *Briefe*, 2 vols (Frankfurt/Main, 1966), I, 351.
9. Lacis, *Revolutionär im Beruf*, p. 46.
10. W. Benjamin, *Briefe*, I, 347, 351.
11. Cf. 'Moscow Diary' (VI, 318).
12. Cf. 'Moscow Diary' (VI, 359).
13. J. Derrida, 'Back from Moscow, in the USSR', in *Postmoderne und Politik*, ed. J. G. Lauer (Tübingen, 1992), pp. 9–56, here pp. 51–2.
14. G. Scholem, *Walter Benjamin: Die Geschichte einer Freundschaft* (Frankfurt/Main, 1990), p. 196. Cf. also *Marbacher Magazin*, 55 (1990), pp. 1678.
15. This probably corresponded to Asja Lacis's view that it was possible 'to teach the entire school programme in the form of theatre'. But it certainly does not mean 'scenic

didacticism', and it is also quite wrong to imply that Benjamin was demanding that children should be enabled 'to think up concrete Utopias and play them through'. Cf. M. Schedler, *Kindertheater: Geschichte, Modelle, Projekte*, p. 247.

16. Lacis, *Revolutionär im Beruf*, p. 26.
17. Lacis, *Revolutionär im Beruf*, pp. 28–9.
18. Lacis, *Revolutionär im Beruf*, p. 27.
19. Fragment 'Zur Erfahrung' (VI, 89).
20. W. Benjamin, *Der Begriff der Kunstkritik in der deutschen Romantik* (Frankfurt/Main, 1973), pp. 54, 55.
21. Fragment 'Zur Geschichtsphilosophie der Spätromantik und der historischen Schule' (VI, 96).
22. Quotations from Hoernle and further details on the agit-prop and children's theatre in Schedler, *Kindertheater: Geschichte, Modelle, Projekte*, pp. 209–12.
23. Cf. the review 'Spielzeug und Spielen' of the 'monumental work' by Karl Gröber, *Kinderspielzeug aus alter Zeit*, (III, 127–32).
24. Cf. the Denkbild 'Übung' (IV, 4067). On this whole complex, cf. B. Menke, *Sprachfiguren: Name, Allegorie, Bild nach Benjamin* (Munich, 1991), pp. 349–60.
25. In the prose piece 'The Carousel' (*Das Karussel*), too, 'life for the child becomes an ancient intoxication of power with the roaring orchestrion in the middle' when it dreams of flying while on the 'board with subservient animals' (IV, 268): 'The music began and the child rolled jerkily away from its mother. At first it [the child] was afraid to leave its mother. But then it noticed that it was faithful itself. It sat enthroned as a faithful ruler over a world that belonged to it.' The relationship of this 'faithful ruler' to the dolls as 'subjects' also forms part of this image.
26. Cf. the review of G. F. Hartlaub's *Der Genius im Kinde* (III, 212).
27. Cf. 'Notizen' (VI, 207).
28. The key word 'signals' recurs in 'Madame Ariane', where the acedia of the man seeking prophecy is opposed to the living presence of mind of the 'courageous man'. But the 'dangerous, brisk movement of the hand with which the courageous man arranges the future' is possible only through an ability to react, not by knowledge, since 'it is more important to observe exactly what is happening in a particular second than to know distant things in advance'. Benjamin formulates the alternative as follows:

'Harbingers, presentiments, signals go through our bodies like waves all the time. The question is whether to use them or interpret them. But these are mutually exclusive.'

The opposite to laziness/indolence (acedia) is liberty. Its courage, however, becomes manifest in the body. For mankind, 'the naked body is the most reliable instrument of divination'. Man is able to turn himself into a 'factotum of his body'. Of course, it is necessary to be taught the innervation of every minute, every fresh day, which has to be 'seized upon awakening', not merely grasped: 'It is precisely in this that the ancient ascetic exercises of fasting, chastity, waking and watching have had their greatest triumphs since time immemorial.'

The historical moment of crisis in which Benjamin sees himself demands no less than the same sort of innervation of danger and appropriate intuitive behaviour. For this reason, he faced the urgent problem of what arrangements could be made to train people in developing this sort of reaction, which mediates between an active defence reflex, child-like innocence, a gift for divinatory observation and an integrity that is just as cold as it is morally courageous.

The child joins the other figures of Benjamin's allegories of a hope against barbarism, all of which imply thoroughly political dimensions. This hope is a flash, transient by nature, an event fusing memory and salvation, and thus, as he hoped, eminently practical and pragmatic.

29. 'Das Recht zur Gewaltanwendung' (VI, 106, 107). This is not the place to discuss the political problems of such considerations, especially not in the context of the Weimar Republic.

30. W. Benjamin, *Briefe*, 2, p. 854.
31. W. Hamacher, 'Afformativ, Streik', unpublished manuscript on Benjamin's 'On a Critique of Violence' (*Zur Kritik der Gewalt*).
32. Cf. Benjamin's essay on educational reform, 'Die Schulreform, eine Kulturbewegung' (II, 15).
33. G. Agamben, 'Noten zur Geste', in *Postmoderne und Politik*, ed. J. G. Lauer (Tübingen, 1992), pp. 97–107, here p. 106.
34. Cf. 'Der Sürrealismus' (II, 305, 304).
35. Cf. the editors' note (VI, 668), where Scholem is quoted as having noted at an early stage 'a strictly amoral element' and 'a not inconsiderable measure of cynicism' in Benjamin. And although Scholem regarded his friend personally as a 'thoroughly uncynical man', he was taken aback by 'a big dash of Nietzsche when he [Benjamin] talked'. We cannot examine here Benjamin's complex thematizing of morality as behaviour, moralizing, cynicism etc.
36. 'Gespräch über dem Corso' (IV, 770). Cf. L. Jäger, 'Dionysus im christlich-jüdischen Gespräch: Walter Benjamin und Florens Christian Rang' (unpublished manuscript).
37. 'Altes Spielzeug' (IV, 511–15).
38. Cf. L. Jäger, 'Dionysus im christlich-jüdischen Gespräch: Walter Benjamin und Florens Christian Rang', p. 11.
39. Agamben, 'Noten zur Geste', in P*ostmoderne und Politik*, p. 103.
40. Agamben, 'Noten zur Geste', in P*ostmoderne und Politik*, p. 105. It is the gesture that articulates 'what remains unexpressed in very expression', hence the exact analogon of the expressionless, the caesura. In Benjamin's famous 'scene' in the essay on Goethe's *Elective Affinities*, the 'interruption by the commanding word' extracts the truth 'from the evasion of a woman' precisely at the point 'where it interrupts'.
41. 'Rückblick auf Chaplin' (III, 159).
42. Cf. Benjamin's text 'Ein Kinderbild' on a picture of Kafka as a boy (II, 416–25; here 418, 420).
43. The German formula is 'Primat des Dinghaften vor dem Personalen' (I, 363).
44. 'Der Sürrealismus' (II, 307).
45. One of the few to recognize this crucial characteristic of Brecht's theatre at an early phase was Loius Althusser. Cf. Althusser's 'Bertolazzi und Brecht', *Alternative*, 97 (1974), 130–43, and the commentary to it in my *Beiträge zu einer materialistischen Theorie der Literatur* (Frankfurt/Main, Berlin, Vienna, 1977), pp. 12–18.

Translated by Olaf Reinhardt (Sydney)

14

Benjamin's Utopia of Education as *Theatrum Mundi et Vitae*: On the *Programme of a Proletarian Children's Theatre*

Gerhard Fischer

I

Benjamin writes his *Programme of a Proletarian Children's Theater*[1] at a crucial time of crisis, both in his personal life and in the long process of what has been called his 'conversion' to Marxism. Asja Lacis, who inspires the *Programme* arrives in Berlin from Moscow in November 1928; her arrival triggers Benjamin's decision to seek a divorce from his wife, Dora. At the same time, it forces the *Gretchenfrage* of his position as an intellectual, 'free-floating' author of bourgeois origin *vis-à-vis* the Communist Party. Lacis is a 'practising' communist; she and Benjamin attend meetings of the League of Proletarian-Revolutionary Writers which has only recently been founded and which may offer the institutional framework for 'officially' joining the movement. Already during his visit to Moscow in 1926/27, under the very vivid impression of a society in rapid and comprehensive change (*Bau* and *Umbau*), Benjamin considers the pros and cons of joining the party.[2] The changed historical circumstances in Berlin two years later, the increasing polarization between Social Democrats and Communists, the electoral successes of the Nazis, as well as the early warning signs of the impending economic crisis, lead him to reconsider his position, especially as the prospect of a continuing relationship with Asja Lacis promises the basis for a private commitment which would seem to suggest a complementary public, political commitment.

The *Programme* is probably written at the end of 1928 at the request of Becher and Eisler, following Lacis's report about her experiments with children's theatres in the Soviet Union. The idea is to try something similar in Berlin, to be sponsored by and under the auspices of the KPD. Benjamin, who is familiar with the Russian developments since he first met Lacis in 1924, is to write a theoretical exposé based on her practical theatre experiences. It is clear, however, that he also uses the opportunity to reflect critically upon his own situation. The essay goes beyond the commissioned brief; it is neither only a 'theatrical model', nor is it restricted to 'proletarian' concerns. It develops, rather, a critique of bourgeois art, education and aesthetics, while it sketches, at the same time, a radical alternative model of education, based on and yet going beyond the examples developed in the early Soviet Union, and as part of the cultural activities of working-class organizations in Weimar Germany. At the same time, the *Programme* reveals the uniquely Utopian characteristic of Benjamin's anthropological materialism. Not surprisingly, the text does not meet the expectations of the cultural functionaries of the KPD.[3]

II

Benjamin's children's theatre is nothing less than a boarding school for young people between the ages of four and fourteen, where the children and teachers live and work together. It is not an institution for socially disadvantaged children, as was the case of the 'children's houses' set up in the Soviet Union after the revolution to integrate the 'wild' children, the *Bespriorniki,* who had lost their families and had become homeless during the war and the revolution. Rather, Benjamin sees his institution as the *normal* school, as the 'centre' and 'base' of a 'bolshevist education' for everybody (II, 765). The school does not constitute a 'pedagogical province' that is removed from the problems and contradictions of the real world; rather, it is part of the social existence of the proletarian class. Social, political and economic issues, the 'contents and symbols' of the class struggle (II, 768) can and 'must be' part of the activities of the pupils of this schools.

There is no formal, planned and prescribed curriculum in this school, either. Unlike the various models of the educational reform movement which seek to offer an alternative school framework and methodology within the guidelines imposed by a state-controlled curriculum, Benjamin's model envisions a radically different set-up in which the pupils themselves determine what they learn. There are no classes in age-based forms as in conventional schools. The school is organized into sections which correspond roughly to the various artistic-aesthetic disciplines involved in theatrical work: music, painting, stagecraft, gymnastics, dance, speech, etc. The role of the teacher is that of a 'guide' (*Leiter*, rather than *Lehrer*), whose job is mainly to assist the children with the technical tasks and skills. The responsibility of the 'guide' is to stay in the background as much as possible, to allow the children to develop their own ideas and initiatives, to observe the children closely, but to become involved only when needed. There is no selection of subjects and subject matters designed to lead to some pre-determined goal that is to be mastered, neither in a pragmatic-utilitarian sense nor in terms of an ideal of *Bildung*. Consequently, there are no tests or exams to be passed. The subject matter which the pupils will appropriate for themselves is the whole world and all of life itself. This is why Benjamin's school must be a theatre: only in the theatre 'does all of life appear in its unbounded fullness' (II, 764).

At the centre of this vision is a notion of childhood that fulfils itself in theatrical play. To play is to learn and to create within a social context provided by the group or collective of children who constitute the artistic-pedagogic community of this institution as a *theatrum mundi et vitae*. Benjamin emphasizes the process of role-playing and play-acting as a continuum of improvization, a course of study that is 'in principle never completed' (II, 765). It is the process that is important, rather than the performance as an end product. In Benjamin's children's theatre, the performance 'happens', as he puts it, almost 'by accident' and 'almost as a piece of folly' of the playful children.

Nevertheless, the performance is an essential aspect. It not only offers a release (*Lösung*) of the creative tension (*Spannung*) that has been generated during the process of learning and playing. Equally important, the performance guarantees the openness of a proletarian public sphere that integrates the school/theatre into society; in order to be fully productive, the children's collective requires as an audience the larger collective of the working class. The proletarian children's theatre takes education out of the closed world of the family and the state-supervised school to return it to the public scrutiny of the social group of which it is a part. And finally, the public performance provides the occasion for a 'great creative break in the educational world' (II, 768), in which the theatrical experience reaches a new height. Benjamin compares it to the 'carnival of the old cults' (II, 768), a festival of unrestrained exuberance and of 'wild delivery of the child's imagination'. It is an experience of the world turned upside-down: 'like in the Roman *saturnalia*, where the master served the slaves', says Benjamin, 'the children now take the stage and educate and teach the attentive educators' (II, 768).

III

A number of influences and sources have gone into Benjamin's *Programme*. Primarily, it is based on the reports of Asja Lacis about developments in post-revolutionary Russia, most notably her own Children's Theatre for Aesthetic Education, which she set up with orphaned children and groups of *Bespriorniki* in Orel in 1918. Lacis's training as a teacher and as an actress provided the combination of theatre and education that constituted the core of her experiment which was to be taken up independently by other educators in the Soviet Union; the organizational model of a children's commune, or 'children's house', became a cornerstone in the new pedagogy that developed under the conditions of wartime communism. The principles involved in these experiments reflect the theories of pre-Stalinist educational philosophy that arose experimentally and spontaneously out of the changing structures of the new society. Schedler has pointed out that this philosophy, far from being theoretically complete and translated into an official school structure, eclectically mixed traditional notions, such as Rousseau's reliance on observation, with reform ideas taken from capitalist education systems, such as Dewey's insistence on allowing children to grow up and develop freely.[4] It used 'pre-soviet, anarchistic notions' that 'presuppose a natural harmony between individual and communal educational aims', defending the priority of a developing individuality *vis-à-vis* the dominant institutions of authority and power. These educators, among them Lenin's companion, Krupskaja, rejected any kind of force or reward and punishment; they were convinced that 'a child growing up in a socialist society will learn by way of a natural necessity to learn to apply and to organize the social instinct inherent in him in the interest of his social environment'.[5]

These ideas of a new, socialist pedagogy were being closely monitored in Weimar Germany. The youth work activities of the working-class organizations, of the unions, as well as of the SPD and KPD, aimed at establishing a socio-cultural infrastructure to counter the all-pervasive dominance of the compulsory state school system, which was seen as an ideological instrument of domination and control in the interest of the ruling class. In children's groups that met after school, on weekends and during holidays, an effort was made to combat the pernicious influence of the divisive bourgeois school system which condemned the sons and daughters of the workers and peasants to 'depravity' and 'exploitation'.[6] The educational aim of the Social Democratic and Communist youth groups was to instil in the children a sense of class consciousness and solidarity.

To Edwin Hoernle, the chief theoretician of the proletarian pedagogy, in Germany with whose work Benjamin was very familiar, the theatre-play of the children was the 'crowning link' of all of the education that was to take place in the proletarian youth collectives.[7] In his report on *The Work of the Communist Children's Groups*, published as early as 1923, Hoernle summarizes a number of points that also appear in Benjamin's *Programme*:

for example, work in sections grouped around the *Schaubühne* as the 'centre of expressive form', the principle of creative tension and release, the emphasis an improvisation, and the rejection of ready-made plays that are part of the repertoire of the bourgeois children's theatre, in favour of realistic subjects devised by the children themselves which reflect their own social environment. A close contact between actors and audience was to provide the unity of a 'collective experience'.[8]

Benjamin, however, goes a decisive step beyond Hoernle by warning of the danger of political instrumentalization of the children's theatres, which was becoming clearly apparent when the party began to emphasize and to develop its propagandistic apparatus. There were numerous children's ensembles among the many agit-prop groups which mushroomed after 1925. Groups like the Young Red Pioneers or the Red Drummers took an active part in electoral campaigns, political demonstrations and public marches, something to which Benjamin was fundamentally opposed. 'Proletarian education', he writes, 'must be built on class consciousness'; however, 'the party programme is not an instrument of a class conscious education', and ideology, albeit important, does not reach children except as a meaningless 'phrase' (II, 763). Elsewhere in the *Programme*, he states that the 'energies of young people can never be animated in a directly political way' (II, 768). The implied criticism of the ideological indoctrination that is part of the KPD's practice around 1928 is consistent with Benjamin's critique of the political instrumentalization of children that he also deplores in Hoernle's theory. He calls for a 'dialectical anthropology of the proletarian child' and a Marxist *philosophy* of education to complement the narrowly-conceived 'political exposé' of Hoernle (III, 209).

If Benjamin uses existing features of children's culture within the communist youth organizations in Germany and the Soviet Union to construct his *Programme*, his own experiences as a student in Wyneken's Free School Community of Haubinda have clearly contributed to the development of his concept as well. The year he spent at the exclusive *Landerziehungsheim* in Thuringia was important and formative in his youth. In Haubinda, Benjamin experienced the liberal structures of a progressive reform school set up as an alternative to the authoritarian, repressive Wilhelminian *Gymnasium* of the kind Benjamin had attended in Berlin, with its stuffy and conservative teachers, bombastic, idealist rhetoric and nationalist-monarchist rituals. Equally important in his youth was the encounter with the charismatic Wyneken, the revered leader of the *Jugendkulturbewegung*.[9] His encounter with Wyneken had a decisive influence that made him become an active and leading proponent in the youth movement scene, both in Freiburg and Berlin. However, in the 1928 *Programme* Benjamin takes great pains to disassociate himself from his teacher, with whom he had already formally broken at the outset of World War I, as well as from the movement which Wyneken represented.

To Benjamin, the notion of *Jugendlichkeit*, social practice and the cultural ideal of the 'youth movement', appears now as only a facet of bourgeois ideology that indoctrinates young people, 'subjugating the child's suggestability' (II, 768) by means of a kind of 'colonialist pedagogy', a term that Benjamin uses elsewhere in a critique of bourgeois education.[10] The 'youth culture' movement, i.e. Wyneken's particular project within the larger spectrum of bourgeois reform pedagogy, writes Benjamin, 'drains the enthusiasm of young people by idealistic reflection upon itself in order to replace, imperceptibly, the formal ideologies of German idealism with the contents of the bourgeois class' (II, 768). Werner Fuld comments on this passage that it is the first public disavowal of Benjamin's earlier involvement in the academic youth movement; it is a piece of criticism and self-criticism in which Benjamin identifies the 'cardinal mistake' of the youth movement that explains the 'pathos of young people's agreement with the martial enthusiasm of the generation of their parents'.[11]

The *Programme* also contains a scathing criticism of bourgeois education generally. Benjamin rejects the disciplinarian pedagogues and their insistence on order and control; discipline is, to him, the 'stigma of shame' (*Schandmal*) of bourgeois education (II, 768). But he also rejects Wyneken's example of the liberal teacher as a spiritual leader, who is able, because of the force of his 'moral-ethical personality', to educate his pupils by 'influencing' – in reality, by dominating and by overpowering them ideologically. Young people need to experience themselves as responsible individuals who will have to freely develop their own individual sense of moral-ethical autonomy, not individually, however, but as a 'collective' process and with reference to the group of which the child is part. To Benjamin, this is possible only in the proletarian children's theatre, where the children's collective will undertake 'all necessary moral corrections and adjustments' (II, 765). Within this system, no teacher would be able to hold his or her own if they were to undertake the 'truly bourgeois attempt' to influence the children directly through the power of their 'moral personality' (II, 765).

Benjamin thus develops a radically different concept of the role of the teacher in his educational model. He speaks of the 'freezing' (*kaltstellen*) of the 'moral personality of the teacher' (II, 766), which alone is supposed to make a true education possible. The function of the teacher is only to observe, on the one hand, and on the other, to mediate, to influence 'indirectly' by way of providing occasions and, in a sense, technical advice for the pupils to become involved with 'materials, tasks, events' (II, 765). All attempts at a direct influencing, even if they are presented under the guise of the teacher's 'love' of his students, are rejected as illegitimate manipulation by an overpowering personality; in nine out of ten cases, says Benjamin, they only betray an attitude 'of knowing better' and 'wanting better' on the part of the presumably superior teacher that results in destroying the child's own courage and desire to learn (II, 766). To Benjamin, true 'educational love' is unsentimental and unconceited, its 'true genius' lies in *observation*, which in turn is given a tremendous boost once the personality of the teacher and his claim to offer a moral example are 'frozen'. Benjamin's reference to love in this context gives some idea, I believe, of the depth of his emotional involvement in these issues, and of the distance he has travelled in the ten years since his own uncritical admiration and 'love' for his own teacher ended in an abrupt rupture after the outbreak of the war. The 'moral' example of the teachers who exhorted their students to volunteer when war broke out in the summer of 1914, and to sacrifice their lives at the front, was the decisive experience which also meant the end of Benjamin's own youth.

IV

Benjamin's radical critique of the 'inhumanity of bourgeois pedagogy' (II, 763) finds a correlative in an equally damning indictment of bourgeois theatre, which is seen as fundamentally corrupt. To Benjamin, the economic *raison d'être* of theatre in capitalist society is profit, which is guaranteed and maximized by sensationalist exploitation, both in front of the curtain and behind it. The dominance of the profit motive also leads to the priority of performance, the show as the marketable commodity, which rules out any true educational development within the bourgeois theatre itself. The work of the bourgeois director, says Benjamin in one of the many scathing invectives to be found in his essay, is characterized as 'overly hasty' and 'lacking in sleep' (*unausgeschlafen*), part of an overall hectic atmosphere that is dictated by the pressure of opening nights and the competetive artistic *Betrieb*. Benjamin also criticizes the 'pseudo-revolutionary attitude' (II, 769) of the most recent left-wing bourgeois theatre in a way which recalls his critique of left-wing journalists, intellectuals and cabaret writers and performers in *Linke Melancholie*.[12] The productions of these authors are dismissed as mere 'propaganda of ideas' (II, 769). Benjamin puts his finger precisely on the weak spot that typifies the contradictory efforts of the left-wing theatre artists who set out to revolutionize society from the stage of the bourgeois theatre. These plays, he notes, 'incite to actions that cannot be executed' in reality; their 'revolutionary impetus does not pass the test of the first sober assessment' and is usually taken 'care of' (*erledigt*) by the time the audience reaches the exit of the theatre (II, 769).

While Benjamin insists that his proletarian children's theatre has 'nothing in common' with the theatre of 'today's bourgeosie' (II, 764), it does exhibit a remarkable degree of similarity with some of Brecht's ideas. The most obvious agreement, apart from a shared dislike of the existing bourgeois theatre, is the concept of a theatre for learners which Brecht develops in his *Lehrstücktheorie*. Both authors stress the unity of education and theatre, of social learning by role-playing in a theatrical environment which functions as a social laboratory and which aims to produce *learning processes*, rather than being oriented towards performances. Both Benjamin and Brecht stress that this is not a didactic theatre of propaganda in which the actors teach the audience, but one of discovery and learning for the actors. In both cases, a performance for an audience is not the essential aim of the process, although the presence of an audience can fulfil a productive function as representing the larger social collective of which the smaller group of players/learners is a part.

In his model, Benjamin emphasizes the importance of 'gesture' (*Geste*) which is to become an important aspect of Brecht's theoretical reflections, as well. Given the fact that the two first met in May 1929 – a meeting arranged by Lacis at Benjamin's request – and that the *Programme* was written about six months earlier, at a time when Benjamin apparently knew only the *Threepenny Opera* and some of Brecht's poetry, is seems fair to conclude that Benjamin's essay anticipates some of the central theories of Brecht's work in the *Lehrstück* phase, which really begins only with his work on the *Badener Lehrstück* in the middle of 1929. It might be academic to speculate on a possible influence of Benjamin on Brecht, but given the controversy within Benjamin scholarship about the role of Brecht's influence on the work of Benjamin (pernicious to some, positive to others), it might be useful to at least state the obvious: namely, that both writers shared very similar concerns and developed very similar conclusions, perhaps independently of each other, at about roughly the same time.[13]

It is, however, more interesting to look at the differences within the similarities in order to more precisely define the special characteristics of each author's theories. Benjamin's educational theatre is characterized by a very distinctive and unique quality, because of his emphasis on improvisation and spontaneity. The elements of surprise and of the child's 'genius of variation' in combination with the rehearsed skills add up to a 'theatrical totality with a thousand surprising changes' (II, 767). The emphasis on unpredictability, in turn, is closely related to the concept of a theatrical *Fest* that is also stressed by Benjamin. The notion of *carnival*, the 'wild' release of creative tension and energy, suggests a theatre that aims at re-establishing links with an archaic form of community steeped in cult and ritual, an irrational dimension of mythological anthropology.

It is here where the distance from Brecht becomes apparent. Improvisation certainly has a place for Brecht within the rehearsal process, but his directorial practice, the insistence on control and precision, for instance the attempt to 'write down' performances by way of exact recording as in *model books*, as well as the highly- formalized textual basis of his *didactic plays,* all seem to point to a direction that is rather different in comparison to Benjamin's model. Brecht's notion of an 'epic theatre', with its claim to represent a 'theatre of the scientific age', underlines the difference. The attitude of *Verfremden,* or 'distancing', of 'cool' detachment and critical observation in a theatre that functions as a controlled sociological experiment, stands in striking contrast to Benjamin's carnival stage, where the children 'free themselves', a theatre of 'fire', in which 'play and reality melt into each other' (II, 768, 765), a theatre of *danger*, likely to frighten the bourgeois pedagogues out of their wits.

V

An analysis of the concept of 'gesture' reveals a similar discrepancy which leads to the last point of Benjamin's *Programme*, the Utopian and Messianic nature of his vision. In Brecht's theatre, *Geste* is a primarily social, even sociological phenomenon. It is the exemplary moment within a theatrical process, achieved through precise observation, arrangement, acting and speech, which reveals the sociohistorical place and background of the stage characters beyond their immediate individual, psychological reality. It is the search for the precise *Gestus* of a scene that illuminates the societal contradictions of the characters, and it is the main task of the director to find a theatrical focus that 'freezes' this gesture, or for the players/learners involved in the self-learning process of the *Lehrstück* to find the gestures that define their critical insights which are the results of their sociocultural/theatrical investigation. Through the focus on the *Geste,* the audience's perception is directed towards recognizing the social context, the characters' embeddedness, as it were, within suprapersonal structures that explain their actions as well as their relationships to each other. Brecht's gesture in his epic theatre reveals that which lies behind the surface reality. The naturalistic work of art is capable only of reproducing this surface, as in the photograph of the Krupp factory that Brecht uses in his famous example.

In Benjamin's *Programme* the concept of 'Geste' is also of central importance, but it is interpreted quite differently. He distinguishes two aspects, both of which are derived from an analysis of the playing child. The first aspect concerns an essential feature within the process of imaginative creation and aesthetic education. The teacher's task is to observe the improvisational play-acting of the children, in which every action, every 'gesture' becomes a 'signal'. These signals capture, in an emblematic moment, how children live and order, arrange and re-arrange their world. It is up to the teacher now to assist the children in their creative expression by way of executing a transformation which 'materializes' the gesture by using the 'material' elements and properties of plot, painting, dancing, reciting, etc. Benjamin refers to Konrad Fiedler's *Schriften über Kunst* to explain the transfer, or 'conversion', from visual perception to creative expression. The artist is not a person who sees more or better, i.e. who sees 'more naturalistically, more poetically or more ecstatically', but rather, a person 'who sees more closely with his hand where the eye grows weak': the artist 'converts the perceptive innervation of the eye muscles to the creative innervation of the hand' (II, 766). Benjamin extends this definition to connect his vision of the imaginative potential of the child at play to provide a basic prescription for an aesthetic education that is based on play as the unifying factor of perception and creation: 'Every gesture of the child is creative innervation in exact correlation with receptive [innervation]' (II, 766). The teacher has to be able to 'read' the gesture in which the children re-create their world in their imagination, and has to help 'convert' the gesture into formalized, material expression: 'It is the task of the teacher to deliver the child's signals from out of the dangerous magic realm of pure phantasy and to commit them to being executed in materials' (II, 766).[12]

VI

The other aspect of 'gesture' is that it also functions as a signal which directs the view of the observer into the child's world. Benjamin speaks of a kind of semiotic language, a 'Lehre von den Signalen' (II, 766), a notion which he insists is not merely a phrase. But this language, the actions and gestures of the child at play, is a secret code that is not easily deciphered; it takes the genius of a Jean Paul to 'open up a view' into the children's world. What, then, does the gesture of the playing child signify? It is not, as Benjamin insists, a psychological signal that reveals a subconscious reality, instances of repression or sublimation. Rather, the child's gesture constitutes the '*secret signal* of that what is to come', and as such, it is the only 'truly revolutionary' language (II, 769).

In Benjamin's *Programme*, the performance which constitutes the essence of his theatrical/educational process becomes a kind of gesture also, a moment that draws together all elements of his pedagogic vision. The performance is the 'synthesis' of gestures born out of improvisation with 'a thousand surprising variations', which 'releases new forces, new innervations' not imagined during the previous rehearsal/learning process; it is controlled by the moral authority of the collective of proletarian children, who display their original socio-aesthetic imagination and creativity, and in so doing present themselves as the educators of their society in the upside-down world and the topsy-turvy atmosphere of carnival play as part of a public *Fest*. The gesture of the performance culminates in the experience of the 'unintentional singleness' (*unversehentliche Einmaligkeit*) of the art of theatre as the transitory art which is precisely for this reason the appropriate art for children (*die kindliche Art*). Childhood fulfils itself for the participating children in this one moment which allows them to become 'free': their creative play 'radiates' and 'calls up' the 'strongest force of the future' in a moment's *gesture* that communicates the 'secret signal of what is to come' to an audience of 'attentive educators'.

This is the bottom line of Benjamin's *Programme*, and it is very clear hat here his concept of childhood and his pedagogy touch upon the philosophy of history that he formulates under the distressing conditions of the later exile years. In one of the preliminary notes to his collection of theses, *On the Concept of History*, he links an aphorism on 'children as the representatives of paradise' with observations on the hunchback dwarf of theology, a characterization of Messianic time as a 'break' in history, and an analysis of the 'history of the oppressed as a *discontinuum*' (I, 1243). The performance of the proletarian children's collective, encapsulated in the gesture of play, becomes one such moment of *profane enlightenment*, the single second 'of the present as the "time of the now" which is shot through with chips of Messianic time'. In this moment, the children emancipate themselves, and the adults turn into perceptive learners; the experience of the performance/gesture is also that of Benjamin's *choc*, by which 'thinking suddenly stops in a configuration pregnant with tensions' and 'crystallizes into a monad'. The audience of proletarian adults, provided they are 'historical materialists', will recognize in this instant 'the sign of the Messianic cessation of happening, or, put differently, a revolutionary chance in the fight for the oppressed past'.[14]

VII

What, then, are we to make of Benjamin's educational-aesthetic-historical Utopia? What, in particular, are we to make of it today, at a juncture in history in which the elements of a proletarian sociocultural infrastructure which Benjamin had discovered as a potential 'frame' or support structure for his own pedagogy have finally become part of the 'rubble' of the 'single catastrophe' that confronts the angel of history who turns his face to the past? Does Benjamin's essay, which was meant to become part of the cultural programme of the Communist Party of Weimar Germany, also belong today to the 'rubble of history' that has been piling up before the eyes of the witness of contemporary history who contemplates the collapse of an ideological system which, for a short while, had become material reality? Digging and sifting through the ruins, are we likely to find something of value to contribute to a debate on the organization of an advanced society held together by parliamentary democracy and a market economy, both of which, to Benjamin, were obviously not the ultimate answers? In conclusion, a few points offer themselves as suggestions that may offer approaches to reading Benjamin's educational theories afresh.

It would be too easy, as Schedler and the proponents of a new anti-authoritarian, 'proletarian' pedagogy in the early 1970s liked to do, either to accept Benjamin's *Programme* as educational blueprint for the construction of a concrete Utopia by children,[15] or to dismiss his visionary conclusion of the child as the messenger from paradise as a remnant of his metaphysical-theological thinking which he allegedly was trying to leave behind as part of his bourgeois heritage in his conversion to Marxism. The Messianic-Utopian quality is a characteristic and consistent feature of his work at large, prior to and after the writing of his essays and reviews on principles of revolutionary-socialist education, just as much as his interest in children, in their work and world, and in their creative-imaginative potential. Even if one admits a trace element of reform-pedagogic idealism in Benjamin's argument which might place him in the vicinity of such bourgeois educational reformers as Montessori,[16] it must be clear that Benjamin's position is different, that this idealism is another side of his Messianic Utopianism. Benjamin's position is thus not that of the intellectual who turns his back on a modernity that is seen as alien and hostile. Neither is his position that of the disillusioned intellectual who is forced to confront ideological defeat in the face of contrary historical forces, and who adopts an attitude of conservative regression, i.e. the attitude of bourgeois intellectuals of Benjamin's (and others') generation, who capitulate in the face of the overwhelming sociocultural, political and economic contradictions of modern society to retreat into a fictional childhood which promises salvation and dispenses with the necessity of *engagement*, postponing any attempts at sociocultural practice or political action.

Benjamin's child is not the child *per se*, who has to be brought up in the protective pedagogical reform province of a Never Never Land that is removed and sheltered from the real world. Neither is his child the individual child envisioned by the bourgeois educators with their curricular demands of socialization and *Bildung*, nor the *abstractly* eternal Messiah who will return in every child. Rather, Benjamin's child is the individual proletarian child as part of a group, the product of very specific sociocultural circumstances and of an educational system that exists only in partial, experimental form within a social system *in statu nascendi*. The insistence on discovering and considering the class basis of education, the material interests of the social groups involved in this process, is to Benjamin an essential maxim of any educational practice, and certainly something that should not be hidden away from children. It is something that he insists on in his suggested proletarian education, just as much as it plays an important role in his analysis of his own privileged childhood in the Wilhelminian West End of Berlin around the turn of the century. The necessity of a materialist foundation of education has 'immense consequences', writes Benjamin: 'The offspring of the bourgeoisie confront their class as inheritors; the disinherited [confront theirs] as helpers, avengers, liberators' (III, 207).[17] Can one deny that this 'drastic difference' is today any less valid and important than it was seventy-five or twenty-five years ago, unless, of course, one claims that with the fall of the Soviet Empire, seen as the eschatological signal, our present-day Western society fulfils itself as the end of history within the *simulacrum* of postmodern and post-historical non-history? Certainly, the materialist analysis of who the disinherited and the inheritors are has become more difficult and complex today, when it seems decidedly unfashionable to ask this question and to consider its relevance within any educational practice.

And what are we to make of Benjamin's Utopianism? The present disintegration of Utopian dreams of socialism, of a just and 'fulfilled' classless society seems to be rather complete, if not final: Utopian thinking as just that, thinking about the impossible, the unreachable, the Never Never. The rest is pragmatism on the part of the pragmatists, i.e. the educators in the guise of economic rationalists and vice versa, and on the part of the left-wing intellectuals it is, if not silence, nostalgia and melancholy dreaming about a paradise lost. Of course, there is nothing new about this: even in Benjamin's own time, some of the contemporaries who wrote about the Utopia of childhood as the promise of happiness invariably did so in a mood of pessimism. Perhaps one needs to be tolerant enough to accept this attitude of the critical theorist who is overcome by melancholy resignation, sacrificing 'childhood for theory', as one critical observer has put it.[18] However, I would argue that this attitude is ultimately unacceptable to the pedagogue who works with children in a daily practice of sociocultural intervention. Benjamin's activist Utopianism is immune to melancholy regret: it does not place the goal of education into an unreachable distance, either beyond the historical horizon or in the irretrievable world of the child as seen from the perspective of the grown-up who has lost all contact with his childhood. Rather, Benjamin places his everyday Utopia squarely in the *Jetztzeit*, the here and now of the child's creative-imaginative potential. For the pedagogue, there is no other space than this time of the here and now as the time of the children.

As a final point, it might be useful to emphasize again the notion of a creative imagination manifesting itself in the child's play that lies at the centre of Benjamin's educational model. In spite of his rejection of a psychoanalytical interpretation, his theory shows a remarkable resemblance to the views of Freud developed in his 1907 lecture on 'Creative Writers and Daydreaming'.[19] Freud compares the imagination of the creative artist to that of the playing child; in his view, imagination is closely related to his concept of satisfaction of needs and wishes. According to Freud, the 'driving forces of imagination' are 'unfulfilled wishes'; every 'phantasy', whether play, imaginative-artistic creation (of adults or children) or day-dreaming, is a correction of an 'unsatisfactory reality'. Both Benjamin and Freud emphasize the close dialectical relationship between reality and imagination. The play-acting child, says Freud, 'likes to link his imagined objects and situations to the tangible and visible things of the real world'.[20]

What I am re-constructing here is, of course, a connection between the theories of Marx and Freud, Benjamin and Marcuse, which became important for the New Left of the late 1960s and early 1970s, in particular the rediscovery of the emancipatory potential of imagination that is embedded in the concept of imagination as an intellectual and social force of production. Phantasy, or imagination, is 'not a special substance, as when one says: "Somebody has a lot of imagination", but it is rather the *organizing principle of mediation,* i.e. the specific work process through which the psychic structure of needs and desires, consciousness and external world are being linked'.[21] It is one of the merits of Benjamin's children's theatre essay that it establishes precisely the notion of an active, *social* imagination that is to be the essential factor in an educational process which is closely linked to the real world.

It is not difficult, then, to understand the rediscovery of Benjamin as an important author in the vicinity of the Frankfurt School by the student movement of 1968, and it comes as no surprise to find that Benjamin's essay first appeared in 1968 in a volume entitled *Walter Benjamin*, the first *Raubdruck* (pirated edition of copyright material) to be published by the Central Council of Socialist Kindergardens in West Berlin, which in turn forced the Suhrkamp Verlag to publish its volume, *Walter Benjamin: On Children, Youth and Education*, the following year. Benjamin's essay played an important role within the short-lived anti-authoritarian movement of the late 1960s and early 1970s, and the *Kulturrevolution* of these years certainly had important and lasting effects on a generation of educators. Of course, what the New Left did not succeed in was the analysis of precisely the 'real world' of 1968. The theorists of the Extra-Parliamentary Opposition (APO) remained caught in patterns of theory and dogma which had by then already outlived their 'use by' date. The attempt to put into practice Benjamin's proletarian children's theatre in the anti-authoritarian kindergardens founded by student activists could not succeed within the borrowed terms of a socialist anti-pedagogy that had no foundation in social reality, then or now.

Does Benjamin's vision, then, of a radically different alternative to educational practice remain a challenge that presents a *viable* alternative? It certainly has not become any easier to locate the potential of children's creativity that Benjamin sees in the real world of the here and now. What are the 'tangible and visible things of the real world' to which today's child who plays with video and computer games 'likes to link his imagined objects and situations'? Benjamin's seemingly old-fashioned children's theatre appears to have become a quaint relic in the high-tech, postmodern age of simulation, of interactive virtual reality, and of instant global communication in a world threatened by the loss of its very life-sustaining material basis through continuing ecological destruction, overpopulation and global conflict. Or has it? What about the teams of young people, computer specialists and software designers, who have set up shop in the labs of Silicon Valleys, where they define for themselves, or are given free rein by their employers to define, their own tasks of creating new systems and applications, not by being told exactly what route to follow, but by exploring the freedom to play and to experiment, their collective creativity finally resulting in a new mode of production (cultural and otherwise) and perhaps products and processes that were not 'imaginable' before? What if we think of these teams as possible examples of Benjamin's 'collective' of young people in non-directed, open-ended and spontaneous learning situations, who open avenues to creative thinking and development that are closed off in traditional educational systems? And, alas, if we imagine that these young creative computer wizards might one day become teachers and educational analysts and administrators, then perhaps we could also imagine that they would set up a structure like Benjamin's theatre, and we would recognize in their own teaching a resemblance to Benjamin's model teacher who has an eye for the playful gesture of the child as part of a language which signifies 'that which is to come', and who might be sensitive enough to help convert the perceptive innervation of the child at play into a creative one that takes the form of material, if electronic, expression.

If this Utopian situation which I have sketched here is the most advanced example of learning situation in practice that is available today, would Benjamin, over a hundred years old today, be happy with it? Of course, he would have asked about the social aspect. One certainly cannot claim that the tremendous leap forward in communicative creativity we have witnessed over the last decade or so as a result of the electronic revolution has brought about a similar leap in our social imagination. This, I believe, is where Benjamin's challenge remains as topical today as twenty-five or six-five years ago. His dream of a non-manipulative, domination-free education which goes beyond 'forming' or 'socializing' children into the straitjackets of conventional wisdom, which not only passes on (or down) known knowledge, but which that creates new knowledge, which liberates original creativity and creative imagination, with regard to our technological, aesthetic as well as our social imagination, remains an imperative that seems no less urgent in the age of electronic communication than in Benjamin's own age of radio and film.

NOTES

1. W. Benjamin, *Gesammelte Schriften*, ed. R. Tiedemann and H. Schweppenhäuser, 7 vols (Frankfurt/Main, 1974–), II, 763–9. All quotations from Benjamin refer to this edition, unless otherwise noted. Abbreviated references in parentheses identify volume and page number.

2. Cf. W. Fuld, *Walter Benjamin – Zwischen den Stühlen: Eine Biographie* (Munich, 1979), p. 188.

3. Cf. A. Lacis, *Revolutionär im Beruf* (Munich, 1971), p. 26, and H. Haus, 'In Memoriam Asja Lacis (19.10.1891 - 21.11.1979)', in *Brecht Yearbook*, vol. 12, ed. J. Fuegi, G. Bahr and J. Willett (Detroit, Munich, 1985), 141–7.

4. Cf. M. Schedler, *Kindertheater. Geschichte, Modelle, Projekte* (Frankfurt/Main, 1977), pp. 242–4.

5. Schedler, *Kindertheater*, p. 242.

6. Edwin Hoernle, in an article on educational work in the communist children's groups, quoted by Schedler, *Kindertheater*, p. 209.

7. E. Hoernle, 'Die Arbeit in den kommunistischen Kindergruppen', in *Der Kindergruppenleiter*, 1 (Wien 1923), quoted by chedler, *Kindertheater*, p. 211. See also Benjamin's review of Hoernle's book, *Grundfragen der proletarischen Erziehung* (Berlin, 1929), in 'Eine Kommunistische Pädagogik' (III, 206–9).

8. Quoted in Schedler, *Kindertheater*, p. 214.

9. Cf. U. Hermann, 'Die Jugendkulturbewegung: Der Kampf um die höhere Schule', ed. T. Koebner, R. Janz, F. Trommler, *'Mit uns zieht die neue Zeit': Der Mythos Jugend* (Frankfurt/Main, 1985), pp. 224–44.

10. Cf. 'Kolonialpädagogik', a review of A. Jalkotzy's *Märchen und Gegenwart* (III, 272–4).

11. Fuld, *Walter Benjamin – Zwischen den Stühlen: Eine Biographie*, p. 61.

12. Cf. 'Linke Melancholie' (III, 279–83).

13. Cf. B. Witte, 'Krise und Kritik: Zur Zusammenarbeit Benjamins mit Brecht in den Jahren 1929 bis 1933', in *Walter Benjamin: Zeitgenosse der Moderne*, ed. P. Gebhardt et al. (Kronberg/Taunus, 1976), pp. 9–36. See also Hans-Thies Lehmann's Chapter 13 in the present volume.

14. W. Benjamin, *Illuminations*, ed. H. Arendt, trans. H. Zohn (Glasgow, 1973), pp. 264, 265.

15. On this point, see also H. Lehmann's Chapter 13 in the present volume.

16. Cf. Maria Montessori: 'The child is the eternal Messiah who always returns among the fallen human beings in order to lead them to heaven', quoted in Schedler, *Kindertheater*, p. 89

17. Cf. G. Schiavone, 'Von der Jugend zur Kindheit: Zu Benjamin's Fragmenten einer proletarischen Pädagogik', in *'Links hatte sich noch alles zu enträtseln...': Walter Benjamin im Kontext*, ed. B. Lindner (Frankfurt/Main, 1978), p. 55. The question may

also be seen in the context of the debate on the *Wertfreiheit* and 'neutrality' of science and educational practice in the Weimar Republic, as well as the notion of the 'free' intellectual, both of which Benjamin criticizes.

18. Schiavone, 'Von der Jugend zur Kindheit: Zu Benjamin's Fragmenten einer proletarischen Pädagogik', p. 45.
19. S. Freud, 'Creative Writers and Daydreaming', *The Standard Edition of the Complete Psychological Works of Sigmund Freud* (London, 1959), vol. IX, pp. 142–53.
20. Freud, 'Creative Writers and Daydreaming', pp. 146, 144.
21. O. Negt and A. Kluge, *Öffentlichkeit und Erfahrung* (Frankfurt/Main, 1973), p. 73.

15

Beyond Benjamin: Performative Artwork and its Resistance to Reproduction

Andrzej Wirth

Benjamin's lucid thesis concerning the reproduction of an artwork needs relativization today.[1] It remains powerful as an early prognosis of a complex development in the arts, but leaves some aspects untouched, exaggerated or underrated. The ideological frame of his reasoning broke down, without affecting the pertinence of his argument. By this I mean his orthodox Marxist illusions: he was expecting the self-liquidation of capitalism, and did not expect that it would happen first to socialism.

Walter Benjamin's central concept of the reproduction of the artwork distinguishes between a purely technical reproduction (e.g. simulacra of multiple film copies or photography stills) and reproduction as an artistic procedure (*künstlerische Verfahrensweise*), e.g. woodcut, lithography, dubbing (in a sound movie). It is clear, although not directly stated, that theatre (as drama or performance) belongs to a domain of reproduction as an artistic procedure.

The status of theatre work, from the perspective of its reproduction (*Reproduzierbarkeit* – as multiple stagings, revivals, reconstructions, model productions, language changes through translation, etc.), receives only marginal attention in Walter Benjamin's master essay. His paradigm is film and the effect it has on other arts. What Walter Benjamin left to one side, I would like to make into a major subject of my investigation. Such investigation profits by applying Walter Benjamin's basic distinctions and intuitions, but also has to make some additions, ameliorations, corrections and revisions.

In theatre, more than in other arts, the placement of an originial work (*Standort*) and its authenticity (*Echtheit*) contribute to its unique aura as a distinctive atmosphere that surrounds sources from which the work of theatre is generated. These sources in theatre are the actors, a defined playing space, and, last but not least, the audience. The changing composition of the audience modifies the acting of the players for every performance. Thus, an interactive factor plays a role which eludes prediction and definition. Walter Benjamin's dictum that 'the work of art has always been reproducible in principle' (I, 436) provokes some scepticism in the case of theatre. A perfect reproduction of a given staging at a different time, with different actors, in another language and with a different audience, means a change in the source from which the theatre artwork is generated.

The unique aura which surrounds the world premiere weakens or disappears on successive nights, especially if the production remains in the repertoire for very long. It seems that the authenticity and uniqueness of an artwork in performance are so feeble and fragile, and only of limited, but not exactly definable, duration, that it is not advisable to talk about a reproduction of a theatre artwork in terms of a transfer to another place and other generative sources. And yet attempts are being made again and again by competent artists to reproduce the initial effect of the world premiere, which is usually the basis of the theatre artwork's reputation. The reproductive revivals try to preserve the charisma of the original staging.

Such attempts, if they are successful, are never really a reproduction, but a transformation of the original work, which produces a comparable overall artistic strength, emanating, however, from changed sources. Attempts by the Moscow Art Theatre to conserve original Chekhov productions over the decades proved that the life of a theatre work has its natural span, which cannot be prolonged indefinitely.

Bertolt Brecht's theory of model productions, which was not intended to produce copies, but to secure his aesthetic orthodoxy, is now only of historical interest. It helped in the initial stage of Brecht's reception as a general orientation concerning Brecht's postulated aesthetics. It did not help, however, the authoritative Brecht stage to preserve or duplicate its master productions over a period of ten years. Attempts to reconstruct productions of historical importance, such as Kandinsky's *The Yellow Sound* or Schlemmer's *Triadic Ballett*, were of museum value for theatre scholars, but are impossible to confuse with live theatre.

Robert Wilson's unique practice of duplicating his own productions intercontinentally deserves our special interest. The practice is new, indicating that internationalization of film production became a model emulated by theatre producers. This is what Walter Benjamin would call technical reproduction as an artistic procedure. Symmetrical examples are the original production of *Golden Windows* in the Munich Kammerspiele (1982) and its revival at the Brooklyn Academy of Music (1989), the original production of *Hamletmachine* at New York University (1986) and its revival in Hamburg's Thalia (1986). Both productions are high-tech theatre with pre-recorded light and sound effects. It would seem that, with the parameters of the staging technically programmed and recorded, an almost ideal condition for the reproduction of a theatre piece has been created.

Nevertheless, a shifting of sources (different space, casting, language and audience) produces different results. Even very carefully coached actors are not capable of creating equal effects, not only due to differences between personalities, but most importantly because of the different cultural conditioning of the player and of the audience. Maria Niecklisch's original laughing aria was composed of quotations of different laughing sequences in her roles from Chekhov through Dürrenmatt to Albee. Such a culturally rich coding, decipherable for a connoisseur audience of the Kammerspiele, was not possible in a reference system of New York actors and theatre-goers.

In the Hamburg *Hamletmachine* (1986), the ideological and political sub-text of the piece (the Berlin Wall) was much more resonant for the players and for the audience than it was in New York. This did not necessarily lead to a better, but to a different theatre event. In my opinion, all examples prove that 'the theatre artwork fundamentally is *not* reproducible'. The technical reproduction of theatre as an artistic procedure is an illusion and a Utopia. In the era of technical reproduction of almost anything, its impossibility gives a special value of exclusiveness, uniqueness and fragility to the art of theatre, analogous to a happy moment in one's life, which can not be programmed. It is unpredictable; it can be remembered, but not reproduced.

It could be considered a paradox that an artist who was so obsessed with a Utopian goal of reproducing his own images globally in a medium which is not suitable for this purpose nevertheless created a pioneering work, pointing towards an alternative. Robert Wilson's installation at the Pompidou Centre in Paris (1991) is a pertinent example. It could be interpreted as an instance of a theatrical *perpetuum mobile*, which reproduces itself continuously through the close proximity of spectators. The large, rectangular space of the Pompidou Centre's mezzanine was used, the sole entrance being at the front, and the only exit at the very end of the space. Admission was controlled electronically so that the number of people moving through that installation was kept constant. The floor of the windowless mezzanine was covered with dark volcanic lava; an impression of traversing the slope of a volcano was created through a light-blue horizon at the end of the long exhibition hall, suggesting illusionistically a blue sky above the top of the volcano. Moving was only possible on the zig-zagging hanamichi bridges, traversing the hall from its entrance to its exit, and making it difficult for a spectator to stop without obstructing the flow of other visitors. Half-buried in the lava of the floor were selected props from Robert Wilson's productions over the last two decades. The preciousness of these pieces of art was heightened by their contrast with the dark greyness of the volcanic dust (alternatively suggestive of nuclear fallout) and by means of precisely-focused spotlights. These objects invited the attention of the spectator as autonomous works of art. For those, however, who had seen them in Robert Wilson's productions already, they were also a means of activating their theatrical memory, of mentally reproducing theatre pictures once experienced.

The constant flow of spectators on zig-zagging hanamichi bridges had another effect. A spectator watching the chosen object saw it in a devastated landscape, with other spectators behind it who assumed for him the role of actors, and complemented the overall picture. The analogy to the dramaturgy of Japanese gardens clarifies the impression given. Robert Wilson's installation thus became an instance of a reductive deconstruction of theatre: theatre without actors as autonomous agents, or better still, theatre in which the function of a spectator is fused with the function of a player.

It is difficult to underestimate the importance of this model of interaction for theoretical investigation. This is, no doubt, a fully-fledged theatre, because blockings and movements are 'remote-controlled' by an invisible director, who is programming and timing the event. He is also choreographing it. The spectator, seeing other visitors, realizes that they assume a certain uniform pose, resembling that of a mourner, standing contemplatively on the edge of an open grave. Such a posture is imposed by the placement of objects of aesthetic contemplation deep under the feet of the spectator. The objects of contemplation are not only stationary and sculptured (Robert Wilson's *Chair* and *Couches*) but also sonorous (a sound track, audible at a certain point of the 'walk'), or moving images in video monitors hanging from the ceiling.

The spectators move through different spheres of light, sound, video images and stationary objects. This creates a complex dramaturgy which has its turning points and even its 'denouement'. Only shortly before exiting does the visitor have a chance to look backwards, and he sees the route he has taken passing through Wilson's 'Japanese garden'. He will discover that he missed one object, standing to the left of the entrance. This object is identifiable now as Saddam Hussein's bunker-like chair, made of concrete blocks. How could one not describe it as the pictorial message of the show?

Robert Wilson's installation at the Pompidou Centre is an instance of a unique technical and artistic self-reproduction of theatre. This, however, does not change my conviction, that the theatre artwork is fundamentally *not* reproducible, and that Walter Benjamin's lucid thesis needs to be corrected with reference to theatre.

The sixty years that have passed since Walter Benjamin wrote his famous essay on reproduction have burgeoned a development weakening the opposition between film and theatre. Benjamin was right to predict that modern mass society will increasingly demand abolition of uniqueness and long for the common and the repeatable (this is reflected in mass tourism, which has abolished a notion of the exotic).

The empirical uniqueness of the world premiere (preserved formally in the ritual of the film release) is nowadays undermined by the internationalization and the spatial dispersion of theatre productions. The best example of this might be the international production of Robert Wilson's *Civil Wars*. International theatre festivals ignore the auratic element of theatre, separating it from its sources. Theatre as merchandise loses its cult value, becomes definitely secularized, and loses its initial authenticity (e.g. Peter Brook's world tour of *Mahabharata*). What Walter Benjamin saw as a unique domain of cinema – persons without role playing themselves in front of the camera – has already been standard practice in multimedia high-tech theatre for a long time (John Jesurun, Sheryl Sutton, Robert Wilson). Today, anybody can be in a movie or in the theatre ('found' persons in Kantor's theatre; Christopher Knowles, Mr Johnson in Robert Wilson's theatre).

The analytical prowess of cinema, praised by Walter Benjamin as its unique feature, came to theatre in the aesthetics of Richard Foreman, Robert Wilson and the new dance theatre after Cunningham. Stress on performance (in terms of perfect execution) became a device of anti-empathy in film as well as in the theatre. Distraction as an element of cinematic aesthetics became a legitimate component of theatrical strategy.

Nevertheless, in spite of all these transformations and an increasingly reduced gap between cinematic and theatrical aesthetics, theatre as such shows a stubborn resistance to reproduction, even in its most secularized, non-cultic, non-auratic, sportive (pure execution as performance) versions. Separated from place and sources, which generated it and catapulted it intercontinentally as merchandise into the international festival trade, theatre remains as it always was: virtually not reproducible. Perhaps this is the reason for its singular place among the arts.

And yet, Benjamin may still be proven right. The development of new technologies – for example, interactive computer-driven multi-media monitors with CD-ROM support – offer opportunities for artistic participation and creation that we have only begun to explore. At this stage, as exemplified by the CD-ROM documentation of Robert Wilson's *Stalin Opera* (edited by Seth Goldstein for the Byrd Hoffmann Foundation, New York 1993), existing computer technology has already created new possibilities for storing, programming and manipulating electronically-reproduced images. Works of art which do resist reproduction – such as improvised actions, performances, happenings, emballages – can now be filmed, documented and stored, not only to keep the memory of the art event alive, but because the electronic material also allows the 'spectator' the possibility of individual creative interaction, of participating in an event in his or her own 'virtual reality'.

NOTE

1. Cf. W. Benjamin, *Gesammelte Schriften*, ed. R. Tiedemann and H. Schweppenhäuser, 7 vols (Frankfurt/Main, 1974–), I, 431–69. All references to Benjamin refer to this edition. Abbreviated references in parentheses identify volume and page number.

Notes on Contributors

John Docker is Senior Research Fellow at the University of Technology, Sydney.

Klaus Doderer is Professor Emeritus of German Literature and Foundation Director of the Institut für Jugendbuchforschung at the University of Frankfurt (Main).

Gerhard Fischer is Head of German Studies at the University of New South Wales, Sydney.

David Frisby is Professor of Sociology at the University of Glasgow.

Michael Hollington is Professor of English at the University of New South Wales, Sydney.

Bernd Hüppauf is Professor of German at New York University.

Manfred Jurgensen is Professor of German at the University of Queensland.

Hans-Thies Lehmann is Professor of Theatre Studies and Director of the Institute of Theatre, Film and Media Studies at the University of Frankfurt (Main).

Gert Mattenklott is Professor of German Literature and Chair of Comparative and General Literature at the Free University of Berlin.

John Milfull is Professor of German Studies at the University of New South Wales, Sydney.

David Roberts is Professor of German at Monash University, Melbourne.

Anthony Stephens is Professor of German at the University of Melbourne.

Margaret Mahony Stoljar is Associate Professor of German at the Australian National University.

Sigrid Weigel is Professor of German Literature at the University of Zurich.

Andrzej Wirth is Professor of Theatre Studies and Foundation Director of the Institute for Applied Theatre Research at the University of Gießen.

Index

Index

Index